"That's What They Used to Say"

"That's What They Used to Say"

Reflections on American Indian Oral Traditions

Donald L. Fixico

University of Oklahoma Press : Norman

An earlier version of chapter 7 was previously published in Donald L. Fixico, *Daily Life of Native Americans in the Twentieth Century*, Westport, Conn.: Greenwood, 2006.

Library of Congress Cataloging-in-Publication Data
Names: Fixico, Donald Lee, 1951– author.
Title: "That's what they used to say" : reflections on American Indian oral traditions / Donald L. Fixico.
Other titles: Reflections on American Indian oral traditions
Description: Norman, OK : University of Oklahoma Press, [2017] | Includes bibliographical references and index.
Identifiers: LCCN 2017006657 | ISBN 978-0-8061-5775-7 (hardcover) ISBN 978-0-8061-8 (paper)
Subjects: LCSH: Indians of North America—Folklore. | Oral tradition—North America.
Classification: LCC E98.F6 F54 2017 | DDC 398.2089/97—dc23
LC record available at https://lccn.loc.gov/2017006657

The paper in this book meets the guidelines for permanence and durability of the Committee on Production Guidelines for Book Longevity of the Council on Library Resources, Inc. ∞

To my cousins

Frank Alexander and Barney Mitchell,

with great respect

Contents

Illustrations

Acknowledgments

A number of people have influenced, assisted, and supported my work. I would like to thank them for their assistance or support in the completion of this work. I am grateful to longtime editor Gary Dunham for reading an earlier draft of this manuscript and suggesting how it could be revised. When I was at the University of Kansas, I served as the founding director of the Center for Indigenous Nations Studies and taught a healthy number of Native graduate students. In one class, Tony Rogers introduced a new word, "storyologist"— a person who studied stories. I credit him with the origin of this term. His thoughts on this word and his broader interests have inspired me to continue to think about the importance of the oral tradition among Indians and its various forms of expression.

Over the past several years, I appreciated hearing the stories of Jim Anquoe, Blue Clark, Lawrence Hart, Ohlin Williams, and many other Native elders. My list of storytellers is long, including Ada Deer, David Edmunds, James Riding In, Eddie Brown, John Tippeconnic, and there is not enough space here to name all of them. I recall one plane trip that James and I were on by happenstance in Phoenix: we told stories for about three hours until we landed in Tulsa. We were two Oklahoma boys returning to our homelands to visit for different reasons. Telling Indian stories does not mean that you have to be Indian. I enjoy hearing such accounts from my good friend and colleague Peter Iverson. Many years ago, I had the honor to hear stories presented by the noted Te Ata, a Chickasaw, who also told stories as entertainment to President Franklin Roosevelt and Eleanor Roosevelt as well as performances for King George VI and Queen Elizabeth II of England.

At the University of Oklahoma Press, I want to thank longtime friend Charles Rankin, editor-in-chief. When I first told Chuck about my oral traditions book at the Western History Association meeting in 2014 and its intended academic nature, he replied that there were already enough academic books about Indian oral tradition and oral history. Chuck said, "What we need is a book about the stories that you grew up with. That would make a good book!" So I listened to his sage advice and over the next two years, I changed the whole approach of the book. My guide and advisor through the process is another wonderful friend, Alessandra Jacobi Tamulevich, senior acquisitions editor. Alessandra has read the manuscript with its new purpose in mind, made suggestions, and shepherded it through the process of making a much better book, and I am very grateful to her. I am grateful for Bonnie Lovell, copy editor, for improving the quality of my writing, and Sarah C. Smith, manuscript editor, for overseeing the production of the book. Bonnie and Sarah, thank you. I am grateful for the reviews and helpful comments from the external readers, Margaret Connell Szasz, Clifford Trafzer, and Tom Holm. I appreciate their knowledge and insights about oral traditions, which helped make this a better book.

At Arizona State University, I want to thank my research assistants, Clara Keyt, Cody Marshall, and Chelsea Mead, for helping me to complete the initial draft of this book. In the revising stages, I appreciate the help of research assistants Brianna Theobald, John Goodwin, and Farina King. And in the final stage, I appreciate the help of research assistants Amy Long and Andrea Field, especially getting things done in a rush with care. Thank you again, Andrea, for helping at the very end in getting the final revision completed. I appreciate my talented doctoral student Grace Hunt Watkinson for producing the artwork for the book cover. Thank you, Grace. I am also grateful to my colleagues across campus for their wit, conversations, and great stories that make ASU a rewarding environment for teaching and discussing history. At ASU, I am grateful for the support of President Michael Crow, Provost Mark Searle, Vice President and Executive Dean Patrick Kinney, Humanities Dean George Justice, Director of the School of Historical, Philosophical and Religious Studies, Matt Garcia, and Head of History Calvin Schermerhorn. I am eternally grateful for my parents, John and Virginia Fixico, as well as my siblings. Over the years, I have heard my mother tell stories about Moccasin Trail in Sac and Fox Country in Oklahoma and my dad render accounts about Indians around Seminole and Shawnee, Oklahoma. My cousins Frank Alexander and Barney Mitchell, both veterans of the Vietnam War, are fun to be with and have shared stories about our relatives, including my parents. I thank them and my parents, especially for their stories, rich in details and cultural importance, which inspired this book.

As I collected photographs for the book, I want to credit Michelle M. Martin for her time and energy for taking great photographs. I thank Rachel Moser at the Oklahoma History Center for the photographs of Wilma Mankiller and Chitto Harjo; Dr. Lee Brumbaugh, Curator of Photographs at the Nevada Historical Society for the Wovoka photograph; my friend Bruce Dinges, Director of Publications, and Caitlin Lampman at the Arizona Historical Society for the Geronimo photograph.

I want to thank my significant other, Michelle Martin, who traveled with me throughout Illinois to collect information and photograph the statues of Tecumseh, Black Hawk, and Keokuk, and who trekked with me up Bear Butte and Black Elk Peak in the Black Hills and the Medicine Wheel in Wyoming. Of her many talents, Michelle is a professional photographer and she has helped improve my own photography, sometimes simply by reminding me to take off the lens cap before I snap a picture. I credit her with many of the photographs in this book. My other photography advisor and traveler on some of the adventures you will read about it is my son, Keytha. At home, I am always thankful for the support from Keytha, who has developed a growing interest in the ways of our people. In my study at home, Josie the cat keeps me company when she is visiting, curled up on her spot at the end of the sofa. My hope is that this volume will help others to understand American Indians and our ways. Writing books is often a lonely experience and one has to enjoy this endeavor. Rewriting and revising is the test of individual stamina to push on, hopefully with the support of others, and I am most appreciative of them. *MVTO.*

"That's What They Used to Say"

Introduction

Being Indian is telling and listening to stories about people, places, things, and experiences in a community of your relatives. Being Indian also encompasses a wide variety of Indianness based on tribes' differing worldviews: Comanche reality is different from Navajo reality, although Seminoles and Mvskoke Creeks have similar realities because they share the same worldview. The goal of this book is to demonstrate how stories in the oral traditions release powerful energies in Indian homes and communities. Native people share stories; some are intended to be told only during the day or at night. Others were, and are, shared only during winter or the other seasons. Most stories, however, can be told anytime. Told in the oral traditions of different tribes, such stories—of myth and truth—make people laugh, cry, and cherish each other's company.

This book is about the oral traditions of American Indians occurring in various forms: legends, creation accounts, oratories, prophecies, and oral histories. It explains the Indian universe via the oral tradition. Although this is not intended to be an academic book, American Indian studies is the first academic discipline to understand the Indigenous universe in a completely organic approach that I have called the Medicine Way, which has existed long before the emergence of Westernization.[1]

In a similar way, other Indigenous communities in the world possess distinct understandings of their worlds and the universe. I have been fortunate enough to observe the oral traditions of Indigenous peoples in my travels to the Samis in Finland, Africans in South Africa, Aborigines in Australia, Maoris in New Zealand, and Ainus in Japan. They share closeness to the earth, their natural environments, and have a non-Western physical-metaphysical reality like American Indians. Their ethoi are expressed in their oral traditions and are internalized within the communities.

Using a metaphorical concept of "inside the lodge" to define internal Native reality, the goal is to share the Indianness of oral traditions, and show how it has perpetuated the connectedness of Indians. "Inside the lodge" implies that oral traditions convey the internal reality of Native communities and, in another way, about being inside the collective Indigenous mindset, respecting that each tribal community has its own set of oral accounts. Stories in this genre of Indian storytelling are what make Indian oral histories different from storytelling in Irish, Jewish, or African American communities, though each group has its own inside the lodge reality of togetherness, belonging, and inclusion in the community that helps to form a group identity. The nature of American Indian peoplehood has been advanced by Native scholars like Tom Holm and Robert Thomas, and in works by non-Native scholars, including George Pierre Castile and Gilbert Kushner.[2] Specifically, Tom Holm maintains that four principles, derived from oral traditions, manifesting sacred history, place, ceremonial cycles, and language, define Indigenous peoplehood.

As a child growing up in rural Oklahoma, I heard my parents and other elders tell stories about a wide range of topics. Stories wove together the social fabric of our community. My elders shared stories about other relatives, things that had happened, and about many things that most people would not believe. Ghost stories frightened us kids, causing us to ponder how anything was possible. To us, the stories were real, although the imagination of children can get carried away. Like children in many cultures around the world, we were told to be good or the bogeyman might get us. Our elders scared us into being good, because if we were not, *hah kv* (the bogeyman) would get us and carry us away, never to be seen again. Needless to say, older children would scare younger ones by talking about hah kv. In my child's mind, I imagined hah kv as very big and hairy, and he would hide until night and then come and try to get me. We were also told by elders not to say his name because that would be like calling him and he would come, *hvmakimata*. That's what they used to say.[3]

Among the Mvskoke Creeks and Seminoles, *ehosa* is a phrase used to describe when a supernatural being or a power has momentarily trapped a person inside a state of mind where he or she loses all sense of direction, place, and time. This state of lost confusion is often characterized by fear or panic because it indicates a greater controlling force at work, sometimes exercised by a very powerful medicine maker. A medicine maker is called *heles hayv* among the Mvskoke Creeks and Seminoles, and some of my relatives are medicine makers.

One morning my dad shared a story as we sat in the den of my parents' house in Sapulpa, Oklahoma. He said that one of his Mvskoke friends told this story that happened outside of Bristow, Oklahoma. His friend and a companion were hunting squirrels in the fall just before sunrise, when night meets day, enabling a surreal transition from dark to light. The two friends walked parallel through the woods, checking the treetops and ground, some two hundred feet separating them. The friend who told this story to my dad said the rain from the night before had made the leaves on the ground smell earthy. Suddenly a musty smell permeated the air and made him stop. He looked straight ahead, then he looked to his right to check on his companion, but he could not see him. It was still twilight as the early rays of dawn pierced the treetops of the woods. The hunter continued staring in the direction of his companion, straining his eyes to see. The musty smell became pungent, and then some twenty feet away from behind a tree what seemed to be a shaggy bear, looking well over six feet tall, walked like a human. Stricken with fear, the hunter squeezed his rifle with both hands, unsure of what he was seeing. The tall humanlike creature with dark brown fur walked through a barbed-wire fence like it was not there. Then, whatever it was sniffed the air, turned, and laid its eyes on my dad's friend and stared at him for several moments. My dad's friend could not move. Only his eyes could follow the massive creature until it disappeared behind a tree. The hunter felt hypnotized, like he was caught in a dream. He was paralyzed, had no idea what time it was, had no sense of direction, and felt trapped by ehosa (confusion). He did not even know his own name or where he was or what he was doing. Then, the creature's entrancing power released the hunter's mind; it was like he had woken up from a spell and returned from a spiritual place. His thoughts returned to his mind as his head cleared. When the hunter found his companion, he asked him if he had seen any squirrels or anything else. The companion replied that he only smelled something bad for a while, something very musty.[4] The hunter had seen hah kv, proving the bogeyman was real.

In the Museum of Man in San Diego, an exhibit displays a creature like hah kv that lived many years ago. Between four hundred thousand and nine million years ago, *Gigantopithecus* lived in what are now China, India, Pakistan, and Vietnam. The creature stood about ten feet tall and weighed roughly twelve hundred pounds, about twice as large as the modern male gorilla. In 1935, G. H. R. von Koenigswald, a German-Dutch paleontologist and geologist, discovered that the Chinese had found jawbone fossils of the animal.[5]

The Mvskokes and Seminoles also call this being *esti capcaki* (Tall Man), and some have seen it. There are many *este cvpcakv,* and they have lived in heavy woods for many years, going as far back as the Mvskokes and Seminoles can remember. Some people say Tall Man is the protector of woods and keeps away those who would damage the forests.[6] In this way, he also protects the earth medicines of plants and herbs found deep in the woods. Esti capcaki likes to be left alone and has the power to disappear. And he watches people.[7] Hvmakimata.

Stories are the sine qua non of Indian life and they transfer knowledge among Native peoples as well as passing this oral literacy to the next genera-tion. Front porches of Indian homes during the spring and summer, or around kitchen tables during the fall and winter months, are intersecting narrative spaces where people consciously share stories that become a part of their sub-conscious. The storytelling occurrences of intersecting spaces become time portals where the past and present interact, creating an inside the lodge sur-realism. In earlier times, Indian people sat around campfires and inside lodges to tell young ears and those interested in the old ways, stories about legendary warriors and stories so they would learn about creation or the future through prophecies. Stories cause us to lose our present sense of mind, simultaneously transporting us into timeless space where we relive the past. This fluctuating space is spiritual energy, which exists in stories, and my life is full of stories.

This book has been a long-awaited project that I have thought about and wanted to write for a long time. Its purpose is to go beyond the old argument about the written word versus the spoken word and the criticism of oral history, a history that includes the oral traditions of Native peoples. Even Sir James G. Frazer noted many years ago, "The importance of myths as documents of human thought in the embryo is now generally recognized, and they are col-lected and compared, no longer for the sake of idle entertainment, but for the light they throw on the intellectual evolution of our species."[8] This study moves to the next important step of sharing insights inside the lodge of Native reality via oral tradition. Conceptually, inside the lodge oneness is pertinent to Native people, according to tribal communities, but this same earthly relationship is experienced by Irish communities in their oral tradition, Mexican Americans telling stories in their cultural realm, African Americans telling stories in their special way, and other people sharing their stories in an ethnic context. This timeless harmony demonstrates all communities manifest a cultural reality that emerges from their oral traditions that transmit their myths and legends.

In this volume, my hope is that readers will hold in their hands evidence of the spoken word that will convince them that the oral traditions of Indians is just as worthy as, and even more insightful than, written history. This book also intends to demonstrate that once written down, stories do not die because their life forces are too great. They possess spiritual energy and storytellers have the opportunity to summon this connected feeling of togetherness. Among the Mvskoke Creeks and Seminoles, the storyteller is known as *empanayv*. In the following narrative, I use my personal voice much like Charles Alexander Eastman did in the nine books he wrote in the early part of the twentieth century. During June 2016 (as I finished revising this book) I attended a two-day workshop on American Indian writers and Indigenous knowledge at Amherst College and my son, Keytha, went with me. I had been told that Charles Eastman, the Santee Sioux physician, had lived outside of the town, and Keytha and I found his house. We drove our rental car up the winding driveway, and the owner and his family invited us inside as I explained who Eastman was. I suggested that Eastman probably drafted some of his books while he lived there, and it was a treat for the family, and for me and Keytha, to experience where Dr. Eastman contemplated and wrote his many books, like *The Soul of the Indian: An Interpretation* (1911), and my favorite, *From the Deep Woods to Civilization* (1916).

This effort is an attempt to buttress the significance of the Indian voice, with hope that it will be received in a respectful way. Within the mainstream academy, the Indian voice is often lost. Furthermore, I have thought it ironic when I have witnessed Native scholars stand when it is their turn and read their conference papers knowing their ancestors relied on an oral tradition for their presentations. Mainstream scholars and students become caught up in the issues and history of the larger American society to the exclusion of the Indian voice. It is there; it has always been there, but the mainstream frequently chooses to neglect and undermine it or even deny its relevance and significance. The following pages explore the presumed subaltern existence of the silent Indian stereotype, and sharing the stories enable it to speak. These stories that I grew up with are accompanied by descriptions of my personal journeys as I visited notable historic places. One might argue this is not objective analysis, but in order to reveal the subconscious nature of oral tradition this volume is more than an academic book. I have stressed feeling the inside the lodge connection, the spiritual power of stories where the mind surreally embraces the past. The connectedness may make you cry, even laugh, or both.

One of the primary objectives of this book is to move the discussion of Indian oral traditions in mainstream academia to Indian academia and tribal communities for all Native readers to understand this inner perspective. This is its proper place—within an Indigenous context—and for people to understand the vibrancy of tribal languages, Native cultures, the ethos of American Indians, as well as their histories. All of this is pertinent to even beginning to understand Indian oral histories. To illustrate this point, I have borrowed a Cheyenne story: "We were sitting about the fire in the lodge on Two Medicine. Double Runner, Small Leggings, Mad Wolf, and the Little Blackfoot were smoking and talking, and I was writing in my note-book. As I put aside the book, and reached out my hand for the pipe, Double Runner bent over and picked up a scrap of printed paper, which had fallen to the ground." George Bird Grinnell wrote these words on the first page of his *Blackfoot Lodge Tales: The Story of a Prairie People*, originally published in 1892. Inside the lodge, Grinnell was at the threshold of Cheyenne reality and in the Cheyennes' ancient space–time continuum in their oral tradition. Other non-Native scholars and writers like Fred McTaggart and Calvin Martin have experienced the same special ethos while entering an Indigenous reality where the physical and metaphysical exist as one spiritual space. Among the Mvskoke Creeks and Seminoles, we would say that they also likely experienced ehosa. Here, orality predominates and its oral history is recorded in the memories of people, including non-Indians. Other scholars like Arnold Krupat have included Indian voices in their works because they believed in Native realities.[9] Simply, you do not have to be Indian to experience Indian things. This Indianness, according to Yellow Wolf of the Nez Perce, is "the story for the people who come after us"[10] and who believe in the inclusive Medicine Way, which contains nature's dichotomies of light-dark, left-right, male-female, happiness-sadness, and Indian-non-Indian.

The validity of oral history is earning respect from the professional history world in academia, but historians will need to become broader minded. Most historians prefer a narrow conventional approach of working with documents. The acceptance of oral history gained important ground some years ago when

Studs Terkel's oral history, *The Good War: An Oral History of World War Two*, won the Pulitzer Prize in 1985. Like the Native oral traditions, *The Good War* consists of stories and storytelling. My book is also not about oral poetry, which Paul Zumthor has superbly written about, nor is it a sociolinguistic study such as Dell Hymes and other linguists, anthropologists, and folklorists might write. Where "folklore indeed is nonfact," according to Richard Dorson in *American Folklore and the Historian*, there are truths in Indian oral traditions that deserve more respect from Native people and non-Natives.[11] At this point, it is pertinent to recognize the early work of Stith Thompson, Franz Boas, and other noted scholars who have promoted the importance of Indian mythology, yet *That's What They Used to Say* strives to reveal the inner contextualization of Native oral traditions.

The foundational sources for this book derive from my own background of being four tribes—Shawnee, Sac and Fox, Mvskoke Creek, and Seminole. My mother was a talented storyteller, especially of ghost stories and accounts that happened along Moccasin Trail near Prague, Oklahoma. My Shawnee grandmother was also a convincing storyteller and shared many Shawnee and Sac and Fox stories with my mother who passed them along to us kids while I was growing up. On occasions, I talked to my grandmother who shared stories about Jim Thorpe, Black Hawk, and Tecumseh. The geographic scope of the book is limited to my four tribal communities—where they originated in North America—and my personal experiences traveling to various parts but not all of Indian Country.

Oral tradition among Indian people is the heart of their collective voice. It is essential to give sufficient respectful attention to this tradition of stories. To understand Indian people is to learn their stories. First, a person has to become a good listener. Removing criticism of the relevance of storytelling and being open-minded are pertinent to realizing the integral role of oral tradition in the fabric of Indian life.

Early Indian academics like Charles Alexander Eastman, Gertrude Bonnin, Ella Deloria, and others were great storytellers who became profound writers. They combined oral tradition and the academia of their times to help establish the Indian voice in the early twentieth century. Even earlier, Alexander Posey of the Mvskoke Creeks expressed Native satire in his "Fus Fixico" letters published in the *Indian Journal*. The oral tradition is the vessel for expressing the viewpoints of many Indian spokespeople and writers. At the date of this writing, several Indian journals include stories from Native oral tradition, such as *American Indian Quarterly, American Indian Culture and Research Journal, Native Studies Review,* and *Wicazo Sa Review.*

There are a number of categories of oral histories. General works in comprehensive collections include all types of oral accounts. Richard Erdoes and Alfonso Ortiz compiled a wide range of tribal myths and legends in *American Indian Myths and Legends* (1984) as a general introduction. Another insightful compilation is Jay Miller's *Earthmaker: Tribal Stories from Native North America* (1992), which stresses the role of nonhuman beings in creation accounts. A similar compilation with wide geographic representation is Terri Hardin, ed., *Legends & Lore of the American Indians* (1914). This broad Indigenous geographic approach is also evident in Lewis Spence's *Myths and Legends of the North American Indians* (2004). Other experts, like Stith Thompson in his pioneering work, *Folk Tales of the North American Indians* (1995), have brought significant attention to Native oral tradition, and as long as Indians are telling stories, the oral tradition continues.

Indian oratory and commentary consisting of speeches on many subjects are found in W. C. Vanderwerth, ed., *Indian Oratory: Famous Speeches by Noted Indian Chieftains* (1971), Colin G. Calloway, ed., *The World Turned Upside Down: Indian Voices from Early America* (1994), Steven Mintz, *Native American Voices: A History and Anthology* (1995), Arlene Hirschfelder, ed., *Native Heritage: Personal Accounts by American Indians, 1790 to the Present* (1995), and Peter Nabokov, ed., *Native American Testimony: A Chronicle of Indian-White Relations From Prophecy to the Present, 1492–1992* (1991). While Calloway's and Mintz's editions stress Indian accounts during the colonial era, Hirschfelder collected more or less contemporary personal accounts about basic areas of life. Nabokov gives the fullest range of individual Indian perspectives from historical leaders to contemporary spokespersons. Native language is imperative to continuing to rediscover oral tradition in Anton Treuer, ed., *Living Our Language: Ojibwe Tales and Oral Histories* (2001). A more recent work on Indian oral tradition and oratory is William M. Clements, *Oratory in Native North America,* which appeared in 2002.

Related to oral tradition are works focusing on the generic Indian trickster. These insightful works are Frank B. Linderman, ed., *Old Man Coyote: The Authorized Edition* (1931), Paul Radin, ed., *The Trickster: A Study in American Indian Mythology* (1956), Berard Haile, *Navajo Coyote Tales: The Curly Tó*

Aheedlíinii Version (1984), Ekkehart Malotki and Michael Lomatuway'ma, eds., *Hopi Coyote Tales: Istutuwutsi* (1984); Mourning Dove, *Coyote Stories* (1990); and Deward E. Walker Jr. in collaboration with Daniel N. Matthews, eds., *Nez Perce Coyote Tales* (1998). Howard L. Harrod, in *Renewing the World: Plains Indian Religion and Morality* (1987), and Michael Kearney, in *World View* (1984), focus on the world at large. The latter concentrates on a model and theories about the worldviews of Native communities around the world. A seminal work often referred to is A. Irving Hallowell, "Ojibwa Ontology, Behavior, and World View," in Stanley Diamond, ed., *Primitive Views of the World: Essays from Culture in History* (1964). To understand how legends and traditions help to explain tribal origin, Harold Courlander's *The Fourth World of the Hopis: The Epic Story of the Hopi Indians as Preserved in Their Legends and Traditions* (1971) remains a reliable narrative description containing valuable insight into Hopi life and the Hopi worldview.

The organization of *That's What They Used to Say* covers the wide scope of Indian oral traditions. It is meant to be comprehensive, with its surrealism exemplifying the past–present existence of Native oral traditions. Chapter 1 addresses the effectiveness of the spoken word—its life force—and explains the significance of the oral tradition among Native people, inside of the lodge, so to speak. Chapter 2 is about the first important category of Indian oral tradition, which is "creation myths" of the earth and people. The purpose here is to demonstrate how Native people are connected to each other, to the past, and to the earth. Chapter 3 discusses legendary warriors in Indian history and explains *why* Indians need Indian heroes as role models. Chapter 4 is about the eloquence of Indian oratory while analyzing noted speeches given by Native leaders throughout Indian history.

Stories about spirits and ghosts are the subjects in chapter 5. An earlier version of this chapter was presented as a paper at the Language, Silence, and Voice in Native Studies international conference at the University of Geneva during July 16–17, 2007. This chapter reveals that Native reality includes both the physical and metaphysical in a combined way. Chapter 6 addresses the spiritual beings, human and nonhuman, found in stories of incidents that happened along the Moccasin Trail. I want to thank Rose Daily for sharing with me her knowledge about Moccasin Trail. Chapter 7 is about Indian humor, explaining what it is and why it is so special to Indian people. An earlier version of this chapter appeared in my earlier book, *Daily Life of Native Americans in the*

Twentieth Century. Chapter 8 addresses the future in visions and prophecies as spoken by Native prophets. Prophecy provides guidelines for lifeways and for all involved to walk the good road. The last chapter is actually an epilogue of three personal stories; it is also a conclusion that needed to be told to help fulfill my quest in writing this book. I invite you to read and ponder them, perhaps benefit from them.

Throughout the following pages, certain words are capitalized to give readers a chance to pause and think about the Native importance of distinct concepts and places such as "Other Side" and "Other Side of Life" pertaining to the spiritual afterlife, "Third Dimension" of Native physical and metaphysical realities combined, and "Circle of Life" as many tribal philosophies involve circularity as a part of life.

Power of the Spoken Word

The whites are already nearly a match for us all united, and too strong for any one tribe alone to resist; so that unless we support one another with our collective and united forces; unless every tribe unanimously combines to give check to the ambition and avarice of the whites, they will soon conquer us apart and disunited, and we will be driven from our Native country and scattered as autumnal leaves before the wind. But have we not courage enough remaining to defend our country and maintain our ancient independence? Will we calmly suffer the white intruders and tyrants to enslave us? Shall it be said of our race that we knew not how to extricate ourselves from the three most dreadful calamities—folly, inactivity and cowardice? . . . Then listen to the voice of duty, of honor, of nature and of your endangered country. Let us form one body, one heart, and defend to the last warrior our country, our liberty, and the graves of our fathers.[1]

A story being told is a body of spiritual energy transporting traditional knowledge and information that passes back and forth between the generations of grandchildren, parents, and grandparents. Stories have multiple purposes of passing along information, presenting values and virtues, reminding us who we are, and giving glimpses into the future.[2] Stories consist of words of power used like the paints of an artist who renders a picture in our minds that resonates with our inner being. When told effectively, stories transcend time; traditional knowledge becomes a part of each new listener and thus a part of the next generation. Tecumseh's 1811 speech to the Choctaws and Chickasaws exemplifies

Statue of Tecumseh in Illinois. Author's collection.

energy released through eloquence and emotions. This energy is akin to that existing in the planting of a seed. The Choctaws and Chickasaws had already planted their corn in their Mississippi homelands, and the following weeks of spring rain would yield crops to be celebrated. The people welcomed the new year with the Green Corn Dance during midsummer, a celebratory affair of social good times and the medicine power that comes from herbs, plants, and the metaphysical world. This was a festival opportunity to share traditional stories and knowledge with adults revisiting the past and the young learning about their people.

I learned to appreciate both the power of storytelling and the way Tecumseh utilized that power from my own family. My Shawnee grandmother, Rachel Dirt Wakolee, proudly claimed being related to Tecumseh. She said from time

Rachel Dirt Wakolee.
Author's collection.

to time that we were related to Tecumseh. Her claim had little effect on me in my youth, but as I grew older and learned more about the great war leader, I gained much respect for him. Grandmother Rachel had married my grandfather Glade Wakolee, who was Sac and Fox, and they lived in Shawnee, Oklahoma, but mostly out in the country on Moccasin Trail, north of town. My mother, Virginia Lee Wakolee, was the first child to survive because her two older siblings had died from pneumonia when they were babies. In this way, my mother was the eldest child, and so am I.

On a cold January night, I was born in Shawnee, Oklahoma, at 12:20 A.M. Several miles down the road lay the town of Tecumseh, so close that old Highways 18 and 177 connect them. During humid Oklahoma summers, we had no air conditioning; we lived at 1420 East Walnut Street in a small three-room gray rent house in town. Those were the days in the early 1950s of the Korean War when you were lucky to have even a fan. We did not. So we kept the windows opened most of the time and hoped for rain. And it did come, but so did humidity. Hot, damp uncomfortable days, but you just learned to live with them. A few years later, we moved out in the country. I was about five or six. My brother Ron was a couple of years younger, though he looked like he was five or six too because he was always big and husky for his age. A few times, our parents took us in the evenings to the south edge of Shawnee toward Tecumseh on

Virginia Wakolee Fixico and John Fixico. Author's collection.

Beard Street where we all got snow cones. This was a big thing because we got to come to town and I remember staring at the snow cone stand and the people lined up. My brother liked grape and I always wanted strawberry. One weekend, a carnival camped next to the Canadian River that separated Shawnee from Tecumseh and my parents took us to ride some of the rides and eat cotton candy. I was filled with excitement; everything looked so big with bright colors, especially at night. At the time, I had no idea that I would grow up and write about Tecumseh like this. The future yields surprising results sometimes. What is personally important is that I feel connected to Tecumseh because of my grandmother Rachel. She always said he was a great leader and we were part Shawnee. Grandmother said Tecumseh was also a great speaker, but she never explained why. "All Shawnees know him," she would say. "He was a great leader, that's what they used to say," she said with tremendous pride and a smile, nodding her head to affirm her comment. Her brown eyes twinkled like she was holding back a surprise.

The Shawnees and Mvskoke Creeks and Seminoles share many beliefs. The Mvskoke Creek–Seminole Way focuses on the Green Corn Ceremony, paying homage to the four elemental powers—fire, water, earth, and wind—and includes dancing from late at night to dawn, a part of Nature's cycle. Some people might call this worshipping Nature, but this Way of Life guided our lives. Several times, my parents took us kids to stomp dances at Little Axe, a Shawnee dance ground, located east of Norman, Oklahoma. The Creeks and Seminoles shared some of their songs with the Shawnees, and Tecumseh's people reciprocated, offering their hospitality. During Green Corn, you never went hungry because people shared their food. This ceremony also enabled my mother to visit some of our kinfolks on her side.

Tecumseh's mother was Mvskoke Creek, so a personal connection bonded the Mvskokes and Shawnees in his family, but in general the two peoples joined often as allies. In his journeys, Tecumseh traveled south with a delegation of warriors from various tribes to visit the Mvskokes in their home area, which became known as Alabama. He delivered a fervent speech to the Mvskokes at one of their biggest towns, Tuckabatchee, trying to persuade them to join him in war against the United States. Both Shawnees and Mvskokes fought for their homelands with other Native groups during the nearly four years of the War of 1812, including the Mvskoke Creek War of 1813 to 1814.

Much of Tecumseh's reputation derived from his passion and the cause to which he devoted his life. No doubt Tecumseh was gifted with oratory, and he was an impressive, stout-looking warrior. I was raised with the Seminole–Mvskoke Creek philosophy that if you were good you might receive a gift in life. This would be a gift that you had to respect or it would be taken away from you by the power that had given it to you. In the speech above, Tecumseh was endowed with the gift of oratory—the power of the spoken word. He fully deployed its power, uttering each word in such a way that it conveyed a spiritual power that could influence others.

Shawnee people believed that Tecumseh possessed great medicine power. His younger brother, Tenskwatawa, or "Open Door," did possess such power, especially demonstrated when Governor William Henry Harrison challenged Tenskwatawa to make the Sun disappear. An eclipse occurred on June 16, 1806, earning Tenskwatawa his English name, the Shawnee Prophet.[3] On the other hand, Tecumseh's personal medicine power manifested itself through his oratory and it is likely that he held an eagle feather or some personalized item that he used while urging crowds to join his campaign with the British and other Indian nations against the Americans. The eagle is the greatest animal that flies, and it is revered among practically all Indian cultures. Whatever the source of Tecumseh's power, there can be no doubt that his gift for oratory enabled him to invest his utterances and stories with meaning and conviction that resonated with his listeners and inspired them to action. History is full of Native leaders like Tecumseh, and often they possessed the spiritual power of the spoken word.

Spoken Word versus Written Word

Traditional Native people and mainstream Americans view history in different ways, especially when their worldviews differ greatly. Based on the tradition of relying on the spoken word, Indian oral history conflicts with the Western training of most American historians. The academic historian works primarily with documented evidence for understanding history. But the differences in historical approaches do not stop here. Professional Western-trained historians define history as events of change over time. In their definition of history, Native people prefer "experience" instead of "history," so that an event is recalled as an experience in a story. The vast difference between the two perspectives comes down to how to understand the past and how to recall it. Furthermore, what is reality? And how is it defined? The linear thinker, like most people in the mainstream, is convinced that history is a measurement of change over time and that each new event becomes a part of the collective past in chronological order. But how is historical meaning important to both groups?

Tecumseh's words to the Chickasaws and Choctaws resonated with an emotional energy of Native patriotism of which Shawnees are proud. Native people can also recall an experience by using words in great detail because of the emotions, vivid colors, interesting smells, familiar sounds, and the people and beings involved. When retold, the experience comes alive again. Storytelling recreates the experience by evoking the emotions of the listeners, transcending the bounds of past, present, and future. Time is not restrictive in a story where the storyteller uses words like a weaver uses threads to construct a tapestry that recreates the richness of a lived experience.

Words become pieces of a puzzle coaxed together to reproduce a picture or mental image of a personal experience. For example, words in the Mvskoke-Seminole language describe the experience of something that has happened or a person or people doing things. The speaker uses intentional words and uses them in such a way to paint a mental image of what he or she reimagines. For the Mvskoke-Seminole speaker, learning the linear way becomes an uphill task because the cultural logic is different. My father struggled with this through his adult years. He completed the fourth grade and his older brother, Telmond, had a grammar school education. Their sisters had about the same amount of education because English was not necessary in a Mvskoke Creek–Seminole farming household. My father became a young man when it was still most important to belong to our traditional community. My mother, who was Shawnee and Sac and Fox, joined the Mvskoke Creek–Seminole community when she married my father.

Many years later, when we moved to Muskogee, Oklahoma, my father became a Baptist minister, the fire-and-brimstone apostle type who believed intensely in the Bible. We lived in a pink rent house on the corner of Callahan Street and North L. On weekends in my teen years, I would come home late, trying to make it in before midnight, which was a house rule for all of us children as we became teenagers. My dad would wait up for us. Friday and Saturday nights in Muskogee were big nights to hang out with friends. I had a black used 1965 Ford Mustang and approached the house from the side street, North L, next to our side of the railroad tracks. Almost a half a block away, I would turn off my headlights and the engine to coast into the driveway. It did not help in that I had replaced the twin exhaust system with two Cherry Bomb mufflers to give my car a loud, rumbling sound that I thought was cool. The only problem was that I clamped the mufflers on because I could not afford to have them welded on, and sometimes one of them would fall off. If I made it past my sleeping dad, later he would wake up and sometimes go outside in the dark and feel the hood of my car to see if it was still warm. This way he could guess about what time I came home.

My father would often stay up reading the Bible, resting in a lounge chair with a floor lamp over his shoulder illuminating the pages. One of his favorite passages was Ecclesiastes 3:2 and 4: "A time to be born, and a time to die; a time to plant, and a time to pluck up that which is planted; a time to weep, and a time to laugh; a time to mourn, and a time to dance." Then he would ask, "Did you have a good time?" If I missed curfew on a Saturday night, he would remind me about going to church in the morning and not getting up late was always about hearing the spoken word.

Sometimes, my dad would fall asleep, the footrest extended as he reclined with his Bible on his chest. If I came in too late, I looked to see if the light was on. I hoped that he would be asleep with the lamp turned off so that I could sneak to my bedroom. Sometimes he would be waiting in the dark and would wait to hear the doorknob click, and just when I thought I was safe, I would hear a voice coming from the dark, "Do you know what time it is?" I would reply, "I think it's just before midnight." And he would say, "You better check again." If I made it past my dad without waking him up, my younger brother, Ron, might wake up and say that he needed a dollar to buy something, so it was like paying a toll for him not to tell what time I actually came home.

On the nights that I made the midnight curfew I said goodnight to my dad as I walked past him to my bedroom as he continued to read his Bible, reviewing the passages he would use in his preaching on the following morning. He would wear his glasses and use his right index finger, underscoring each word as he pronounced it softly in a whisper. "For the Son of man is come to seek and to save that which was lost," which he highlighted in yellow and underlined in blue ink in Luke, chapter 10. He liked the New Testament and preferred it over the Old. A few years later, I realized my father was teaching himself how to read words that were unfamiliar to him. I asked him one day about teaching himself to read English and he replied, "You can do anything if you put your mind to it."

On an unexpected November day in 1986, my father handed me the same Bible that I saw him read on those Friday and Saturday nights. He said, "I want you to have this." And as I held it in my hands, it felt like it weighed as heavy as the Ark of the Covenant. Inside the cover in faded blue ink: "To our Beloved Son, Donald L. Fixico, Our Love and Blessing Always." The book is black with a white-laced border around its edges. Pencil marks, inked underlining, and yellow highlighted passages mark contemplative moments and prayers throughout with Scotch tape holding together well-worn pages. Now more than thirty years later, this gift is sacred to me.

This well-traveled Bible was the one my father preached from for many years, from the pulpit, at weddings or funerals, while standing in church, in rain, snow or cold. Many called him Brother John. Younger relatives called him Uncle John. To us kids, he was Pops. He would often return home from an afternoon winter funeral. Sometimes it was a long drive for him; sometimes I would go with him, or my mom, or one of my siblings. But most of the time, he went alone. He would be tired. We would ask, "How did it go?" He would answer with a few details, saying someone had to lead the services and comfort the family. This is what he thought needed to be done: to take care of people, especially in their times of grief.

One winter afternoon, I drove with my dad to a funeral he had to offici- ate. He coughed so badly that I said he needed to see a doctor. So I took him to the hospital and a doctor said he needed to stay a couple of days. When I arrived home, the family members asked where was Pops and I said I took him to the hospital because he had pneumonia; they thought I was joking and expected him to walk through the door. So they waited; I watched *Gilligan's Island* on television. They went outside to look for him, came back in, and said, "You weren't kidding." Years later we laughed about the incident, how every- one thought my dad and I were playing a trick on them when he was actually in the hospital with walking pneumonia.

Stories bond families together. The hospital story was one of many that came up at the dining table years later when we would gather at Christmas or when I would come home on visits several times a year and my brothers would come over from their homes in the Tulsa area. We recalled and retold stories following breakfast until it was time for lunch. Sitting at the oval dining table, we laughed until we cried, bringing the past back to life. We imitated people's voices, using the same words they used in telling stories and using colors to vividly describe things and places; we were not just recounting anecdotes, but using an entire way of thinking like old-timers or how Indian people do cer- tain things.

The vehicle for transmitting this oneness of past and present is the spoken word. Oral tradition differs from oral history. Oral tradition is an interaction with and understanding of the world; oral history is an event told orally. Oral tradition, thus, includes oral histories because it involves the verbal recounting of events. But oral history is not a part of oral tradition. In an oral-tradition- based community, people think and act according to what has been said. Daily communication is imperative for the community to function successfully, and cooperation is essential. Orality is the process of the Indigenous mind taking in information and transmitting it to other people in the community. In this light, non-Indians can learn much about Indians by listening to their stories, for example, what Shawnee people remember about Tecumseh. But the con- text of the spoken word is very important, like knowing the background of a conversation or the circumstances of Tecumseh's speech. As folklorist Barre Toelken has noted, "You will have little difficulty learning about Indians and their culture if you simply listen to their voices and watch their performances, their expressions . . . in the routine of their normal lives."[4] This is why the Shawnees are different from the Sac and Fox who are different from the Mvskokes and Seminoles.

When discussing Native oral tradition, various kinds of tribal realities make it not always possible to compare it to the mainstream views of history and oral history. Various tribal worldviews help to determine realities that encompass human living. Different values in communities consisting of personalities and relationships profoundly influence how people function within each worldview. For example, Germans and Chinese think differently from Americans because their logics and pasts are different due to different values arising from their realities.[5]

While oral tradition and oral history are two different things, both privilege the spoken word. In addition, due to the unreliability of human memory, the recorded spoken word in oral history is criticized by mainstream historians. The debate over written history versus oral history is a continuous one. Many academics argue that recalling the spoken word is not as reliable as history documented by written evidence.[6] History based on documents is called "empirical proof," where only the facts matter. But how are the facts perceived and understood? In the case of the spoken word, oral history has the advantage because it uses the physical senses of human beings that become a part of the memory process. In this light, a great memory of an experience can become remembered more vividly than by reading about the same account in a book. For example, to have heard John F. Kennedy or Martin Luther King Jr. speak in person is a much greater experience than reading about either or both of them giving their speeches.

The passionate words of Tecumseh were remembered and continued to inspire the Choctaws and Chickasaws. And his reputation continued to be remembered in many circles, even to the present. His historical presence has been imprinted on the minds of the Shawnees at a subconscious level. Such an impression lived in the memories of those in attendance that day when they heard him in 1811. Tecumseh made his listeners realize that freedom was not free: "Let us form one body, one heart, and defend to the last warrior our country, our liberty, and the graves of our fathers."[7] We know this to be true because the power of Tecumseh's oratory convinced many Indians from more than a dozen tribes to join him with the British against the Americans in the War of 1812.

Oral Tradition and Oral History

Despite facing skepticism about their belief in the legitimacy of the spoken word, oral historians of the mainstream have argued for the validity and recognition of oral history. As a result, general works written by mainstream oral historians have set standards for obtaining and using oral history.[8] The methodologies involved have been written down so that oral history has become more formal and organized through the Oral History Association. But non-oral historians and scholars of other disciplines did not recognize oral history as a legitimate field until after World War II. The perspectives of America's war heroes and politicians seemed important enough to collect before such noted men died. Every presidential library has stressed the importance of oral history collections of officials who served in presidential administrations and at other high levels of the federal government.

Perhaps the ultimate mainstream example of oral history is Studs Terkel's *The Good War: An Oral History of World War Two*, which won the Pulitzer Prize in 1985.[9] That is, if winning awards is indicative of a level of importance. Unfortunately, another decade and more elapsed before women began to be seriously given the same recognition that male politicians and heroes received. A scant number of oral histories of women received recognition in academia by the end of the twentieth century. One might think that this could not be true, but a quick computer survey or look in bookstores reveals a limited number of women's oral histories. Indian oral histories did not receive recognition until the post-activism years of the 1960s. Indian protests aroused public interest in Native perspectives just as other ethnic groups also attracted attention due to their civil rights protests. This helped Dee Brown's pathbreaking book, *Bury My Heart at Wounded Knee: An Indian History of the American West* (1970) to become the most well-known book on American Indians. This magnum opus has been published in seventeen languages and has sold more than five million copies.[10] Ironically, Dee Brown is not an Indian.

But this also means that not all Indians protested. My uncle Telmond served in World War II in the 101st Airborne Division. He returned home, but he never talked very much about the war. My uncle won some awards for his service, but he wanted to return to the old ways, and he did. He followed in the footsteps of my grandfather Jonas Fixico, who had served in World War I. More importantly, my grandfather was the keeper of the stomp ground at Gar Creek in Seminole County and as I type these words a vivid memory comes to my mind of seeing him sprinkling the ground with medicine before the dancing and singing began. He was a heles hayv—medicine maker—and so was my uncle Telmond, who later became Gar Creek's keeper of the stomp ground. Both served our people and protected them spiritually, and fought to protect all Americans when they served in the armed forces.

Narrative and oral tradition are essential tools for building a bridge between the mainstream and Indian oral interpretations of history.[11] In theory, oral history has certain attributes related to oral tradition. They can be used to discover Indigenous views. From a Native perspective, American Indian history is a collective of tribal histories based on oral traditions. Many of the current 567 federally recognized tribes have written histories published mostly by academic presses, but others still do not have written histories.[12] More than twenty tribes have no written history at this date, and this is likely an undercount. Yet oral history has long been a part of cultures around the world.[13] Mainstream scholars do not usually include Indian oral tradition when writing about American Indians, and it is important that they should in order to fully understand Indian lives and history. Many scholars choose not to talk to Indians while writing articles and books about Indians, for fear of negative feedback. However, since the mid-1980s younger non-Indian scholars have begun to make an effort to interview Native peoples as a part of their research, which has led to some improvement in the inclusion of oral tradition. These interviews are oral histories that often contain oral traditions such as a creation story or trickster story. In specific cases, the interviews focus on stories told in the oral tradition of a community, and this becomes an integral part of the research to understand the history of a community from the inside.

Understanding the actions of Native people when writing and learning about them from the inside out reveals insights as one writes. For example, rather than defining history, understanding it is more appropriate for Indigenous people. The worldview of each people's community produces an understanding of the past. Among my tribes, the Shawnee, Sac and Fox, Mvskoke Creek and Seminole of Oklahoma, worldview, Indigenous logic, reality, and causality interact for their understanding of history. Similar to what happens in other tribes, mine depend on oral tradition to inform them about the past by using stories, legends, myths, and songs.[14] These forms of oral tradition enable people to visit the past and contextualize their lives within their tribal communities.

Formal and Informal Stories

Storytelling is an inherent sharing among Indians. For example, stories continue to be told among the Shawnee about the legendary Tecumseh and what he means to our people. Stories function like quilt patches sewn together to form the fabric connecting a community. The storyteller is the key, and sometimes he or she embellishes past accounts to create a humorous story to make listeners laugh, and at other times the person might be more serious in order to convey a cultural lesson to children. The nature of storytelling includes telling "formal and informal performance stories. Through the years, the American Indians' stories that have mostly interested scholars have been formal performance stories such as the great tribal myths and cycles of trickster tales."[15] In contrast, the stories told to small gatherings for entertainment or as teaching tools to impart a moral or lesson about cultural norms are informal narratives.

Oral tradition includes the forms listed, while oral history is the spoken record of events. Furthermore, the oral tradition does not function with the sole purpose of becoming oral history, although mainstream academics typically classify it that way. As mentioned, the oral tradition becomes a sociocultural history of the community. And it may contain biographies, hero accounts, women's studies, environmental updates, and metaphysical experiences. Various stories constitute a body of knowledge that provides a communication network within the community.

Oral tradition is the connecting force among a people. On a daily basis, stories are told linking people to the past. It is imperative to be connected to one's people. Oral tradition in the form of stories, such as in Tecumseh's speech, spins off related stories. These accounts are about people and what happened to them, perhaps about "what they did," but not necessarily about "what they accomplished." In listening to stories about Tecumseh, people might think of other great leaders like Martin Luther King Jr. or John F. Kennedy and recall the power of their spoken words and where the leaders spoke. I recall hearing King and Kennedy on television when I was a young teenager. They were mesmerizing. Tecumseh had the same effect on his many followers. All three orators represented different racial groups, separate causes, expressed distinct worldviews, but they all had a hypnotic effect on their listeners.

This kind of Native oral tradition appeals to curious listeners, telling us about human beings, animal beings, and spiritual beings. As certain stories are repeated, and others are not, community members undertake a sorting process to determine what is most relevant. In other words, certain formal stories among tribes are carried on as they become classic tales. Important values, perceptions, and understandings are reinforced by the popular stories. One can imagine that those who heard Tecumseh memorized much of his speech and shared his words with their various communities. Like a ripple effect, such an energy-charged speech created oral accounts about the great Shawnee leader that made him a legend and respected by many admirers. Over the years, people have named towns, schools, and communities after him and even taken his name as their own. Ironically, a notorious Indian fighter of the West and against the Florida Seminoles was named William Tecumseh Sherman, who was a commanding general of the U.S. Army. Sherman's father admired Tecumseh and named his son after the Shawnee leader. Raised in Ohio, Sherman was born only seven years after Tecumseh's death and the end of the War of 1812.[16] And it is interesting that William Tecumseh Sherman carried his full name proudly throughout his life. On a personal basis, this story is meaningful because Sherman fought against my Seminole ancestors in the Second Seminole War (1835–1842), so Tecumseh's name has served both sides of Indian wars.

Oral tradition is at the heart of worldviews. It is where Indian oral tradition resonates. Stories in the Native oral tradition have purposes and convey lessons about morality or the future. They offer lessons in life about vanity, pride, showmanship, hidden danger, and how life can be lost–all as a part of the natural laws of the universe. Among Indians, stories are a part of growing up like I did in rural Oklahoma during the 1950s.[17] Elders told stories; even visitors and distant relatives talked mostly about "what happened" to someone that everyone knew.[18] They described in detail who these people were related to and why a particular incident happened. Stories sustained life; life inspired stories, and stories inspired people.

Storyology

Indians tell stories to share information, pass time, communicate positive feelings, and reassure listeners, especially children, that things are all right, making them feel safe and secure. Storytelling is enriched by the person telling the story. A good storyteller is known for providing a brief history of kinship of the person(s) involved, presenting the plot of what happened, and usually speculating about why it happened. Sometimes the stories are serious, like a mystery unveiling danger or bad things happening. Sometimes they invoke laughter. Such humor breaks tension and solidifies people as a group. A good belly-laughing story makes you snort and your eyes fill with tears from laughing so hard. Such a funny story places the group of listeners into a shared space as the people identify with the story. Everyone can relate to it, and they remember that shared special time later as the years go by.

Narrative is powerful and it remains evocative among the Seminoles, Mvskokes, and many other tribes. Indians laugh a lot; they are masters at teasing and hilarious joke telling. The average person laughs seventeen times every day, and I would bet dollars to doughnuts that Indians laugh more than that. There is indeed such a thing as "Indian humor," which will be discussed later, and it is also a way of introduction between strangers, and Indians meeting other Indians in particular.

Non-Indians believe the "stoic Indian" stereotype, but Indians talk a lot, especially my people, the Shawnees, Sac and Fox, Seminoles, and Mvskokes, and I am sure that others would say the same about their tribes. Storytellers use narrative as an effective tool in the multiple forms of legends, myths, and stories. Furthermore, those people who lived during the times of the stories provide a great depth to the accounts. The late Jean Hill Chaudhuri described the importance of such stories in the following way. She said, "The full-blood storytellers, using Creek language through the late [nineteen] forties and early fifties, were the intellectual guardians of a major watershed in Creek history. They were connected with the Trail of Tears themselves or in their immediate family circle."[19] Their elders had walked the Trail of Tears and recalled graphic descriptions of the suffering due to removal and being exiled from their homeland. They established a context like being inside of a lodge where Indians remained in their natural world consisting of physical and metaphysical realities, while surviving and believing in their medicine ways to protect them.

Word choice is very important in oral tradition, especially in Tecumseh's speech to recruit the Chickasaws and Choctaws. In the passage that opens the chapter, Tecumseh contextualizes the overall situation of the two groups of people caught in the wave of white expansion "unless" they do something about it. Tecumseh urges, "We support one another" because the whites are too many for one tribe. Which words to use, how to use them, delivery, and logic are critical parts of his speech. His speech was about the present and the immediate future as he challenged the Choctaws and Chickasaws to take notice of other tribes and what happened to them. The rest of his speech contains Tecumseh asking his listeners at the council of other tribes, "Where today is the Pequod? Where the Narragansetts, the Mohawks, Pocanokets, and many other once powerful tribes of our race? They have vanished before the avarice and oppression of the white men, as snow before a summer sun."[20] Tecumseh also incorporated past stories within the story he was telling about the present and the future, while simultaneously drawing on emotional poignancy.

Story is the heart's expression via oral tradition. Due to its complexity, a story can be best understood when dissected into parts. "Story" among American Indians consists of at least five parts: (1) time, (2) place, (3) character(s), (4) event, and (5) purpose. Together, they are the sum of an "experience."[21] Each of the five parts connects with the other parts as the storyteller weaves his or her story in the art of storytelling. The outcome and objective is poetry, fine entertainment, or knowledge sharing in Indian communities. Robert M. Nelson, a professor of American Indian literature, described the creation of these stories as requiring a "cultural literacy—a process of learning or re-learning, living or re-living, the stories and lifeways . . . and thereby identifying themselves with a particular cultural milieu."[22]

Time and Place

Tecumseh used the past to focus on the present. Time, the matter of when something happened, tends to become less significant as a particular story is shared among people. For example, Tecumseh described the process of white settlement as a living energy that would continue. He described the past becoming a part of the present. Tecumseh breathed life into the message by describing the Indians and whites involved and vividly argued what he thought should happen. He masterfully laid out his plan to the Choctaws and Chickasaws as they listened intently. Tecumseh portrayed the Choctaws and Chickasaws— and all Indians—as one people because he wanted each listener to see this in his or her mind. In his speech, Tecumseh described the situation like a story in which eastern tribes had been defeated individually because they did not unite; however, the solution was to bring all the tribes together, united, as one massive Indian army.

"Place" has a fundamental role in storytelling by providing a foundation for the account. Without place, a story becomes abstract and more difficult for people to relate to. Without a place named or described, the listeners imagine their own place, which results in possible confusion in understanding the story. Tecumseh familiarized the listeners with the place and explained why it was special. Supplying details about the place provided the backdrop for Tecumseh to complete the verbal vision he wanted them to see in the same way he did.

In our personal lives, place becomes a necessary reference point so that we know where we come from and who our relatives are.[23] Stories themselves are also reference points that connect us to various sites or places within our communities. Such reference points are relevant to people; they are a part of us and help to form our identities. They become landmarks in our lives; they help to organize our memories. Even mundane things such as trees, rivers, and mountains are like touchstones for our mental mapping. On the whole, our lives are like mental puzzles with stories as reference points establishing our human experience. Tecumseh's words connected places and people.

Shared Experience

The presentation of the story is the "experience" shared by Tecumseh with the listeners. Storytelling and listening form a reciprocal partnership that becomes the third entity, "shared experience." The shared experience is central to oral traditions for Native peoples. The listener's role is equal and reciprocal to that of the storyteller. Listening allows the potential energy of the story to come alive. The responsibility falls to the storyteller Tecumseh who must convey the correct knowledge in such a way for proper understanding of the story's message.[24] When Tecumseh used words effectively, they became powerful, and his speech empowered its listeners by touching their emotions and increasing their awareness about what was happening.

The results of telling a story about the Indians' dilemma—white settlers encroaching on Indian homelands—involved another element that can be referred to as "interpretation." While interpretation arises as a result of sharing a story, it becomes the foundation as the story is retold. How we hear a story and interpret it needs to be contextualized within cultural values for the same interpretation to occur consistently. Basically, the same message needs to be the takeaway for all listeners or else the interpretation will distort the original story. In this cultural context, it is possible to guide the interpretation of listeners who listen sincerely without taking away only what they want to hear. Interpretation is as much of an active process as telling a story. Telling and the listening combine to make oral tradition and both are dependent on each other for the story to be told as a part of tradition. This balance of telling and listening is precarious in this shared experience of oral tradition because some people get more out of a story than others.

Power

The power and influence of a story within oral tradition-based cultures are vastly underestimated by those unfamiliar with oral traditions. Storytelling is the central means for disseminating local history, sharing genealogical information, spreading gossip, and establishing a network of communication as a part of a community's infrastructure. A story's power is contained until the storyteller releases it by telling the story, thus addressing cultural elements that are a part of life in Indian realities.[25]

Native reality is inclusive of all things in existence within a community, including nonhuman beings. Indian people believe in the importance of relationships and strive to understand them. We should know all of our relations; all things are related, hvmakimata. This also means including nonhuman entities in our understanding of the complexity of life. Excluding the roles of flora, fauna, and other nonhuman entities dismisses most of life.

The totality of Ibofanga (inclusion of all known and unknown things) among the Mvskoke Creeks and Seminoles deems that all things contain spiritual energy, and that the release of such power can be unpredictable. The Mvskoke Creeks have the concept of Ibofanga where all that is known and unknown exists in their world. Stories within the Indian oral tradition have the power to transcend linear time, which is governed by the power in the story itself and the storyteller's effectiveness. Each story possesses spiritual power to draw the listeners into an inside the lodge feeling. Each word is a measured body of energy placed in proper sequence by the storyteller. From a traditional perspective, one might say that the story is spiritual in the form of released power or energy having its effects on listeners in the audience. The story's quality and being told by an effective storyteller determines the strength or intensity of the story's reception. A story should be told in its cultural context because when the storyteller shares a story "it cannot be called back."[26]

The power of words, like those of Tecumseh speaking passionately, has the potential to inspire a person to visualize Tecumseh actually giving the speech. In the mind, a person can imagine him raising his hands, making his plea to a crowd of Indians to fight, if necessary to save their homelands. Indeed, Tecumseh convinced many; they agreed with him. They responded with approval, saying yes, shaking their heads and gesturing in agreement. The power of the story does not always come from hearing it firsthand because one can read Tecumseh's words and visualize him speaking them.

Yet despite the power of Tecumseh's words, not everyone followed him. The Choctaw orator and leader Pushmataha also spoke at the same gathering. Tecumseh was the outsider and most of the Choctaws and Chickasaws sided with their leader; they decided not to join Tecumseh and remained neutral, despite the prophetic plea from the Shawnee leader. But Tecumseh proved that the power and persuasiveness of a story comes from who is telling it, not just from the story's content. In this case, the oratory of Pushmataha was ultimately more persuasive to the listeners, not based solely on the words or the story but instead based on the position of who uttered them. Pushmataha reminded his Choctaw people and Chickasaw allies that Tecumseh's fight was far from their homelands and that they had no quarrel with the Americans. Tecumseh left frustrated and warned the Choctaws and Chickasaws that he would stomp his foot on the ground and they would feel his anger. A foolish gesture? On December 16, 1811, a massive earthquake occurred in the Lower Mississippi region covering thirty thousand square miles and producing fifteen-foot waves. It even made the Mississippi River flow backwards, thus creating Reelfoot Lake in northwest Tennessee.[27]

Spirituality

Time is a measurement of life that has no bearing on spirituality. In fact, the spiritual nature of stories allows them to travel through time. All three parts of linear time—past, present, and future—are a part of the American Indian circular understanding of a life experience. Told again and again, the story's power becomes known and acknowledged, much like a person of known reputation, as a good or bad story, interesting or dull, short or long, and so forth. These binaries are a part of Native life, and people strive to find the balance in between by understanding both sides. Finding the balance between two opposites is capturing the momentum of peaceful inactive energy.

In addition to being an orator, Tecumseh was a skilled storyteller who possessed the ability to empower his listeners with visual imagery. In this way, Tecumseh brims with energy. The styles of storytelling vary and the most effective can electrify their listeners. Successful storytellers are powerful, like Tecumseh, and transfer their own spiritual power into the story itself. In this sense, the storyteller awakens the story's encapsulated spiritual power.

During the summer of 2006, I met regularly with other Native scholars and experts to help to design the Oklahoma Indian Museum and Culture Center in Oklahoma City. On this warm afternoon, Ohlin Williams, a Mississippi Choctaw, told our group about the importance of basket weaving among his people. Holding a basket in his reddish-brown hands, he talked about his grandmother weaving and demonstrated how the weaving begins with the bottom and what each strand means in Choctaw belief. We listened intently to Ohlin speak slowly and deeply, using Choctaw words at times, which helped to release a captivating spiritual power. He spoke of this way of weaving as a part of Choctaw life and how this tradition moved with the Choctaws on their Trail of Tears of removal to Indian Territory (Oklahoma). The power of Ohlin's words embedded his narrative in our subconscious so that we would never forget this experience of his storytelling and seeing in our minds his elderly grandmother weaving the basket. It was as if her presence was in the room with us. This telling released the inside the lodge spirituality and it felt like even the basket had power—and it did. All of us who listened to Ohlin that day are now connected by this optimal experience.

Personal storytelling talent, experience, and cultural knowledge are significant factors in practicing oral traditions—expression excites the emotions of the listeners. An inexperienced storyteller or poor orator will leave listeners indifferent and likely bore them. Experienced and talented storytellers can paint visions in listening minds with their voices. Listeners can see the characters and envision the place, the smells, and the colors, as well as the emotions of the actors.

Listening

As a body of collective spiritual energy, a group of listeners waits to be inspired. The audience, like the Indians listening to Tecumseh, is essential for the story to live on as a part of the circular time continuum. Like a chain reaction in a cycle, the storyteller and listeners are engaged in a symbiosis. Both parties are needed in this Indigenous nature of oral tradition called Indian history. In this inside the lodge realm, "listening" is imperative to the cycle and success of each story retold. Without listeners the story is powerless.

All stories possess spiritual power, which rests until a storyteller engages it with his or her own spiritual power. The two spiritual powers must connect and the better this is done, the better the results. When the connection is made, a flow of energy occurs from the storyteller to the story, like it did in Ohlin's description of the basket. During the story, the flow ebbs back and forth like an ocean tide and the context is the place, providing a geocultural contextual reference to the listeners. In the end, the power of energy flows back to the storyteller and to the listeners who have been empowered or inspired by the energies of the story and the storyteller in tandem. The geocultural context of place is important for the listeners to know where the story occurred. In the account of Tecumseh's speech, the story takes place in the homeland of the Choctaws and Chickasaws near the Mississippi River within their worldview.

Linear listeners need to understand the cyclic continuum of storytelling and respect the spiritual power of Indigenous oral traditions. Karen Gayton Swisher, Standing Rock Lakota and former president of Haskell Indian Nations University in Lawrence, Kansas, noted, "Among the current methods being used to attempt to capture authenticity is: listening to the voices of the people and making sure they are heard through the writing; telling the stories of the people as metaphors . . . and presenting the perspectives of others in an attempt to encourage readers to see through a different lens."[28] A master Indian storyteller can use the imagination of listeners to enable them to hear the distinct voice of each character in the story in their minds, while also transmitting ideas, emotions, and knowledge to those who are receptive inside the lodge.

Untold stories contain an emotional energy that remains at rest until the power is released by the storyteller, making people feel happy or sad, laugh or cry. Among my four tribes and among other Indian communities, stories are generally about ordinary people and their interesting experiences. They are not typically about someone's great deeds of personal victory or a battle. They do not have the historical significance of Tecumseh's speech, but they are important to communities on a daily basis. Stories told at a local level help people to know their roles in society and provide them membership in a tribal community. The stories represent an accessible trove of memories that all of us can relate to and feel something in common.

Listeners can feel the emotional energy in a story as they relate to the characters involved. The more believable the storyteller makes the story, the more the momentum rises and falls in rhythm, sometimes unexpectedly, as the storyteller takes the audience by surprise. As more energy is expended with each spoken word, the listener feels involved and pulled into the story. At the same time, the storyteller applies his or her craft to recreate the past memory into reality where past and present blend. At the story's end, the spiritual energy bonds the storyteller and listeners as they feel an inside the lodge togetherness. This shared experience is shared energy.

Some stories are classics. And as they are retold, the characters, beings, or places become well known. Spirits and Indians share the same space on earth. Spirits are among us and sometimes allow themselves to be revealed. They remind us there is another dimension that is metaphysical, and they compel the living to ponder our relationships and to contemplate how they are important to our roles in the community.

By learning about the oral tradition of a community, scholars can begin to understand the surrealism, the spiritual feeling of the past and present combined. This crossing the threshold into the reality of the Native community demonstrates why it functions as it does. Listening carefully is imperative to understand each story. In his work on oral poetry, Paul Zumthor wrote, "The listener listens, in the silence of the self, to this [storyteller's] voice that comes from elsewhere; lets the sound waves resonate; and, all judgment is suspended, . . . all in the space of a single listening."[29] The story's energy and power is received during this telling. The oral tradition is like a metaphorical key for opening a door to understanding a community and how its people think, how they conceptualize within their logic, and how they draw conclusions based on their prior knowledge. In this light, this is a cultural reorientation toward the reality in which the people and their community exist, and it reconfirms who they are. All things are connected, hvmakimata.

A part of passing through the door to the Other Side includes understanding the thought process of Indigenous people. So the Other Side of the spiritual and abstract is always nearby. For Native groups who are closer to their historic traditions, their sense of logic is related to a circular thinking process.[30] The circular process addresses realities as to their relationships within a system or base of knowledge in a different way than does the linear process of Western society. Basic elementary functions of perception, causality, and reality work in a circular fashion that does not differentiate time and historical events so that conscious knowledge becomes a part of subconscious knowledge. This is a part of the continuance that Black Elk, the Lakota holy man, described as he stood at the top of Black Elk Peak in the Black Hills. He lamented, "Then, I was standing on the highest mountain of them all, and round about beneath me was the whole hoop of the world. And while I stood there I saw more than I can tell and I understood more than I saw; for I was seeing in a sacred manner the shapes of all things in the spirit, and the shape of all shapes as they must live together like one being, . . . And I saw that it was holy."[31] In 2016, Harney Peak was renamed Black Elk Peak out of respect for the Lakota holy man.

This kind of circular thought and inclusive logic influences the thinking of Indian people and how they "see" and "understand" the world. For them, reality combines the conscious and subconscious in one mindset. For them, the mind combines the physical and the metaphysical to achieve a balance that influences Native logic or action and reaction to stimuli. The real world and the surreal world are one due to the metaphysical forces that have power over human life.

In addition to what has already been mentioned above about listening, hearing a story can be considered a gift of knowledge and information that increases the awareness of those listening. Listening is not a passive activity, but rather a participatory one that is mandatory if oral tradition is to live on. A good listener is a partner with the storyteller as a part of the symbiotic process and must be receptive to the story.

Memory, Trust, and Community

The ability to think about things is based on memory. There are three basic kinds of human memory: sensory, short-term, and long-term. Sensory is the shortest type of memory dealing with the five senses of sight, hearing, smell, taste, and touch. It lasts about a second, whereas short-term memory lasts from fifteen seconds to a minute and is sometimes referred to as working memory because it can only remember several items at a time. Short-term memory works with long-term memory as instances or experiences remembered in the short term can become long-term memories that last a lifetime.

Memory is an integral part of the oral historical process and the transmission of traditional knowledge.[32] At the same time, memory makes oral history vulnerable due to the limitation of recall and accuracy. This is the point that historians use to criticize oral history and American Indian oral history specifically. But mainstream academia is also fallible due to the limitations of memory. Historian David Thelen explained that a person's memory of past experiences is a combination of "basic identities of individuals, groups, and cultures, [and] the study of memory exists in different forms along a spectrum of experience, from the personal, individual, and private to the collective, cultural, and public." He stated, "At one end of the spectrum are psychological issues of individual motivation and perception in the creation of memories. At the other end are linguistic or anthropological issues of how cultures establish tradition and myths from the past to guide the conduct of their members in the present."[33]

In the Western world, the printed word carries much weight and supersedes a verbal agreement and a confirmed handshake. People would rather have a contract in writing than believe a person's verbal promise. In this view, the printed word is more reliable than the spoken word.[34] In Native societies, trust among people remains an important virtue and essential for positive communication. Thus, the sociocultural practice of trusting the spoken word enhanced Native oral traditions, as they were the primary means for people understanding each other.

For American Indians, oral tradition is imperative to uniting communities. A story unites people with a common understanding of kinship, giving us a common experience and creating a collective ethos. This combination explains how Native people think. Community is central to Indigenous societies and holds more importance than individual status. Community is the most important social unit among Native people.

Identity

The presence of community is important among American Indians for a sense of identity. Where the people of a community come from is relevant to the group identity of Indigenous people with a sense of place of origin. Stories provide this knowledge, which is passed down to each generation.[35] Group identity is more important than individual identity because in the past sheer survival depended upon protection by others who were kinsmen. A sense of togetherness is pertinent for security as iterated by Tecumseh in his 1811 speech.

Spoken words are a part of the process of sharing oral tradition, and events or experiences are essential for reference. When the words in stories cease being told, a serious disconnection is likely to occur that severs the current generation from the past generations. To be Indian is to be connected to one's people and to know who one's people are. Like a large puzzle, words are pieces of a creative lexicon and as people hear the words that construct stories, they begin to realize the full account of their people up to their present time. Being connected to our personal pasts provides perspective and connects us to our communities.

On June 12, 2013, Michelle Martin and I rented a silver Chevy Cruze to go to the Absentee Shawnee tribal office in central Oklahoma. While driving through Shawnee on Beard Street going south I pointed out where my family used to go for snow cones. They used to cost five cents each, which was a lot of money in those days, a luxury to a kid. I recalled my childhood and what my grandmother Rachel had said about Tecumseh. The Absentee Shawnee tribal

Keytha Fixico and Michelle Martin. Author's collection.

office is actually located in the town of Tecumseh. Upon arriving at the tribal office site, I had an opportunity to speak with Ester Louden, who is Potawatomi and Osage and works for the tribe. Although Ester is not Shawnee, she was well aware of the Shawnees' reverence for their great leader of the past. Tribal officials speak respectfully of Tecumseh, and he is a role model for Native leaders. To them and to me, Tecumseh embodied what it means to be Shawnee and this feeling manifests community identity.

Sacred Places and Sacred Words

Words become sacred when they carry special meaning and understanding of an important past, whether good or bad. In fact, such words do not have to be spoken because they connect with the inner feelings of a person—a moment of realization that some people might call an aha moment. I have walked the battleground along the Wabash River in western Indiana four or five times. And each time, it is as if *ecuna* (the earth) spoke to me, not in words, but in feelings of understanding. Listening to a bird chirp, hearing the wind in the leaves of the oak trees, and kneeling to pick up a small handful of dirt—all allowed my senses to hear and feel the sacred. This is when understanding supersedes language. For this is the same place where Tecumseh walked, rested, and contemplated what was to come. This is where he made his most difficult decisions in his life, and when you think about what he might have gone through, you can imagine the pull in many directions of his thoughts, with people and other forces trying to influence him.

For the Shawnees and other tribes in the Ohio region, the Tippecanoe area in Indiana was important to them with its tall trees, lush meadows, and wide flowing rivers. Stories involve place, usually homelands with deep human attachments. Homelands, especially in Native minds, can never be taken away as long as the Indian mind wants to recall such places. Identity is influenced and often grounded in place. Home is also place. Such place is embedded in the subconscious for all of us have a home place, and for those who say, "I don't have a home," think about where you live now.

On earth, ecuna, there are many important places, especially for the Indigenous. For Indian people, hundreds and thousands of sacred places, like the Serpent Mound, exist throughout Ohio and the rest of Indian Country. It is important for Native people to know and understand their relationships with these special sites. This way of knowing all of one's relationships is the natural-ness of traditional Indian life for all tribes.

Such experiences and places are important to Indians in life. Places become significant in personal ways, and there are places with power, such as sacred sites. Natural sacred places to Native people are special for their earth knowl-edge. This knowledge is understanding and learning about life, and it is an ongoing process that includes finding out why certain places, such as the Blue Lake of the Taos, Mackinac Island, Mount Rainier, Mount Taylor, and Bear Butte, are important.[36] Other sacred places include Uinta in Utah, Tucumcari in New Mexico, the Black Hills in South Dakota, and the Four Corners area of the Southwest, which held special meaning for the Hopi, the Diné (Navajo), and early Spanish peoples.[37]

Such places of power contain knowledge and the spoken word about these places becomes sacred. By understanding the spoken words' relationship within the natural environment, important information can be accessed. Per-sonal experiences of encountering sacred places are the means for receiving sacred knowledge. Listening to the wind create songs passing through pine trees in the Black Hills, observing the waves rushing to shore at Taos Blue Lake, or focusing on your feelings at other sacred places channels nature's knowledge from ecuna, the earth. We are connected to all things, hvmakimata.

Pictures Are Word Documents

Images from the past carved in rocks or etched on the surfaces of rocks are Indigenous documents that can reveal much information. A Navajo sandpaint-ing, Lakota winter count, and medicine wheel are pictures that possess the same importance as written documents. Such images are documentary evi-dence that relates to storytelling and what stories it holds. Learning how to read images left by ancient ones requires a visual logic for understanding how people are connected to the earth. This is one way and other methodologies need to be found to discover the relevance of the past. Each carved or painted image contains a story of how a person experiences something relevant as he or she made record of the experience. This process is a cyclic continuum that the old ones left behind for us in rock art, petroglyphs, and on hide paintings and story robes or in wampum belts. Sequoyah's clever invention of the Chero-kee syllabary of eighty-six characters emulated the writing of white Americans.

Other sources of Indigenous writing occur in the form of images of Navajo sandpaintings, designs on Ojibwe baskets or Pueblo pottery. All of these images come from the memories of individuals who conveyed something relevant to them that they wished to share with others in the future. Indigenous-made objects are empowered by the energy from a dream, vision, or experience that the object creator wanted to share with family members, other relatives, or simply with other people who would understand the story left behind.

Native people left image documents behind for us to decipher. Whether in the form of winter counts, designs on wampum belts, carvings on a wooded staff, or figures on a basket, these created documents left knowledge behind about the supernatural phenomena, dreams, visions, or positive or negative accounts.[38]

As the oral tradition is practiced, over time the stories add to the Indian point of view. Actually, the stories become a sociocultural history about the community in general, conveying values, ideas, beliefs, and providing much insight about the Native people. As a result, cultural information or ethnographic data can be a product of the oral tradition and can be interpreted and read through the documentary evidence left by that tradition.

Men and Women Using Words

Indian men and women tell stories in their own gendered styles. Generally, men are more direct in staying with the plot of the stories. Typically, women are also as concerned with the tone of the words as they are used in telling the story. Details are stressed, whereas men might overlook them to get to the gist of the account. Women's stories are more family oriented. Female storytellers are more apt to insert little stories that help to clarify the original story.[39] Men's stories are less complex and shorter in storytelling time, but there are always exceptions.

Among the Mvskoke Creeks and Seminoles in Oklahoma, women experienced a different reality than their men.[40] Female perception and male perception are not the same, even among different tribes. Here is what I mean. When I was baby, my mother was holding me as my dad drove us home late one night from a stomp dance. While rounding a curve on a gravel road outside of Shawnee, the car's headlights shone on a field of tall grass. My mother (Shawnee and Sac and Fox) told my dad (Mvskoke Creek and Seminole), "Look over there. Do you see that?" My father looked just at the same moment. He saw a large animal like a dog. My mother saw something like a white bedsheet floating up from the grass.

Since few historical documents accurately convey how Native women view things, trying to research their perspectives is even more challenging but is necessary to fully understand the importance of oral tradition among Native people. Chickasaw scholar Amanda Cobb has highlighted the significance of historical consciousness and continuance through stories about her grandmother. She noted, "There is a need to touch . . . an attempt to know my grandma better, to reach through time, to listen to and touch the past."[41]

Often men tell stories when they are doing something, while working, hunting, or perhaps even on the eve of a battle. The stories bond them, making them feel as a collective, as one force. At the same time stories are told to relieve tension and stress, especially before going into battle. Stories are also told about metaphysical beings or spirits or visions that invite divine support. Stories are often related to each other in the context of oral tradition, as the storyteller moves from one account to another. The shared experience between storyteller and audience is primarily based on the storyteller's individual perspective interacting with the body of oral traditions.

Ethos and Reality

The words chosen in telling stories convey this reality of spiritual beings interacting regularly with people. Nature and its phenomena of metaphysics interact with people in a nonconcrete fashion that Western society usually dismisses. This metaphysical and physical combined reality is natural to traditional Indians. It shapes their lives and the realm in which their community functions. In the equation of Indian-white relations, the "other side" of the equation is the theoretical right side of Indian-white, or the white side. The Other Side is the Other Side of Life in a spiritual dimension. Indian plus white equals a shared history, but the Indian side means a context of Native worldviews.

Conceptually, oral tradition has been a conduit for connecting families, groups, communities, and tribes. The oral tradition of Native groups in the multiple forms of oratory, myths, legends, songs, parables, and prophecy helps to present the reality of the Indigenous community. Yet oral history is the non-Indian interpretation and understanding of Native oral tradition. Oral historians (not oral history itself) often practice a non-Indian interpretation and understanding of Native oral tradition or their study of oral history often includes a non-Indian interpretation and understanding of Native oral tradition.

The oral tradition of story remains one of the essential elements bonding the various entities of Indian communities. Due to the lack of a written language and the power of the spoken word, the oral tradition historically was the essential means for communication. Although current oral tradition seems unimportant to most people, what is said today in the form of the story will become increasingly relevant as the mainstream knowledge of Indigenous cultures increases.

Other events such as Indian-Indian encounters have also been passed along to succeeding generations in what might be called the Medicine Way.[42] In the Medicine Way, all things, human and nonhuman, are connected with a mutual respect for each other, and understanding these relationships is important. But this is not always easy. In a historic confrontation between the Lakotas and the Crows in the nineteenth century, Thomas Leforge, a white Crow Indian, noted the dire situation for the Crow warriors who were fewer in number that day against their archenemy. He explained, "Our Crow warriors were doing their medicine, each according to his own way of imitating the vocal noises and the actions of his own special animal-friend which he believed protected him in time of danger. There was a tumultuous mingling of whoofing [*sic*] like a bear, talking like a magpie, howling like a wolf, screaming like a curlew, hooting like an owl, mimicking the sounds and movements of a crane, a badger, an eagle, and elk, of many varieties of lower animal life. I was wearing dangling from my long black hair my red plume that had been given to me by a medicineman. Yes, I believed in it as a helpful charm."[43] That day in battle was lucky for the Crows. After some sparring between the Lakotas and Crows riding the line in front of the enemy and drawing their fire of arrows and bullets, the Lakotas decided to retreat. The Crows had fewer warriors, but they upheld their pride that day. This oral history account told in the Crow oral tradition is a prime example of the relevance of understanding the inside the lodge context of being Crow. Simultaneously, the same account could be told from a Lakota point of view as it was remembered and recalled in a story, which would differ from the Crow story.

Wisdom represented power stored, to be used when needed and when it would be most effective. In the same context of Tecumseh challenging the Chickasaws and Choctaws, Leforge described the Crows and Lakotas challenging each other. A part of the decision of cultural logic was to challenge the pride of the other person(s). The idea of cultural logic being different among tribal communities, however, allows both perspectives to manifest in the Medicine Way of the ethos and reality of Indigenous people.

The use of oral traditions has been a means for tribal prophets to report their visions and messages from the Other Side, the afterworld. Oral history has been the Indian counterpart to the "white man's" written history of Indian-white relations. The practice of oral tradition accounts for the same historical events as written documents, and although the memories of individuals are depended on, the events are relived. This spiritual quality gives oral history greater dimension than written history. But one can also argue for a distinction between history written down in the first person (memoirs, letters, diaries) and historical documents and records. First-person written historical documents share something in common with oral history in that the individual writing is reliving and recreating experiences for the reader, whereas third-person historical documents and records do not have that relived dimension. Memories of past events include the emotions and intensity exhibited during treaty making, battles, and the telling of stories that describe vividly Native leaders and their peoples. Elders shared their knowledge via the oral tradition, passing down historical accounts of the people from one generation to the next. Whether myth, legend, tale, or song, oral tradition was a means of sharing knowledge, and it served several purposes. Oral accounts contained parables and lessons, and the young people learned from them; morals of stories told by their elders enlightened them as to virtues, values, and the importance of respecting taboos. Stories and tales also served in other ways. Although they were entertaining, frightening stories were used to discipline the young when they misbehaved. At the philosophical level, the oral tradition explained the origins of the people and the creation of the universe, and it was a vehicle for prophesying the future.[44]

Words convey certain places as important in Native cultures. Word usage has multiple purposes for learning and sharing traditional knowledge. The words of a story possess power and lives of their own; they transcend time as an experience comes alive again in the minds and ears of listeners when the storyteller evokes the emotions of those hearing the account. Stories permeate the mind and soul. Story is the heart of the Indian oral tradition, and Indians enjoy a good story. Yet it is much more than hearing a fine entertaining account. The story has power and energy, and it brings the past to the present. Oral tradition is not oral history; rather it is the process of oral expression via speech, oratory, argument, and story. Oral tradition weaves stories together to construct the historical record of tribal communities. Story is much more than oral history. For Indians, stories live and live on. Oral tradition weaves stories together to construct the historical tapestry of tribal communities. Story can be part of oral history, but it is also more than oral history. For Indians, stories live on, and they will live longer than all of us. This is the way it was meant to be, hvmakimata.

TWO

Creation Myths of the Earth and People

Long ago, before there was light, the Mvskoke Creek people lived underground where it was dark and they were cold. Feeling along the damp walls, the people realized they were moving upwards. Slowly they emerged from the earth and a misty fog blinded them. Unable to see and stricken with fear, the people and even strange beings called animals cried out until the wind blew away the fog so that they could see. In all four cardinal directions, the forces of fire confronted the people, and they had to make a decision. From the south, a yellow fire faced the people, a black fire burned in the west, a white fire was aflame in the east, but the people chose the red fire from the north.[1] The northern fire warmed the people, lighted the world, and enabled the plants to grow; the Mvskokes learned to respect all the elements of life. They celebrated the harvest of the green corn in ceremonies. Should the people fail in their respect for nature and forget the Green Corn Dance ceremonies, the people would disappear from the earth, and all would fall beneath the waters of the ocean. People respected the animals. The Mvskokes named groups of people after animals and the wind, calling them clans. The savior wind became the highest recognized clan.[2] The Mvskokes stressed the importance of community and generations practicing ceremonies reinforced the importance of the clan system. As this became ritualized, the Mvskokes developed ceremonial laws to maximize and confirm the success of the community's ceremonies, and thus confirm that the Mvskoke way of life was the right one.[3]

Everyone is of the earth, which the Mvskoke people call ecuna. Made of dust and other essential elements in a finite space in different forms of energy, all people are born to live. All of us have this heritage in common. Yet Indigenous peoples have not forgotten this fundamental principle, which is steeped in their traditional cultures and oral traditions. Native peoples perpetuate this knowledge. For Indians, knowing the origin of one's people is imperative for remaining connected to one's ancestors. Being Indian means knowing one's people. Mine are Shawnees, Sac and Fox, Mvskoke Creeks, and Seminoles.

Being connected to one's people means coming to the *totkv* (fire) to take one's place, especially around the ceremonial fire, *totkv etkv,* which is central to the community. The totkv etkv is the focal point of the camp or *tvlofv* (town) in the Mvskoke Creek–Seminole tradition. My community is a Seminole ground called Gar Creek in Seminole County in Oklahoma. I remember as a young boy, our family camped near my grandfather and grandmother's camp on the west side of the fire, but at a distance because dances would be held around totkv etkv. The Creeks used the term "grandfather" to pray to the totkv etkv, and continue to address it that way today. It has always been done this way going back to the days when the Seminoles lived in northern and central Florida in the late 1700s before it became a state. And the Creeks were actually known as Mvskokes, "people living in swamp areas," which included streams and creeks. European traders arriving in the area of Georgia and Alabama called my ancestors "the people who live by the creeks," or "Creek People." Later we began to call ourselves Mvskoke Creeks, or just Creeks or Mvskokes. But in the late 1700s, when we were still called "Creek People," some of our people migrated and moved their fires to northern and central Florida, and formed an offshoot group called the Seminoles.

The story of how we received totkv is told in the tale of the trickster, Rabbit, who swam across the great water to the east and brought it to our people. The Mvskokes were now warm and could see, so they held a dance around the totkv because they were happy and wanted to celebrate this new gift. They shared the new gift with all the families. Rabbit was a hero and he danced too. He danced too close to totkv and his head caught on totkv, and he ran to the water and began to swim to put totkv out. He returned and so the Mvskokes received the totkv from the East because of Rabbit.[4] Hvmakimata.

Being connected to one's people is knowing totkv, which also symbolizes the powerful force of life. The Mvskokes first became connected to totkv long ago, after having come from somewhere beneath the unknown, perhaps from a cave or crevice in the earth that would have been located somewhere near present-day Macon, Georgia. If you consider that is the place of origin, it would have been at or very near the elaborate Ocmulgee complex of mounds. Ocmulgee was the original central town center and all representatives from other towns came to meet there at least once a year. They celebrated the harvest of corn in the Green Corn Ceremony that honored fire, water, wind, and earth. This grand gathering of Mvskokes announced the cycle of a new year of summer, fall, winter, and spring.

The oral tradition of telling stories is the process for passing along pertinent knowledge from one generation to the next. Stories about human creations are the most important of all accounts told in the story form. While origin stories exist about all Indian groups, the origin accounts of the Mvskoke Creeks, Sauks and Foxes, and Shawnees are those of my ancestors. The creation accounts of these groups represent various types of origin stories from different Indigenous cultures. Whether coming from under ecuna or from the sky (or *Speh min kee*, meaning "up" in the Shawnee language), it is not most critically important that we believe these accounts, but that such accounts connect us to a known understanding of the past since the door of believing or not believing in them is already open. People do not just come into existence from nowhere, and our origin stories help orient us to who we are. There are believers and nonbelievers, and Mvskoke believers believe in the old ways, hvmakimata.

In analyzing creation stories, one notices that migrations are almost always involved. Such movements may take the form of emergence from beneath the ground or the earth, emergence from the sky, or movement from one place to another. Nonhuman entities are often involved, such as a Supreme Being of many names. Indians have humanized the Creator in their origin stories so that communication is possible. In these accounts, the Creator speaks to people when it wishes, but people cannot always speak to it. In addition, one single Creator does not always reign, but dual Creators like Sun God and Water God in the Navajo Rainbow Bridge myth,[5] or those of lesser status also sometimes have creative powers. Sometimes animals also are involved, such as culture heroes, who possess the ability to speak to humans and engage in conversation with the Creator. Finally, the purpose of creation is a vital part of these stories, and sometimes creation myths also contain valuable insight into the correct way of life by providing a code of conduct for people to follow.[6] The Mvskoke Way is the *Heles* Way (Medicine Way).

The most significant aspect of origin myths is "place." All origin accounts focus on a geographic or metamorphic place from which people emerged or to which they arrived. The geographic place is realistic, consisting of rivers, valleys, and perhaps mountains. Sometime long ago, the people forgot the names of such places, as in the Mvskoke Creek's account. Yet "the sense of place, is a phrase that privileges the process of human identification *with* place that informs American Indian cultures" and links them to their point of origin.[7] Such places continue to be acknowledged, even by people of different cultures and languages. For example, the Ocmulgee Mounds have become a national monument and recognized by the State of Georgia, whose government workers have learned about the significance of the mound complex to the Mvskokes. The same comparison can be said about the Kiowas and Devil's Tower, the Lakotas and Black Hills, the Taos Pueblo and Blue Lake, the Yakamas and Mount Adams, and so on.

In each place rests power. For Native groups, their genesis is a place of empowerment. Spiritual power connects all community members to the same point of emergence. Yet this link differs from physical power. Spiritual power is pertinent to the people from the area of their origin place for it bonds them together in a shared experience, thus sustaining their relationships and identities.

Symbolism of place is essential to oral tradition; it fulfills the human need for a reference point and requires celebration on a regular basis. We need to know where we come from. All people need to have an attachment to a site, like a birthplace or where they grew up, because this point of reference helps to form their identities. I have always been struck by the story that Peter Mac-Donald, former tribal chairman of the Navajo Nation, told when he spoke at the University of Oklahoma during the 1970s. I was a student there when he talked about enrolling at OU to become an electrical engineer. He spoke about his homeland in Arizona and said that he was born near Teec Nos Pos, the mountainous summer home of his family, in 1928. His mother went into labor and an aunt assisted her. The aunt placed a goatskin on Mother Earth, and Peter MacDonald was born on the ground, not in a bed at home, not in a hospital.[8] This way of coming into the world shaped the way he thought and how he was connected with the earth.

As people travel and leave home, the symbol of their place of origin remains strong in their minds and hearts. It becomes an instinctive memory, a part of their intuitive logic of how to relate to others. In this way, homeland is the heartland of the people and evokes a powerful memory. Thus, information about one's homeplaces tells much about the person and their natural environment. Their values, views, and virtues derive from their birthplace and the site of their community's creation.

These places are all around us and become a part of our cultures, rendering meaning to people. For example, in the Seminole-Mvskoke tradition each of the four elements essential for life—fire, water, wind, and earth—is incorporated into Native oral traditions. Furthermore, the elements become symbolized in religious imagery and in designs for clothing and art, thereby reflecting the things most pertinent to Native people. Important in tribal cultures, such symbols act as codes connecting people to the past and where they come from. Certain colors chosen by a people also represent their identity and how they wish to present themselves to other communities. Symbolism is all throughout Native existence. Among the Mvskoke Creeks, for example, the mist metaphorically represents children at birth opening their eyes for the first time. And in all origin accounts, the most powerful symbol represents the Creator.

A Supreme Being exists among almost all Indian groups. All Indian nations have their own words for the Supreme Creator. The Apaches call the Creator "Ussen." The Ojibwes (Chippewas) of the Great Lakes call the Supreme Being "Gitchi Manitou." "The Great Mystery," or Creator, is known as "First Maker" or "Person Above" to the Crows of Montana. "He-ja-va-ne-au-thau" is "The Unknown One on High" to the Northern Arapahos. "Dam app pit see" is "Our Dear Father" to the Shoshones. "Nuakolahe," or "One Who Made the Earth," is the name for the Creator among the Kiowa Apaches of western Oklahoma.[9] Indian people know the same Supreme Being; most full-bloods and traditionalists recognize that the white man's name for God is the same Creator for all people. Among many Indian groups, other deities—good ones and evil ones— exist alongside the Supreme Being. They were and are a part of the metaphysical world. At the same time, the metaphysical world is a part of the physical world, and the Creator is seemingly everywhere. Each tribe has its metaphysical understanding of the roles of the Creator and other deities. Among the Mvskokes, the deities are wind, also known as the Master of Breath for all who live; fire, who controls light and warmth; water, who provides the source for life; and earth, who houses the natural environment.

The culture hero is similar to the Supreme Being in that both are fundamental elements of Native oral traditions. The culture hero is represented in stories told in the oral tradition. Even today, individuals struggle according to nature's plan of evolution and they need a hero to serve as a role model. Because of such a need, the culture hero often looks like or performs the actions of a human. The culture hero is a figure in Native oral tradition that can change the world. In this way, Native people have personalized nonhuman entities such as animals, plants, trees, mountains, and rivers. They believe that, like the living, nonhuman entities have a spiritual life. For example, the Cherokees call a river "the long man." In this spiritual realm, Native people talk to the entities and often give them human names. They talk to them as if they were people, asking them to share their knowledge, for a blessing, perhaps, or to give them refuge if they are traveling. While this may seem abnormal to the mainstream of society, many people who have pets talk to their cats, dogs, and horses. While language is important, understanding is more important because two people speaking different languages can understand each other by using hand and facial gestures.

After an extended time with animals, people are convinced that they can communicate with their animals and believe that their pets can understand them. "Our fellow creatures can tell us the most beautiful stories," said Konrad Lorenz, Nobel Prize winner for medicine.[10] Most culture heroes are animals who act like humans most of the time. If people can train their minds, they can begin to interpret what their animals are trying to communicate to them. I believe this is true; it is not so much a language, but an understanding occurs between people and animals. And a horse whisperer or someone who trains dogs would likely agree. Lori Alvord, the first Navajo woman surgeon, described her dad who had a special talent for talking to animals. She described the dogs on the Navajo reservation where they lived. The dogs were always attracted to her father—"rez dogs, chocolate and black-splotched or the color of coyote and mesa and riverbed mud." Crows were attracted to him and would land on a fencepost near him. She said, "Sometimes I'd turn a corner and find my father standing deep in a philosophical discussion with a crow."[11] Nor is it so strange to think about a kind of communication between humans and elements of nature or a kind of personification of those elements. When we are drawn to a particular place or have a sentimental attachment to a certain feature of landscape, we, in a sense, have a communication with nature. Something about that place or mountain or river speaks to us and we develop a relationship with it. The best example is our home place, where we come from and with which we develop a deep attachment, at least most of us do. It is interesting that we do not explore this relationship and what home really means to us. And this relationship is tucked deep into our subconscious, for home place is a part of our core identity. I come from a state that has had a difficult history involving American Indians. Oklahoma has a long history of oil, football, and Indians, but I feel a resilient pride because this is where I am from.

Climate

The elemental powers of the world interact with the natural environment that produces climate, and this interaction is recorded in oral tradition. This kind of knowledge through stories is Indigenous knowledge, and people have learned to respect this system of relationships. The climate of the world is a complex system of different spheres influencing the weather and cultural development, and thus, how we think. This is certainly the case with Indians and even today; climate is underestimated as a part of life in general, especially for the American mainstream. But weather affects human attitudes and feelings, thus influencing human relations and communities. It is important that we know this. As a child growing up in the Seminole-Mvskoke tradition, an old saying I used to hear concerned common knowledge for one's own safety and well-being. This saying is "Hesaketvmese, vnvtaksetv," which means "Master of breath, look up at the sky," hvmakimata. The Master of Breath controls breath for all living beings but does not produce breath. Many years ago in Oklahoma, most roads were not paved or even graveled. As one traveled, especially the back roads or less traveled roads, it was wise to look in the direction you were going. You watched the sun and clouds for a possible change in weather that might mean taking cover from a rainstorm, hail, sleet, or even a tornado. Water, known as *eauwa*, is one of the central powers that governed all life. The human body needs eauwa and about 70 percent of our bodies consists of water. In the form of rain, water makes things grow, such as corn, which is so important for life among the Mvskokes and Seminoles.

Just as climate affects the natural environment and human relations, it also shapes the oral traditions that are an expression of a community's ethos. Undoubtedly, the following creation stories involved the climate that instrumentally shaped the natural environment for each Native group. Climatic systems involve the interaction of the atmosphere, hydrosphere (oceans, lakes, and rivers) and biosphere (the earth's living resources). These large systems create the natural world, producing the natural environment for humans and nonhumans. In addition, the cryosphere (particularly sea ice and polar ice caps) and lithosphere (the earth's crust and upper mantel) interact with the atmosphere, hydrosphere, and biosphere. A continuous series of interactions defines the climate for various sectors of the world.[12] These systems, in addition to the natural environment, establish the foundation for human life and cultural development everywhere, and this fact does not go unnoticed in Indian Country.

As Native peoples made adjustments to their natural environment and climate, their cultures developed accordingly. Climate produced the four seasons, causing Native people to "see" things in cycles as they observed plants grow and animals migrate during different times of the year. As a result, Native people depended upon the migration patterns to know what time of the year it was and what circumstances to expect. The consistency of the migration patterns of animals and cycles of plant growth became common knowledge to Native people. As a child of six or seven years old, when I was visiting my grandparents, a storm might be on the horizon. I remember my grandfather would look up at the sky and study the clouds, watching for the movement of an approaching storm. He would put his arm around my shoulder, and say, "*Cepvne* (little boy), we better get to the house." I would go, but always looked back because he would be standing there speaking Mvskoke to Hesaketvmese, "the Master of Breath." My grandpa was a heles hayv (medicine maker) and although I could not hear him, I suspect that he was asking for us to be safe from the approaching storm. Our way was holding a sharp object like a knife (even a sharp stone, if you did not have a knife) toward a threatening storm like a tornado, and praying to The Master of Breath to divide the wind to go around the people and allow them to be safe. In Oklahoma, storms can easily occur because of the warm and cold air masses coming together that changes the weather. In the panhandle of Oklahoma, the average rainfall is seventeen inches, and in the southeast, fifty-six inches on an annual basis. In the western part of the state, thunderstorms occur forty-five days out of the year and fifty-five days in the eastern part, with fifty-three tornadoes occurring across the state every year.[13]

The evolutionary actions of nonhumans might be called plant knowledge or animal knowledge. Plants know when to grow in the spring, trees lose their leaves in the fall, and the most common time of blooming is late spring or early summer. In North America alone, an estimated twenty thousand species of flora are known to currently exist, and scientists continue to collect data on even more species.[14]

Through instinct, animals know when to migrate. Birds fly south, bears prepare to hibernate, squirrels store acorns, and other animals act in concert with the approaching of winter. As the cold leaves in the seasonal cycle, animals mate and the young are born mostly in the spring months. In North America alone, there are 400 species of mammals; 340 reptile species north of Mexico; 90,000 insect species north of Mexico; 230 amphibian species in the United States; over 700 species of birds in the United States and Canada; and with the 20,000 species of flora there are roughly 112,000 known species total.[15]

Climate influences the seasons with the rotation of the earth, and Indians have always known this and adjusted to the seasons. In some regions, winter was the harshest season of all. Winter evenings became a good time to tell stories inside the lodge. Plains Indians, particularly the Lakotas, created winter counts to record one significant event per year. Each band had an official winter counter who made drawings of key events and experiences that served as reference points of knowledge. In this record keeping, the winter weather often dictated the recording of human experiences, like the recording of blizzards when people went hungry. In Seminole-Mvskoke philosophy, the approach to solving problems is to do something to prevent the problem from happening. For example, although we can only control what we can, this philosophy mandates that you do not put yourself in harm's way. Problem prevention calls for examining and being proactive to prohibit bad things from happening.

Should one have to deal with a problem, then one relies on his or her wisdom, experiences, resources, and decision-making skills. Problems that are greater than one's abilities to solve are presented to individuals with the power to provide a solution.

Native people, as a result, have always understood the importance of human relationships and the various roles of individuals involved in the accounts that people tell. Climate governs life, including the seasons, and stories about those who have lived, and even when such stories are to be told. Some stories are told during the winter, and some stories are meant to be told at night. In cold regions, the majority of oral tradition is influenced by the climate. Stories about birth, origin, and the young are commonly told in the spring. Summer is the time for stories about the harvest of corn among the Mvskokes and Seminoles.

Mother and Grandmother

Native people believe in a circular philosophy that is based on the changing seasons of the year, the cycle of day and night, migration of animals, growth patterns of plants, and birth and death. Rotations and cycles are told in the oral tradition to illustrate how the earth and the universe work together. Stories convey this earth knowledge to Native youth, as they will one day pass this information to their children when they are adults. As children, they ask questions and stories hold the answers. Why is there day and night? In the Medicine Way, day and night is a universal dichotomy, natural opposites, where the spiritual balance hangs in between. In this Indigenous thinking, the same holds true for light and dark, male and female, sadness and happiness, good and evil, and so forth.

The traditional Indian woman represented the heart of her people. Her role was often mixed with the symbolism of the earth in the philosophies of many tribes. In the oral tradition of many tribes, the earth is a mother nourishing her human children and animal children alike. Native writer Jane Katz noted, "Most Indian societies acknowledged woman's vital role in the creative process. In tribal ceremonies and lore she was portrayed as the giver of life."[16] In this light, earth and the mother are the same.

The Native woman retains this special status although much has changed in modern times. Due to the flexibility of Indigenous cultures to adapt to new circumstances, the Native woman remains the central figure in communities. Simultaneously, the traditional role is changed by surrounding influences from outside of the Native community. Thus, the Native woman has learned to adjust to both internal changes, such as relationships within the family when a husband is lost and a son or daughter. She is flexible in meeting these changes in her immediate family and external changes. These adjustments are a part of her cumulative experiences that become wisdom, enabling an even greater role for her as a grandmother.

The grandmother is the matriarch of a family or more than one family. With many years of experience and collected wisdom, the grandmother is admired and respected by her family and friends. To be called "grandmother" is an earned position based on respect from younger women and relatives in the community. Possessing years of experience, the Native woman elder commands respect, especially within communities, although she also may be

Wilma Mankiller, Principal Chief of the Cherokees. Courtesy Oklahoma Historical Society.

heavily criticized for her personality and actions. A great-grandmother possesses even more respect than a grandmother.

My grandmother Lena Spencer Fixico was full-blood Mvskoke Creek. She was a matriarch and the clan elder as I remember growing up and spending a lot of time at Gar Creek, the last practicing Seminole stomp ground in Oklahoma. As a child playing and watching the elders, I learned that my grandmother reigned over the women in her camp. Her many years of wisdom and experience were recognized throughout the Gar Creek ground and she was very mindful of her children and grandchildren. At the same time, if we were causing mischief, she scolded us, saying *"Ae lv mecekot!"* Don't do that!

I revered my grandmother. Often she would take me and one or more of my cousins with her into the woods to look for herbs. She knew where to look for red root, which was used in the purification ceremony of the Green Corn Celebration. Most of the time, she would carry a paper sack as we looked for herbs and other healing plants. She would point out the different plants, including poison ivy and poison oak, and warned us to stay away from them. My grandmother always wore a long cotton dress down to her ankles and most of the time a long apron with what seemed to me a dozen or so safety pins at the top right corner of her apron. If she did not have a sack, she would pull up her apron by the bottom corners to make a temporary carrier for the herbs that we collected. She seemed to be connected to ecuna and knew its ways. In fact, my grandmother had such earth knowledge that she seemed to be a part of the earth, and I am a part of her like her children and my cousin relatives. On February 22, 1989, my grandmother returned to ecuna.

Via this assumption of responsibility, the grandmother became a social magnet for relatives to rally around when necessary. She symbolizes strength and safety for all around her, and they look to her for security and protection. She is protector, discipliner, and teacher.

Traditionally, a grandmother has a collective wisdom of political and medicinal experiences that helps to protect her relatives. As head of the extended family, the grandmother wields an impressive amount of influence and political power. People listen to her, and the more articulate she is, the greater her status. Respect for elders is a part of traditional Indian life, and listening to grandmothers presents an opportunity to gain wisdom and knowledge.[17]

In addition to her respected status, the grandmother draws upon her wisdom to care for sick and suffering members in the extended family. Her many years of experience include a storehouse of cures and means for improving the health of those who become ill. Armed with a collective knowledge of more than 170 known medicinal herbs and plants on this continent, the grandmother draws upon her knowledge of ecuna to enable her to be a provider of good health and to maintain the well-being of her loved ones in the community.[18] Naturally, granddaughters and daughters defer to their grandmother's expertise. In time, their turns will come when they will become grandmothers and perhaps even take on an extra role as the grandmother to children outside of the family. The grandmother is aged, wise, witty, sometimes mean, and has much knowledge, like the earth. The creative power of grandmother, like that of the earth, is passed on to her daughters so that earth-knowledge stories are a part of the transition of the Native woman to becoming a grandmother and even more like the earth.

My grandmother was very watchful and reminded me when I was a child about being careful where I stepped. Her cautious nature made her watch not just for *chittos* (snakes) but also for certain wild plants and herbs that we should not step on. It was like walking into a store where you should not touch certain things, or you would pay the price: playing around poison ivy or poison oak, getting into goat heads if you were barefoot, and touching certain other plants would cause a rash. Even so, as a boy, playing barefooted was more fun and it was allowed, but it also saved wear and tear on our shoes so that they would last longer.

Power of Creation

Grandmothers are symbols in a way, elders to be respected. Grandmothers have multiple meanings, and their knowledge, wisdom, and experiences are like the earth itself. Grandmothers know about life—how it comes to be and how it ends and begins again, like in the Circle of Life. This is the continuum of birth, child, adult, elder, and it starts all over again.

The immense power of creation cannot be underestimated. The source of this power derives from the Other Side of Life. It is most important to understand that this source is beyond human potential. And there is more than one power at work. At the same time, each tribe has its own interpretation and understanding of the power of creation and all things that are involved. At this point, it is best to be more specific.

The Creator is everywhere. In reference to the Creator or Mystery of Mysteries, some Native peoples have visualized the Great Spirit in human form. In this way, they established a personal meaning of the Creator in order to better understand this Great Power. They prayed to a Great Being or chanted a song. Simultaneously, they knew the Creator is not always human but can appear in human or spiritual form. The Creator is in everything and it is everything, according to the Mvskoke Creek. Their term for "everything" in this sense of "totality" is *Ibofanga*, meaning "all that is." In this thinking, the Creator is always everywhere in a nebulous existence that permeates everything.

Mvskoke Creation

Originally from the Southeast, the Mvskoke Creeks tell a story of creation of the people coming or emerging from ecuna—earth. The Creeks are speakers of the Mvskoke linguistic family, as are the Choctaws, Chickasaws, and Seminoles. Their history, as previously mentioned, dates back to early historic times and places their point of origin near the Ocmulgee Mounds near present-day Macon, Georgia. The Creeks lived in towns, each with its own leader. The Creeks lived along the Chattahoochee River and were divided into an upper and lower division. Common political interests enabled them to meet on a regular basis or at least once a year during the summer at the harvest time of the green corn.[19]

According to their origin story, the Mvskoke Creeks were within the earth or underground in the dark and cold. They wandered blindly, hearing only their own voices. They were lost and confused because they had no light, for it had not yet been created. They were cold because the sacred fire had not yet been given to them. Cold and afraid, the Mvskoke people huddled together for warmth and to console each other as the darkness imprisoned them under the earth. At some particular point, without knowledge of time or even the conception of time, the opportunity for creation occurred. The Mvskokes realized an opening and felt a draft of air that compelled them to follow its source. They tried to find their way from the darkness toward the air that had established a presence. They followed in that direction, hoping to see. Without light, the gift of sight had not yet been given to them. As they emerged from a cave or hole in the ground, they stepped into a new darkness that they could sense, but they still could not see, although they could feel ecuna, the earth. Because they could not see, as they emerged they asked their leaders what was happening, but the leaders did not know. First, a veil of mist kept them blind; then, *hodalee,* the wind, came and swept the mist away so that the first people could see. They were like newborn babies opening their eyes for the first time. The first Mvskoke people became known as the Wind Clan, and as the first ones to see certain animals and plants, they took the animals' and plants' names for the powers and strengths of the animals: the Bear Clan, Tiger Clan, Alligator Clan, Deer Clan, and so forth. The Mvskoke learned that they, like all living things that breathed the air called hodalee, were a part of ecuna. And that a Great Power called Hesaketvmese breathed hodalee into all that lived. Hesaketvmese was the "Master of Breath."[20] This was told earlier, but it is important to repeat so that it will not be forgotten. This is a Mvskoke way of learning by hearing important knowledge again and again and observing things that occur in cycles and patterns.

The animal world intersected with Mvskoke Creek life, becoming an important part of it. Person and clan correspond to one's identity. In this way, the

Mvskokes became close to nature, shaping their culture according to the earth's systematic cycles and patterns. Plants were equally important and respected by the Mvskoke for they were and are a part of ecuna. In the eyes of the Mvskokes, all things are related and connected to the earth. All is connected. We, meaning all people, should not forget this so that we can take care of the earth. Hvmakimata.

Shawnee

Among the Shawnees, there are two Supreme Beings or supernatural beings. One is the Supreme Being often referred to as the Great Spirit. His name is Muyaataalemeelarkwau, who is also known as Mutetelemilakwau, or the "Finisher."[21] The other supernatural being is a female deity who is responsible for the second creation, which included people.[22] They are like helpers who assist the Creator or the Supreme Being. They appear in tandem as dual great powers that balance each other, meaning they are equal to each other in the eyes of the Shawnees.

The female Supreme Being among the Shawnee people is one whom they call Grandmother. The Grandmother's common name is Kokomthena. An early traveler, C. C. Trowbridge, mentioned her as the Shawnee female deity by the name of Waupoathee. Trowbridge described Waupoathee as "this old woman [who] seems also to have charge of the affairs of Indians, and is allowed to be nearer the residence of the Great Spirit than her grand child, whose location is immediately above the Indians and so near as to enable them to distinguish them & supply their wants."[23] The Old Woman Waupoathee was the Second Supreme Being and had considerable status, acting as the liaison for the Shawnees to the metaphysical world.

James Clark, an Absentee Shawnee of the Kishpokotha division, gave the following rendering of our people's origin. The Shawnees say that in the beginning the Great Spirit existed in the form of wind and was invisible. He appeared sometimes in the shape of man and lived above the sun. At this time, there was only space, no earth and no water. The Great Spirit commanded that there would be a woman and as soon as he spoke these words there appeared a being shaped like a woman. To this woman, the Great Spirit gave the responsibility of creating the earth, light in the form of the sun, water, people, and the animals. She became known as Grandmother and lived on earth, as did the Devil and her grandson and the great giants. The woman is the one the people saw and believed in. The first people lived a long time and died four times in their lives. Afterward, the Grandmother Creator made the rules for all people to follow.[24]

The Shawnees' Kokomthena is a female deity who acts as a teacher, mentor, and caregiver to the people. She is responsible for everything and sometimes acts as a trickster. The Shawnees have humanized her in the oral tradition so that they can better understand and learn from her actions and relate to them as deeds that they should remember. In this way, Kokomthena guides the Shawnees and challenges them to learn to live. They learn from their mistakes, yet she comes to their aid when she believes it is necessary. Stories among the Shawnee people of tragedy and triumph indicate the resilience of the Indians. The stories are told so that the oral tradition does not let the Shawnees forget their Creator and lessons in life.

Unfortunately my Shawnee grandmother, Rachel Dirt Wakolee, did not tell this creation story to me. She believed in the Medicine Way as a traditionalist, but at the same time she was also very modern. Grandmother Wakolee loved shiny new cars that she could afford to make payments on since she worked for the Indian Health Service in Lawton, Oklahoma. Interestingly, because she married my Sac and Fox grandfather, Glade Wakolee, she learned many of the ways of his people and passed them to my mother, who passed them to her children.

Sac and Fox Creation

The Sac and Fox were originally two different peoples who joined together as one nation in approximately 1804 by treaty with the United States. However, as early as 1733, the two groups had become one people, meaning they lived side by side.[25] The Sacs, whose original name was Sauk, were known as the people called Asakiwakis, meaning "people of the yellow earth." The Foxes, also known as the Mesquakies, were called the Meshkwahkihawis, meaning "People of the Red Earth."[26] According to the Sauks and Foxes, hundreds of years ago the world was inhabited by animals and manitous that were also known as spirits. Gisha Manitou, the most important of the deities, had a wife and four sons. The two eldest sons, Wisaka and Kiyapatha, were blessed with their youth, and it was apparent that they would have powers much greater than the other manitous. All of this led to the manitou Wisaka meeting with

Glade Wakolee. Author's collection.

the animals, and with the help of the turtle, buzzard, muskrat, wolf, and other beasts, he shaped the various parts of the earth into all of the mountains and valleys.

Jealous of their older brothers' gifts, the two younger brothers, with the help of their grandmother, Mother of the Earth, plotted against their brothers, killing them. Gaining dominance over the other manitous, one of the younger brothers killed more of the manitous. He drove others underground or into the sky. There in the sky at night, their campfires can be seen distributed all along the Great White River called the Milky Way. Some became the Thunderers, who rode the south wind and were appointed guardians of the people.[27]

The Sauks lived originally near the Saint Lawrence Seaway in Canada, according to oral tradition. Europeans and other Indians forced the Sauks to move to Saginaw, Michigan, then to Green Bay, Wisconsin. Finally, the Sauks claimed a new homeland called Saukenuk where the Rock and Mississippi Rivers meet. The Sauks consisted of a system of patrilineal clans of the bald eagle, bear, potato, black bass, deer, great lake, panther, ringed perch, sturgeon, swan, thunder, and wolf. Old-timers have estimated that the Sauks in early years consisted of twelve hundred people.[28]

The Foxes consisted of arbitrary, black-and-white divisions that provided a balance so that one kind of people would not presumed to be better than the other. They were further divided into patrilineal clans: bear, fox, wolf, swan, partridge, thunder, elk, and black bass. Knowing one's clan is a part of Native identity. Clans exist in many Indian tribal societies and they are the next important sociocultural kinship unit after the extended family. I was born into the Fox Clan from my mother and I learned as a youth to watch and study the fox for its strengths and weaknesses. The fox is my guardian spirit like the wolf would be the same for someone who is of the Wolf Clan. In this ethos, for example, you learn to think like the fox; its many centuries of survival and instinct will help you to survive. Learning the logic of the fox becomes learning about yourself. According to this belief, you develop a fox personality and you can tell the clans of others by their actions, especially those who are four legged and related to the fox like a wolf or bear.

As a youth, I was told that I would never be alone because the fox spirit would always be with me. If I heard something in the dark at night, I should not be afraid because it was the fox spirit letting me know that it was there. As my guardian spirit, the fox spirit is a part of my subconscious and I would instinctively know what was right and what was wrong, what to do and what not to do. To feel the connection to another being was and is like a part of the universal dichotomy of yourself and your alter ego. And as a person lives each day with decisions to make and responsibilities to be met, the guardian spirit helps the individual to find balance in his or her life.

The fox is an interesting animal. Kin to other four-legged creatures, especially the wolf, the fox has learned to negotiate its way in the animal world where some beings are bigger and more powerful. The fox is wise from its experiences and from observing other animals. For example, the name Wakolee means a fox that does not take the straight route of going from one point to another, especially in an open field. Wakolee means a fox that takes the half-circle route to get to its destination. This is what I was told as a teenager by my Sac and Fox grandfather Glade Wakolee when I visited him. He was in a nursing home near where we lived on the corner of Callahan and L Streets in Muskogee, Oklahoma. For most of his later adult years, he worked as a laborer in southern California. After he had a stroke late in his life, he returned to

Oklahoma since my mother was his oldest daughter. My grandfather had trouble speaking due to the stroke, so he used the palm of his left hand to illustrate an open field and with his right hand he showed how the fox trotted in a half circle around the edge of the field to get to the other side of it. My grandfather liked to smoke cigarettes, so my mother would buy them and sometimes I would take them to him. She sewed a second pocket on some of his shirts and tried to find material that kind of matched his shirt. He did not care how his shirts looked as long as he had double pockets. Grandfather liked to have a pack of Camel cigarettes in each front pocket of his shirts so he would not run out. Grandfather said to watch animals and you can understand them because they watch people and they understand human beings. In fact, they know us better than we know them. On April 24, 1975, my grandfather walked toward the West for the last time. Sometimes I think of him and recall the meaning of Wakolee when I gaze at the family photographs on the wall of my study. I most vividly remember him being in a wheelchair when I would push him down the hall to the dining room at the nursing home in Muskogee, or outside to check on the weather. I suppose being Indian is always looking at the sky and checking on the weather.

Long ago, the Foxes numbered as many as sixteen hundred people. They lived in the vicinity of Lake Winnebago near the Fox River. When the French Jesuit missionary Claude-Jean Allouez met them, he found them living on the bank of the Wolf River in this area that they called home. Of the western Great Lakes region, the Foxes engaged the French in two major wars from 1712 to 1733 to the detriment of their people because many of them died.[29]

The Sauks were in a similar situation in the eighteenth century, having waged war against many tribes and the whites called Europeans. The overall condition of both groups forged a natural alliance that brought the two peoples together permanently, but it is not known for sure when they began to consider themselves as one people. They had fought as allies against other groups in many instances, and they lived near each other.

Together, the Sauks and Foxes forged a single identity as one tribe. As Alqonkian speakers, they share a similar origin. They have not forgotten their roots as two distinct groups, although in modern times they have one defined identity. They are an excellent example of alliance and how important partnerships have been formed in the past and in the present. Their shared experiences in the past have resulted in a shared modern identity that is true for other groups, like the Southern Cheyennes and Arapahos, and Shoshones and Northern Arapahos. Other groups are more than two nations joined, such as the Klamaths of Oregon and the Confederated Tribes that make up the Colvilles in Washington.

Creation stories are told again and again to remind Indian people who they are and where they came from. To them, it is important to remain connected to the past, which sustains their connectedness to their ancestors. In this same way, the stories about creations explain how tribes are different. The recounting of creation stories is in all tribes a source of identity for each person in the tribal community. Not just knowing one's history but where one's people come from is valuable knowledge regarding personal identity and community history.

All cultures have creation stories. Creation stories are reference points in one's life. In each person's life, he or she comes to the central question: where did my people come from? For Native peoples, the creation story tells how people came into existence and where. Again, place is important. In such stories, humans are involved and sometimes, animal beings are also.

In these stories, humans and animals can communicate and understand each other. In this way, they are equal beings with established relationships between them that are a part of the oral tradition as told in stories. Hence the first and perhaps most important kind of oral tradition among Indians is the creation story. This is where oral tradition and oral history begins for Indian people who are close to their traditions. Like the Mvskoke story of creation told earlier, the role of human beings is set, the place is usually identified, and the way creation occurred is the objective of the story. A part of this important place is the natural surroundings or environment, both physical and metaphysical. While origin stories may not make logical sense to non-Indians, Native people accept them for they demonstrate where they came from. To understand the creation stories in the Native oral tradition, one must remain open-minded and consider all the possibilities that influence one's belief system because there is so much more about life than what we know now.

THREE

Legends of Warriors

Samuel E. Kenoi, Chiricahua Apache, said in 1932: "I was born in 1875. I remember the last time Geronimo went on the war-path. That was in 1885, but I had heard about his taking the war-path before this. . . . He . . . was called a human tiger. He would rather be on the warpath than anything else. He would advise his parents' group, and his wife's relatives, and any other relatives, to leave and he would take them out with him. . . . Then somebody would say, 'Geronimo is out again,' and there he would be with a small band of about forty men up in the mountains."[1]

Geronimo. This name is perhaps the best-known Indian name in history. Three years after I moved to Arizona in 2004, my young son, Keytha, and I took a road trip to explore the southern part of our new home state. I wanted to experience the land that Geronimo had fought so hard to protect. I wanted to know what it felt like to touch the same earth space that was his homeland. Many years earlier, my grandmother Rachel Wakolee had told me about Geronimo when she worked as a nurse's aide at the Indian hospital in Lawton, Oklahoma. She lived in Lawton, and Fort Sill, an active military base, was several minutes away on a less busy highway than I-44. Army officials kept Geronimo as a prisoner at the fort after he surrendered for the last time in 1886. Geronimo was very well known around Lawton, especially among the soldiers who trained at Fort Sill. The soldiers learned to parachute from a high platform and it became tradition to yell "Geronimo" when jumping to add to one's courage. Two or three sources explain the origin of yelling "Geronimo" when doing something

Geronimo, Apache war leader. Courtesy of Arizona
Historical Society.

death-defying. The most likely story occurred in August 1940 when the parachute was modified for soldiers to learn to jump at Fort Benning, Georgia. To
settle their nerves the night before making their first jump, soldiers watched
the 1939 movie *Geronimo.* They saw the ferocious Apache leader attacking
his Mexican enemies with only a knife. Private Aubrey Eberhardt was afraid
of heights and very nervous about making the jump. His friends teased him
relentlessly that he would not even be able to remember his own name. The
young private replied, "All right, dammit! I tell you jokers what I'm gonna do!
To prove to you that I'm not scared out of my wits when I jump, I'm gonna
yell 'Geronimo' loud as hell when I go out that door tomorrow!" When it was
his turn the next morning, Eberhardt yelled some war whoops as he shouted
"Geronimo" and he jumped. Other soldiers did the same and the contagious

practice of yelling "Geronimo" to summon one's courage began, becoming a tradition. And the U.S. army's first combat-ready parachute unit, the 501st Parachute Infantry Regiment, 1st Battalion, in 1941 made Geronimo a part of the insignia on the upper arms of their uniforms.[2]

Born a Bedonkohe Apache in about 1827, Geronimo was initially called Goyathlay (One Who Yawns). But he became the most well-known warrior of all and certainly legendary. At about the age of seventeen, Geronimo joined his people's council of warriors. He soon married and his wife gave birth to three children. During the summer of 1858, Geronimo traveled to the small town of Kas-ki-yeh to trade pelts and horses for goods. While away, Mexican soldiers attacked the Apache settlement and killed his mother, his wife, Alope, and his three children. From that day forward, he lived a life of revenge against anyone who was Mexican.[3]

From 1859 to about 1873, Geronimo fought alongside Mangus Colorado who led raids against Mexican settlers and soldiers. On many occasions, Geronimo led only a handful of warriors, and they traveled on foot into Mexico to raid. Geronimo terrorized the Mexicans who retaliated by attacking the Apaches. In 1873, Mexican troops attacked Geronimo and the Apaches turned them back. The Indians' success led to the Battle of White Hill where two companies of Mexican soldiers confronted Geronimo and sixty warriors. Geronimo and his men won a decisive victory. In 1880, twenty-four Mexican troops surprised Geronimo and forty Indians at Casa Grande. On this day, Geronimo and his warriors won the battle that resulted in an understanding meant to lead to peace between the Mexicans and the Apaches. During these years, American settlers and miners began building homes and prospecting in the Apache homeland. The Mexicans used the agreement as a ruse and gave the U.S. military permission to cross into Mexico to defeat the Indians. Apache leaders Victorio and Juh joined Geronimo in trying to protect their homeland from Mexicans and Americans. In Mexico, American soldiers surprised Victorio and killed many Apaches in the Tres Castillos massacre on October 14, 1880. In the same year, American soldiers captured Juh and Geronimo with 108 Apaches and took them to San Carlos, only to have Geronimo to escape. Other warriors like Cochise and other Apaches rose to lead their small bands to strike against the Mexicans and Americans.[4]

In his many attacks, the Mexicans wounded Geronimo eight times. He had vowed to kill as many Mexicans as he could for the rest of his life. In war,

Geronimo's medicine protected his life, and other Apaches witnessed the power of the medicine. The fighting continued after Geronimo's escape, but with Americans, as settlers moved into the Apache homeland now called Arizona Territory. Geronimo, who had fought with Cochise, became identified with the Chiricahua Apaches in raids and clashes with the U. S. military for the next several years. Other Apache warriors, Juh, Nachise (Cochise's son), and Chato joined in leading the Mescalero Apaches on raids. Finally, several Apache leaders surrendered in March 1884. The balance of power had tipped against the Apaches and Geronimo's medicine had weakened. On September 4, 1886, the legendary Geronimo surrendered for the fourth and final time.

Having heard of Geronimo when I was a boy, I wanted to know where he lived, now that I had moved to Arizona. My son and I drove past Tucson, through Tombstone, Mule Pass Tunnel, and Bisbee. We should have started out earlier in the day. We live in northeast Mesa, one of several bustling suburbs of Phoenix. On this spring weekend afternoon, we underestimated the amount of highway we would meet in pursuit of Geronimo to the extreme corner of southeast Arizona. We searched for the Geronimo Surrender Memorial and I glanced at the map now and then. I had no idea that my new home state was so large, the sixth largest in the Union. One mile led to another on the two-lane asphalt, as our destination on Highway 80 climbed higher near Apache, Arizona. Our destination seemed like the football goal line, moving farther and farther away. Finally we reached it with less than an hour of daylight as I fumbled for my camera on the floorboard in the back seat. The 9,000-feet-tall Chiricahua Mountains surrounded us, nature's ancient giants that tested anything that lived—the heartland of the Apaches. I stared at the six-foot-high rock memorial, studied the mountains in more than one direction while my impatient son whined it was time to go. Actually, Geronimo surrendered in Skeleton Canyon where it meets the South Fork River, not too far from the rock memorial. My young son was more interested in driving in the car, turning to the radio stations that he liked, and eating candy. I must admit I sugared up with Mountain Dew and M&M's to stay awake. As I turned the car around to drive north, the intersecting moment of day and night began to happen. When light and dark meet; this is a powerful moment, hvmakimata.

The long drive back to Mesa started with the last rays of sunset. The mountains stood silent, but they held memories of the past battles when Geronimo and his people waged war against Americans and Mexicans. I thought of the stories that these mountains could tell. The earth experiences everything.[5] I wondered about the trauma and pain that the mountains and surrounding area had experienced. In particular, I wondered about the trauma and pain suffered by Geronimo's wife, his three children, his mother, and the other women and children, who had been massacred by Mexicans near Janos, Chihuahua, Mexico. Geronimo had joined the men who decided on that dreadful morning to trade horses for food supplies and goods that they badly needed. I thought about the trauma in the land of the Chiricahuas that would be analogous to other places. I had sensed the same kind of pain when I visited places like Wounded Knee, Sand Creek, Washita Battlefield, and Civil War sites like Gettysburg, Vicksburg, and Wilson Creek—all had witnessed horrible killings. The historian Dominick LaCapra writes in *Writing History, Writing Trauma* that all people likely will experience trauma in their lives. Indians and other Indigenous people know this too well. Trauma is something most people do not think about even though we live through it without realizing its lingering hauntings. Navajo surgeon Lori Alford has written about this kind of trauma, calling it "historical grief." She wrote, "Navajo children are told of the capture and murder of their fore-fathers and mothers, and then they too must share in the legacy of grief."[6] She was angry about the past when the famed Indian fighter Kit Carson and the military killed her people and forced the 8,500 survivors on the Long Walk of three hundred miles to Bosque Redondo, a prisoner of war reservation in New Mexico. One can only imagine feeling Geronimo's pain of discovering his family murdered and retreating into his own suffering, then lashing out against all who were his enemies. He knew no fear because his spirit had died with his family.

The story of Geronimo does not stop in Arizona. It is as if Geronimo lived another life while a prisoner of war. The U.S. military held him as a prisoner in Pensacola, Florida, and at Fort Sill in Oklahoma for the rest of his life. The military believed that if he were allowed to return to Arizona he would lead another Apache war. His status as the last fierce warrior made him a living legend who people wanted to see. In 1889, Geronimo was allowed to attend the Omaha Exposition in Nebraska and in 1901 he was a part of the Pan-American Exposition in Buffalo, New York. Three years later he appeared in the Saint Louis World's Fair and he rode in President Theodore Roosevelt's inaugural parade in 1905. His twenty-three years in captivity make him the longest-held prisoner of war in American history. If asked who is the best-known Indian in history, many Americans and Mexicans would undoubtedly say "Geronimo."

Many noted warriors have been written about, sung about, and told about through stories. For the following individuals, tribal accounts offer insights into their lives and help those of us who are outsiders to understand their causes. The warriors fought in small and major battles to defend their people— Black Hawk of the Sac and Fox, Osceola of the Seminoles, Crazy Horse of the Lakota, Phillip Coon of the Mvskoke Creeks, and my uncle Telmond Fixico. Tribal elders, including some of my own, have shared stories about their people's greatest warriors. All tribes tell stories about their heroes and their brave deeds in battle. Even in defeat, to die on the battlefield was preferred to capture, according to the general code of warriorship.[7] Death for the cause of one's people rendered glory in the afterlife and gave social status to one's relatives. These warriors represent various circumstances and different ways of being immortalized. Some are more well known than others and have had books written about them. Remarkably, they have also achieved recognition from many people and have been chronicled in the history of Indian-white relations.

These individuals represent a warriorship respected by relatives, friends, and enemies—one facet of this warriorship involves being a warrior among one's own people, and the other involves being a warrior in the mainstream, such as serving in the U.S. military. To be accomplished among one's own people is significant, but to be recognized by one's enemy means that he or she has impressed others according to another set of cultural values. In either case, these warriors risked their lives to protect their people and defend their homelands. My relatives of the past were also warriors who fought for their homelands, but were removed to Indian Territory. All four tribes were not originally of Oklahoma and moved their fires to new treaty homelands where my grandparents met.

My grandmother Rachel was glad to be married to my grandfather Glade Wakolee, who was Sac and Fox. Grandmother Rachel and my mother visited with each other a lot, which meant lots of shared stories. They talked about who we were related to. My grandfather's father was Jackson Wakolee; he was one of the original allottees to receive 160 acres in the old Sac and Fox Nation in Indian Territory before it became the state of Oklahoma in 1907. The Sac and Fox were not allotted lands via the Dawes Commission. Instead, they received separate lands when the president of the United States pronounced a proclamation on September 1891 that called for allotting tribal lands to the 448 tribal members, 220 males and 228 females. The Sac and Fox had survived at least three major removals that ended in the central part of Indian Territory. Fortunately, the majority of my tribe arrived during a mild winter in 1869, only four years after the Civil War that had spun all of the Indian nations into turmoil since the majority of the tribes had fought for the Confederacy.

Accompanying the removals of the Sac and Fox were memories of the past life at Saukenuk and of Black Hawk of the Thunder clan. Saukenuk was the sacred land of the Sac and Fox, located on Rock Island in western Illinois. By the end of the eighteenth century, Saukenuk was "the most imposing town in the Northwest, Indian or white. This magnificent town hosted more than 100 wickeups (lodges extending 60 feet in length), and an estimated 3,000 Sauks lived there from April to October."[8]

In earlier times, the Sacs were known as the Sauks and they were the People of the Yellow Earth due to the color of the clay soil in the Saginaw Bay area, and the Foxes were the People of the Red Earth because of the color of the soil in Iowa. On my mother's side of the family, the Sac and Fox hold Black Hawk in great esteem for his patriotism. Born at Saukenuk in 1767, Black Hawk's parents named him Makataimeshekiakiak, which means Black Sparrow Hawk in flight.[9] Black Hawk was the son of Pyesa, a medicine maker.[10] Black Hawk grew up during turbulent times when American settlers poured into the western Illinois area and eventually wanted Saukenuk as they pushed westward. As events unfolded, Black Hawk became fraught with despair. In a treaty in 1804, the Sac and Fox ceded their cherished homeland to the United States when William Henry Harrison and other American officials lured a delegation to Saint Louis and tricked the five Indians into signing the agreement when they tried to respond to the charge of the murders of four trappers. The delegation had no authority, could not read or write, but they made their marks, signing away Saukenuk for a new homeland west of the Mississippi River in Iowa.[11]

For the rest, the removal proved to be devastating. I can only imagine what it must have been like to feel the anger that Black Hawk felt. Black Hawk stared across the river to watch the settlers. He declared, "They are now running their plows through our graveyards, turning up the bones and ashes of our sacred dead, whose spirits are calling to us from the land of dreams for vengeance on the despoilers."[12] I have tried to find where he may have stood and looked across the same river. Angered by this desecration, Black Hawk rallied warriors and they struck the war pole. Such action publicly designated that each one had declared to fight, thereby committing their loyalty to take back their homeland. On April 5, 1832, Black Hawk led an estimated 1,800 kinsmen, including warriors and their women and children, to cross the Mississippi to take back their cherished Saukenuk.[13]

Rumors had already spread about the angry Black Hawk and his talk of going to war. The United States prepared to meet the invasion to reclaim the Sauk and Fox homeland, which would become known as the Black Hawk War. Black Hawk and his followers won the first battle against the Americans at Stillman's Run on May 14 but lost at the Battle of Wisconsin Heights on July 21. Weary from fighting and the lack of food, Black Hawk and his people made their last stand at Bad Axe River. The battle, which started on August 1, turned quickly into a massacre. Black Hawk wanted "to die with my people, if the Great Spirit would not give us another victory!"[14] For the rest of the day and into the next, the U.S. soldiers hunted down the Sauks and Foxes and many of our people drowned in the river or reached the other bank only to find themselves at the mercy of Sioux, their sworn enemy, who scalped them.[15]

Black Hawk had fought against the odds and lost, but his passion and commitment to winning back Saukenuk made him a hero in the eyes of many tribesmen then and now. This admiration, however, was marred by the rise of another tribal leader, Keokuk, of the Fox people. Black Hawk led his followers in flight from the troops and state militia. During the turmoil, Keokuk comforted his people and decided to negotiate a peace talk for the well-being of those with him. Ten years younger than Black Hawk, Keokuk seized the opportunity to become leader of the Sauks and Foxes. With the defeat of Black Hawk, American officials found Keokuk quite willing to negotiate treaty agreements. These hurried negotiations involved extra provisions, which provided Keokuk with fine clothes, a white Arabian stallion, and other goods for his group of warriors who protected him from his critics, some of whom had threatened to kill him. People were gossiping about him because they did not trust him. A treaty in 1832, a council in 1838, and a treaty in 1842 called for the ultimate removal of the Sac and Fox to Kansas and then to Indian Territory. Black Hawk disliked Keokuk, and stories about the two different personalities and their different kinds of leadership have become a part of the oral tradition among the Sac and Fox.

In spite of his failed effort, Black Hawk won the respect of both his people and non-Indians. Admiration of the Sauk leader convinced the sculptor Lorado Taft to design *The Eternal Indian*. This statue, standing forty-eight feet tall, overlooks the Rock River, near where Taft founded a summer artist colony.[16] In 1927, Illinois state officials purchased land near Saukenuk and opened a historical museum to the public in 1939. Many Sac and Fox returned to Saukenuk to dance at the annual Labor Day powwows during the 1940s and 1950s.[17] The legacy of Black Hawk and admiration for him continued with Black Hawk College founded at Moline, Illinois, in 1946. The Chicago Black Hawks professional hockey team founded in 1926 was named after the Blackhawk Division, a machine gun battalion in World War I. Black Hawk has been the subject of at least four biographies and towns have been named Black Hawk.[18] And among the Sac and Fox people, Black Hawk remains a celebrated hero forever. My grandmother Rachel was also very proud of Black Hawk and so are many people, including non-Indians. In her later years, my grandmother moved to Prague, Oklahoma, in the heart of the Sac and Fox Country. She kept a picture of Black Hawk hanging on her wall in the living room. And if you visited the Sac and Fox Nation complex in Stroud, Oklahoma, you would see a painting of Black Hawk proudly displayed in the room leading to the library.

In August 2013, I fulfilled a lifelong ambition by making a pilgrimage with Michelle to Oregon, Illinois, to see the forty-eight-feet-tall statue of Black Hawk. I had wanted to see this large statue since I first learned about it many years ago and kept waiting for an opportunity to go there. That never happened. So, I made that opportunity possible. As we journeyed to western Illinois, I imagined what it was like during the prominence of Saukenuk in its glory in the late 1700s on Rock Island. I agree with Lorado Taft, who made the statue a reality, when he realized during one of his many walks that Native people likely gazed at the sunset as they stood on the bluff of Rock River. I stood there on the same bank, looking westward; wishing that my mother and my Sac and Fox grandfather could have had the same chance to look at what was once Saukenuk. Taft wanted to commemorate this experience and thought that Black Hawk himself likely enjoyed many sunsets, perhaps where his statue stands. *The Eternal Indian* is the second tallest concrete statue in the world. Although in need of some repair from decades of storms, seasonal changes, and natural deterioration, Black Hawk continues to watch over the region known as the West.

On that partially cloudy day as Michelle and I ate a Subway lunch and listened to visitors reading the signs about the Black Hawk War of 1832, I recalled my grandmother's words of pride about the great leader. A slight breeze pushed

the clouds steadily along. I ate slowly while thinking about how this coura-
geous warrior fought for a just cause, attempting to regain his sacred homeland,
my homeland. I left a small part of my sandwich and poured some of my drink
on the ground. The Sac and Fox believe in sharing food and drink with the
spirits and showing them that you are not selfish and only think of yourself. I
wished that all my relatives could be there. I took many photographs of Black
Hawk, including this one, on that August afternoon. The warm air currents carried an unexpected visitor as I took in all the ambience of Black Hawk's historical presence. One could imagine this was a response to my gesture of sharing
some of my food and drink (and I love Dr. Pepper almost as much as Mountain
Dew). A black sparrow hawk arrived and circled several times high above Black
Hawk's statue, and then three more appeared, making this day even more special to this enrolled member of the Sac and Fox Nation. Four hawks that day;
four is a good number, hvmakimata.

I wanted to know the extent that the local people acknowledged the famed
Sac and Fox war leader. I had heard of Black Hawk College when I saw a decal
on the rear windshield of a car while driving through Illinois more than twenty
years ago. In the afternoon, we found the college and saw signs of many types
that had Black Hawk's name on buildings, stores, and the like. My grandparents Glade and Rachel would have been very proud, but they never had the
opportunity to travel to this part of the country, so far away from Oklahoma.
As I typed these words for the first time while flying back to Phoenix, I thought
about the four black sparrow hawks hunting that day, circling high above the
Black Hawk statue. I write with my laptop and think a lot on airplanes and
in airports, something that has become habit when there is time alone in a
crowd to reflect on the past and share it with others on these pages. On this
occasion, as I thought about those black sparrow hawks, I also thought about
several things. I thought about the efforts of Black Hawk leading our people in
three battles, especially the last one at Bad Axe where survivors swam to the
opposite bank, the enemy Sioux waited to club them to death and take some
as prisoners. I thought about the suffering in removing two times to end up in
Oklahoma, how our people rebuilt their community and government in the
twentieth century. In a small contributing way, I have given some of my books
to the Sac and Fox National Public Library.

The Sac and Fox Tribe sometimes charters a bus for kinsmen to visit their
ancient homeland and to see the tall statue of the one called Black Sparrow

Black Hawk, *The Eternal Indian*, Rock River, Illinois.
Courtesy Michelle M. Martin.

Hawk. If their visits are like mine, they enjoy a life experience of visiting our
homeland and understanding why Black Hawk fought so hard to try to win
back the beloved Saukenuk. And I think about many Sac and Fox who lived in
Oklahoma and never got a chance to see Saukenuk, like my mother and grandfather Glade Wakolee.

Osceola and the Second Seminole War, 1835–1842

A warrior of grand repute rose through the ranks and made his way toward
leading his people in war in spite of traditional protocol. In times demanding
leadership, one cannot help but think that destiny crowns certain individuals.
Osceola emerged from turmoil involving a loose group of refugees called the

Seminoles to ascend to the status of important warrior.[19] History would bestow upon him even greater status.

Osceola was born in 1804 in Talisi, a town near Tallassee, Alabama, into the highly regarded Bird Clan. The Seminoles are an offshoot of the Mvskokes, originally located in the central parts of Georgia and Alabama, who moved to northern and central Florida. In his time, Osceola would only know war: as a child in the Creek War of 1813–1814, and as a teenager and adult in the Seminole Wars, 1817–1818 and 1835–1842.

As a child, Osceola learned about the strengths of his totem clan animal—Bird. One's clan totem came from the matrilineal descent and Osceola obtained his clan identity from his mother, Polly Coppinger. The Bird Clan represented the second most important clan next to the Wind. The Bird people oversaw the laws of the community; they made them and they enforced them. According to their creation story, the Wind blew the dark mist away, allowing the people emerging on ecuna to see and hear birds flying above them. Birds were the first animals the people saw when they were no longer blind. The ability of birds to fly over us, to observe, and carry messages was a good thing. And to be one of the Bird Clan, one is said to have a good outlook on everything going on.

Osceola's childhood name was Cepvne, meaning "little boy" in the Mvskoke language, which the Seminoles spoke. This was my name too, as I played at my grandparents' house. I followed my Seminole grandfather, Jonas, who plowed the earth with a horse; my job was to try to help remove the rocks that he uncovered, at least the ones I could carry. My grandparents lived at the Old Place, on my grandfather's allotment of 120 acres in Seminole County, Oklahoma. Mostly I remember my Creek grandmother, Lena, saying *"Wiketv, cepvne!"* This meant "Stop doing that, little boy," and I was in trouble again, throwing dirt clods at most anything, instead of helping. Grandmother would motion with her hand that I needed to walk along with Grandpa to help remove the rocks he uncovered with the plow. At six years old, I was full of energy and wondered about everything I saw in the country where my grandparents lived. None of us knew at the time that my grandfather would die the following year on August 25, 1958, at the age of sixty from a stroke after working in the sun too long. He was number 945 on the Dawes Roll for Seminoles, which meant his place on the roll to receive an allotment of tribal land, and he was the youngest child of Aharlock and Nelsey Chupco Fixico of the Okoske Harjo Band that became a part of the Thomas Little (Ceyvha or Wolf) Band.

In my lifelong research on the Seminoles, I learned that my oldest relative is Tustennuck Hajo, who had three sisters and was the fourth person on a "List of Seminole Prisoners" of Coe Hadjo's town scheduled for removal in 1841.[20] I remember that so well on a late morning on February 16, 1982, sitting in the Saint Augustine Historical Society's library when I opened the folder and read the list. My ancestor, as far back in time as I could find, was not a relative of George Washington or any other founding father of this country. The United States regarded my oldest ancestor as an enemy to be defeated and moved away. Holding the paper, I felt stunned and then a flood of anger hit me. I thought this must be how Osceola felt when the U.S. military was trying to kill and drive our people from our homeland—the same rage that Black Hawk felt. I thought that I needed to do something with this information, something positive; to tell people how Indians felt trying to protect their people and save their homelands.

Osceola was a well-liked child among his relatives and friends. Full of energy and possessing athletic ability, the happy brown-eyed child soon witnessed troubled times. The turmoil in Creek Country found young Cepvne's community at risk. The Red Towns, which produced warriors, and White Towns, which supplied peace leaders, were constantly at work to stabilize and calm the people who were war ready. At the age of four, Cepvne's father died in battle. By tradition, a favorite uncle or one of the grandfathers began to teach Cepvne about the virtues of becoming a man. Many of his relatives died in the Mvskoke Creek War of 1813–14 and he heard stories about the great battle at Horseshoe Bend, which he carried into his teen years. Such memories sustained his efforts to become a great warrior, so that Horseshoe Bend would not happen again. In his twenties, young Osceola distinguished himself as a warrior and had to fight to prove his worthiness. As a mixed-blood, part of his heritage included a Scottish trader, and full-bloods reminded him of this fact. He vented his anger toward the whites to prove that he was all Seminole. In the following years, Osceola encountered more strife between his people and white settlers as he honed his warrior skills and became more knowledgeable in medicine. During these years, Osceola learned that he was gifted with an ability to speak impressively about the wrong of settlers taking Seminole lands. In his early thirties, his talents as a warrior and speaker gained notice among whites.

At the Seminole Agency located at Fort King in Florida Territory, Wiley Thompson, an Indian agent, called an important gathering of Seminole leaders and warriors on October 23, 1835. The U.S. military had built Fort King in the heart of the Seminoles' homeland in north central Florida. On a spring day in May 2006, I visited the site of Fort King and stood on the same sandy earth where Osceola stood many years ago. I felt connected to the earth, lamenting about my grandfather Jonas Fixico, great-grandfather Aharlock Fixico, and great-great-grandfather Tustennuck Hajo. Tustennuck was forced to remove with other Seminoles to Indian Territory, which became Oklahoma in 1907. Just four miles northeast of old Fort King rested the original ceremonial ground of my Seminole people from where I get my last name, Fix-i-co, pronounced in the Native language "fik see co," which is actually a title of war, meaning "Heartless in Battle."[21]

The fateful meeting at Fort King in 1835 began at 11:00 A.M. Thompson reminded the Seminoles of the previous signing by their brethren of an agreement at Fort Gibson in Indian Territory. Thompson said that some Seminole leaders had visited Indian Territory and agreed for all of the tribe to remove to new homelands there. Agent Thompson asked if the Seminoles would accept the invitation of the Creeks in the West to live next to them in Indian Territory. He asked if they wanted cattle or money upon their arrival in the West. He wanted to know if the Seminoles wanted to go by boat or travel overland. Lastly, Thompson wanted to know if they wanted their next annuity in money or in goods. And then he motioned to them to sign the treaty.

The Seminoles wanted to talk among themselves and meet with Thompson later, possibly the next day. Osceola grew furious at the idea of giving up his people's homeland and being moved to some strange land in the West. Watching an angry Osceola inspiring other warriors, Thompson forced his own agenda and asked each leader to step forward to confirm the Treaty of Fort Gibson by making his mark as an added signer. Several leaders angrily proclaimed that they had nothing to do with the treaty and that they did not authorize the delegation to go west, much less sign any treaty! The tension mounted; anger filled the air among the tall oaks and shrub trees surrounding the Indian agency. When Thompson told Osceola to step forward, Osceola paused. Standing still, he simmered with anger at what was happening—his people agreeing to another meaningless treaty that only took Seminole land and did nothing to protect Seminoles from the encroaching settlers. Writers of this famed incident say that at this decisive moment Osceola approached the treaty lying on the table. Legend has it that he unsheathed his knife and with one quick thrust, he stabbed the treaty, stating angrily that he rejected it by yelling at Thompson, "This is the only way I will sign this treaty."

During the summer in 2007, I went on a research trip to the National Archives to see the original Treaty of Fort Gibson. Finally obtaining permission after a couple of months, I waited outside of the vault as an archivist retrieved the treaty from a box and presented it to me by laying it on a table. At my instruction, she unfolded the treaty, which had been folded to fit the archival box and had been folded for well over a hundred years. Was the legend of Osceola stabbing the treaty true or not? There it was—a hole in the paper. I leaned over to inspect the hole to determine if indeed Osceola had stabbed the treaty. But it could not have happened the way the legend described it. If Osceola had approached the table head-on and if the treaty was placed exactly in the middle, he could not have stabbed the treaty this way. Rather, it is more likely that he stabbed the treaty as he approached from the side of the table. I realized Osceola would not likely have approached the table head-on if the treaty lay in alignment with the table because the hole was an angular cut.

Legendary or not, a small triangular hole shaped like the point of a knife blade is in the middle of the Fort Gibson Treaty now preserved in the vault of the National Archives in Washington, D.C. Osceola's knife could have made the hole. The impression that this is likely what happened is made all the more vivid by the vision that that hole evokes in my mind. The enraged warrior felt that his people had been tricked into the Fort Gibson agreement. Most likely, the delegation had become hostages and were forced to sign before the members could return to their families. In Osceola's mind, the white man's shrewdness had to be challenged. To threaten a small number of his people to sign away their land while they were not even in Florida was wrong. Nonetheless, Osceola was angry at the delegation too and called them traitors for signing the treaty. Osceola's outspoken words made him the most well-known Seminole opponent to the United States. His words became a clarion call for others to join him, including Mvskoke Creek and black allies who were former slaves. More blood would stain the sandy brown soil at Fort King.

At this point, Osceola addressed his fellow Seminoles with an emotional speech. He called out to all of the Seminoles as his brothers. Osceola blamed the white people for getting some of the Seminole leaders "to sign a paper to give our lands to them." He said that the leaders did not do as they were told to do by the Seminoles and they had done wrong. Moreover, he said that he and the other Seminoles must do right. Osceola criticized the agent Wiley Thompson for saying that the Seminoles must leave their lands—"our homes and the graves of our Fathers"—and go west of the big river called the Mississippi. They would be among bad Indians. At this point in his speech, because he loved his homeland and did not want to leave it, Osceola expressed his hatred for Thompson. To add to his position, Osceola said that he would only go to the West if the Great Spirit told him to do so. Osceola then made his famous statement: "but I have a rifle, and I have some powder and some lead. I say, we must not leave our homes and lands. If any of our people want to go west, we won't let them; and I tell them they are our enemies, and we will treat them so, for the Great Spirit will protect us."[22]

From 1835 to 1842, the diverse Seminole bands, including communities of Creek allies and escaped African Americans, fought twelve generals of the U.S. Army in eight major engagements until they accepted removal to the West. Of the several Seminole leaders involved in the Second Seminole War, including Alligator, Coe Hadjo, and Coacochee, Osceola emerged as the most well known. How to end this guerrilla war in the swamps and in the Everglades received high priority in the American government.

Capturing Osceola was the army's strategy to end the war. The treachery of having captured the great leader under a flag of truce made Osceola a hero for both Indians and whites during the 1830s and even to this day. The unwillingness to recognize the international recognition of a white flag of trust vilified the U.S. army. The army could not defeat the Seminoles, thus forcing army officials to resort to trickery, including the use of bloodhounds to track Seminole men, women, and children. Until his capture, Osceola led his bands to victories for almost two years. Captured in 1837, Osceola caught pneumonia while imprisoned. He died from his illness in the following weeks. Coacochee was the last Seminole leader to surrender, ending the Second Seminole War in 1842. By war's end, the United States had spent a sum of $15 to $20 million to defeat the Seminoles. The plan to alleviate Florida of all Indian presence failed. As many as 350 Seminoles remained in the state to fight a Third Seminole War from 1855 to 1858, led by Billy Bowlegs.

Throughout the state of Florida, including all private and public schools, there are five elementary schools, four middle schools, four high schools, two combination schools, and two adult learning schools that have been named Osceola. At this date, the total is seventeen schools named after Osceola in the same way that such schools are commonly named after U.S. presidents.[23] In Florida, one county is named Osceola, but no incorporated towns or cities carry his name in the state. Since 1965, there have been 984 incorporated businesses in Florida that have Osceola as part of their name.[24] Outside of Florida, seven states (Indiana, Arkansas, Iowa, Missouri, Nebraska, Wisconsin, and Pennsylvania, but not Oklahoma) have incorporated municipalities named Osceola. Michigan and Iowa have Osceola Counties.[25] In addition, the well-known resistance of the Seminoles led by Osceola became known in Hollywood, and at least three movies have been made about the Seminoles and their famous warrior. He became a legend even in his own lifetime, and both Seminoles and non-Seminoles knew him for his bravery in defending the homeland of his people.

Stories about Osceola have been told by Seminoles, Mvskoke Creeks, and other Indians and non-Indians. In an interesting way, an uneven oral tradition exists among people in northern Florida who know something about their state's history, especially if they went to a school named after the great leader. By reciting the history, they share this information with other people. And the point of this oral tradition is that Osceola was a Native patriot to his people who fought to defend their homeland.

Crazy Horse of the Oglala Lakotas

In the vicinity of the Bear Butte just north of the Black Hills in about 1840, a light-skinned child of yellow-brown hair was born to an Oglala medicine man and a Miniconjou woman named Rattling Blanket Woman. He would become an enigmatic individual, almost ghostlike to settlers, and powerful in war. Mystery shrouded the warrior, and white settlers knew little about him except for his feats in attacks during the Lakota war on the northern plains in the 1870s. Crazy Horse possessed a hair texture that earned him the name of Curly. It has been said that his mother committed suicide when Curly was a boy and that his father married two sisters of the famed war leader Spotted Tail.[26]

In 1876 the Lakotas, Cheyennes, and Arapahos engaged U.S. forces in the Battle of the Rosebud and the Battle of Little Bighorn, two of the best known battles in U.S.-Indian history when the noted leaders of the Lakotas and the U.S. military met on the battlefield. At the Rosebud River, Crazy Horse led seven hundred Lakotas and Cheyennes against General George Crook's one thousand soldiers, including three hundred Crow and Shoshone auxiliaries. The U.S. military responded with General Alfred Terry issuing a war declaration against the Lakotas and their allies, resulting in six battles and the defeat of the Indians. On June 25 and 26, General George Custer led his 647 soldiers to defeat against the Lakotas and their allies in perhaps the most famous Indian battle in American history. About one thousand Northern Cheyenne suffered serious defeats in 1876, at War Bonnet in Nebraska in July and at the Battle of Dull Knife in Wyoming in September. In the same month, Captain Nelson Miles defeated American Horse's Teton band at Slim Buttes, South Dakota. In the following year, Miles defeated Crazy Horse's band at the Battle of Wolf Mountain in a cold January, and in the spring Miles won against Lame Deer's Miniconjou Tetons in Montana in the Battle of Lame Deer.

Legend has it that Crazy Horse was protected in battle due to a vision that he had of a horse dancing in a strange manner. People who know of Crazy Horse also understand how he came by his name. He had protective medicine in war. In numerous battles and attacks against the U.S. military as well as against traditional enemies (Crows, Shoshones, Pawnees, Arikaras, and Blackfeet), Crazy Horse was wounded only twice. His vision protected him in battle: it came to him in the image of a great warrior riding on a spirited dancing horse poised to ride into battle.

During the fall of 1877, Crazy Horse surrendered after realizing it was necessary to save his starving people; more than one thousand Indians, mostly Oglalas gave themselves up and joined him. He had lived a life of violence on the battlefield. In talking about the past, Crazy Horse explained that he did not hate the white man, but that sometimes young white men would attack Indians and take their ponies. Crazy Horse said that his warriors responded in the same way by raiding for horses since this was the way of life on the northern plains among Indians. Horses were essential for hunting the buffalo. He described eloquently that on the reservation his people had no buffalo to eat and no hides for clothing or for making their tepees. But the Lakota did not want these government handouts. They preferred hunting to doing nothing on the reservation, but they were forced to accept the assigned area in which they were to live. Crazy Horse said that his people preferred their own way of living, especially when they cost the U.S. government nothing. "All we wanted was peace and to be left alone," said Crazy Horse. He described soldiers who were sent during the winter to destroy his people's villages who were led by Colonel Joseph Reynolds of the

Third Cavalry. He said that "Long Hair," the soldier leader known as George Custer, attacked too, Crazy Horse said, "They say we massacred him, but he would have done the same to us had we not defended ourselves and fought to the last."[27] He added that his people's first reaction when Custer attacked was to escape in order to save their wives and children. But the soldiers had blocked their paths, so they had to fight. Crazy Horse said that after the battle he went to the Tongue River with a few of his people to find peace.

Yet the U.S. government would not leave him and his people alone. Ultimately, Crazy Horse returned with his Oglala people to Red Cloud Agency where the Indian agent who was in control of the reservation lived. The Oglala leader was exhausted and tired of fighting. Crazy Horse went to the Spotted Tail Agency and asked to be allowed to live in peace. He wanted to talk to agent Jesse Lee, but was denied the opportunity. On September 5, 1877, the army escorted Crazy Horse to Fort Robinson in Nebraska where it had been arranged to send him on a train to Florida. At the agency, a guard and Little Big Man escorted Crazy Horse, and a scuffle occurred in front of the small detention building. Crazy Horse tried to escape and pulled out a knife. One of the guards fatally stabbed the famed warrior with a bayonet.[28]

On August 28, 2013, Michelle and I visited Fort Robinson to see where Crazy Horse was kept as a prisoner during the last days of his life. After landing in Denver on an early morning flight, we drove a small gray rental car, making the long steady climb up Highway 25, then, traveling south into Nebraska. Michelle loves to drive long distances, which make me sleepy. Fort Robinson is near the small town of Crawford, Nebraska. Today, Fort Robinson is a well-maintained historical facility. And Michelle thoroughly enjoyed Fort Robinson. She also loves marching around old forts and inspecting everything.

The Nebraska Historical Society reconstructed three log houses at Fort Robinson; the first one was where disobedient soldiers were kept and was divided into two parts. Days before his death, soldiers guarded Crazy Horse outside, fearful he might escape as they watched him pace back and forth in the 18 x 18-feet-square room. To his small advantage, the prison building faced north with two barred windows toward the east and one toward the west. He could pray, perhaps sing, to the morning sun and do the same at day's end with the sunset, the two times of day—day to-night and night-to-day—when light and dark intersect. About two hundred yards to the left, the military kept its horses. Crazy Horse likely imagined his escape to the white limestone hills toward the west. Disappearing into the pine forests, he would be free again. But as he gazed out the east windows, his eyes saw the officers' row of several white houses, whose occupants rendered him powerless. His supernatural power was sustained by nature, but such a high level of power as he possessed cannot manifest itself forever. For just like the seasons passing, cycles of nature also have their ways where even sacred places like the Black Hills, home of the legendary Lakota warrior, pulsated their power, as it was meant to be. For like the seasons, these powers are cyclical, and even in sacred places like the Black Hills, the home of the enigmatic warrior, they wax and wane. Now, the noted warrior was dying.

Several hours passed, and around midnight Crazy Horse finally died from his stab wound. Crazy Horse's father and others took the body and buried it at an undisclosed location, perhaps near Wounded Knee, South Dakota. The legend of Crazy Horse fighting for his people and homeland proved so great that the artist Korczak Ziolkowski decided to make it his life's work to sculpt a giant figure of Crazy Horse in the Thunder Mountain of the Black Hills. He started on June 3, 1948, with a Budah compressor, a machine run by gasoline to power his drill. Still unfinished and carried on by the Ziolkowski family members, the granite memorial will be 563 feet tall and 641 feet long. More than a million people visit Crazy Horse Mountain every year. In 1982, the U.S. Postal Service commemorated Crazy Horse with a thirteen-cent stamp.[29] As the work on Thunder Mountain continues, so grows the legend of Crazy Horse preserved among the Black Hills, the sacred area of the Lakota.

I have seen Crazy Horse Mountain four times, observing over the years the progress of this massive sculpting of this granite space. It will be the largest monument in the world when completed, but that will be at an undetermined date. What is more important is what Crazy Horse has become, and to all people. Indeed, Crazy Horse has become a legend, something that I am sure he would never have thought about. To the Lakotas, Crazy Horse will always be admired and looked upon as a hero. But the legendary Crazy Horse is not the same as the warrior Crazy Horse. Since the twentieth century, Crazy Horse has been used, even exploited, to the commercial advantage of many non-Lakotas. The warrior Crazy Horse would likely not have wanted a mountain carved to exemplify him, especially in the Black Hills that are sacred to the Lakotas, Cheyennes, and other Indian nations. As a warrior, he did not want attention drawn to himself, although stories about him as a powerful force at

Monument to Crazy Horse in Black Hills. Author's collection.

Rosebud, Little Bighorn, and other battles he fought in—all secured his place in the Lakota oral tradition of their great leaders.

The last time I checked on the legendary Crazy Horse Memorial was in late summer of 2013. The face of Crazy Horse and his outstretched hand indicated that his land was out there in the Black Hills where his people were buried. As a hero to many Lakotas, Crazy Horse has become a legend. And Crazy Horse still has an everlasting presence.

Uncle Telmond and Phillip Coon in World War II

Some warriors do not exist only as legends or as celebrated and well-known figures of the past, but rather many individuals who do not have monuments or have not been widely celebrated as warriors have possessed the warrior spirit, which continues to persist within them. Uncle Telmond was my dad's older brother by more than several years; he was born on February 12, 1919. At the age of twenty-three, he was single with no dependents and listed himself as a semiskilled mechanic with a grade school education. He enlisted on February 25, 1942, trained at Fort Sill, and joined the 101st Airborne Division. Uncle

Telmond Fixico, Frank
Alexander, and Otis Harjo.
Author's collection.

Telmond was a private, and his unit parachuted as a part of the second wave
at Normandy. I am sure that he yelled "Geronimo" when he trained and when
he jumped out of the plane over France. He survived in Europe and mustered
out of service on December 3, 1945. When I was a child, Uncle Telmond would
bounce me on his knee and ask me if I had been good. I would respond, "Yes, I
have been very good." He would ask me how do you say "very good" in Indian,
and I would reply, "*estv mahe.*" He would repeat it to make sure that I got it
right. Then, he would reach into his pocket and give me a penny. Uncle Telmond was a hero in my young eyes; he died on December 24, 1999. My parents
gave me a small metal piggy bank when I was a child and I can only wish that
some of the pennies still in it were from my uncle. Uncle Telmond.

A warrior's luck is not just luck. For those who believe, they have protection medicine power like Crazy Horse and Osceola, who followed the ways of
their people. Although one prepares to meet death with honor, such warriors

believe their medicines will protect them against the enemy when needed. This power in war is a part of the spiritual traditions of Indians whose warriors have died with dignity on the battlefield for their people, including in the United States. This is why when most people think of warriors, they think of American Indians.

Each tribe has its war heroes, and stories about them in battle have been told continuously. One generation shares these hero stories with the next one. This is a good practice for each community needs heroes, individuals to look up to. The warrior heroes become legendary as their names stand out because of their characteristics and deeds. Within tribal histories, these warriors are well known, perhaps famous. In this way, this oral tradition has been carried into the twenty-first century. Service in the American armed forces in modern times has enabled the continuance of the tradition as in the case of Ira Hayes (Pima), Ernest Childers (Mvskoke), and other war heroes. The Mvskoke Creeks are quite proud of Ernest Childers who won the Medal of Honor for his bravery in Europe during World War II. The Muscogee Creek Nation government has honored him with a statue of his likeness at the tribal government complex in Okmulgee, Oklahoma. I have met some of the relatives of Ernest Childers, and I have talked with Phillip Coon on three occasions before he passed away in 2014. My dad knew Phillip Coon and his wife, Helen, as friends and invited him to come over to the house to tell me about his serving in the army during World War II. My dad told me, "You gotta meet this man. He's a *tvstvnvke* (warrior)." Phillip Coon told the most bizarre true story. Like Childers, Coon was another Mvskoke Creek who entered the war and he experienced extreme hardship, but he had good medicine that guided him. That afternoon in my parents' living room, he said he was from Okemah, Oklahoma, and raised in the area. He went to Haskell Indian boarding school in Lawrence, Kansas, like a lot of Indian boys and girls from the state. When the war broke out in Europe, the country stayed neutral, but then the United States entered immediately following the attack on Pearl Harbor. That is when Phillip Coon joined the army. The good luck kept him alive when fellow soldiers were killed; many of them were his friends. In one situation, he got up to get a drink of water when a shell hit the area where he had been with his friends, killing them.

Bad luck occurred when the Japanese captured him as a prisoner. He was one of several hundred American and several thousand Filipino prisoners forced to endure the Bataan Death March of seventy miles on April 9, 1942.

Before the march started, most prisoners already suffered from malnutrition. Each was allowed to carry one canteen of water. Many died from lack of food and water; others were bayoneted to death by the Japanese. The enemy guards forced prisoners to march four abreast. Sometimes watching Japanese citizens gave them water, for which the soldiers punished the prisoners and the civilians. The temperature soared to 104 degrees under a torturous sun. April is in the hottest season in the Philippines, and the days are sultry. As the Japanese soldiers forced the march to continue, many men dropped from exhaustion and dehydration. They were forced to get up to continue walking. Many died on the spot where they dropped. As they struggled along, Phillip Coon thought he saw a ghost. One soldier look somewhat familiar and he thought his weary eyes deceived him. He struggled over to the fellow soldier, who was looking down at the ground. Coon bent down and looked into his face, and said, "Alex, it's me, Phillip Coon. We were at Haskell together." The stricken soldier, Alex Matthews, a Pawnee from Oklahoma, turned his head toward Coon and shook his head "yes" and they hugged each other until the Japanese guards motioned for them to keep walking. They whispered to each other and made a pact of trust—that they would not drop at the same time for fear that they both could not get back on their feet. So if one fell, the other would pick him up so that both of them had a better chance of surviving the death march. Coon related that it was better to march in the middle as the second or third person from the edge because the prisoners on the outside were easier targets for being prodded by a bayonet.

As I sat mesmerized by Phillip Coon's story, he said it did not stop there. After surviving the Bataan march, the Japanese forced him to work as a slave in their mines with other American soldiers. Bad luck struck again when the Japanese forced him with others to board Hell Ships that took him to Japan. As a prisoner of war for three years, his weight dropped from 145 to 90 pounds. Finally, the war ended and he was rescued with other survivors. He told how he was afraid to go home, back to his Mvskoke homeland in Okemah, because he had lost so much of the language. As he took the bus home, he practiced the Mvskoke language, trying to remember it. He got off the bus and hoped no one saw him, walking down one side street, he turned the corner only to meet face-to-face one of the Mvskoke elders, a woman who had known him since he was a child. Wearing a black scarf wrapped around her hair worn in a bun, she greeted him in Creek and asked him how he was. Tears came to his eyes and he replied in Creek that he was *e the ma he.* He was feeling good and felt lucky to be home. The elderly Creek woman hugged him and said she knew he was good because she and many Mvskoke Creeks had prayed for his safety and used medicine to help keep him alive so that he could come home.

The United States government alone has authorized 1,679 battles, skirmishes, and wars against Indians throughout the history of Indian-white relations. Often timing enables a leader to rise to prominence, and this has occurred with Indian leaders. Most important, stories are told about them in oral traditions. Indian warriors served their communities as they risked their lives to protect their people and homelands. For their brave deeds, stories have been told about them in oral traditions and this continues today among Indian people. In this way, the warriors of the past live today as examples and role models for Native youth. It is important for Native people, like people of any culture, to remember their heroes as examples of leadership and who often earned the respect of those they fought against.

We who are Mvskokes and Seminoles will always remember Osceola through our oral accounts about him and the wars in Florida. On the same trip to Fort King in central Florida, I found the original ceremonial ground a few miles away where Tustennuck Hajo (Fearless Warrior) sang and danced as a member of the Coe Hadjo band. A newfound friend that day led me to the ancient stomp ground that rested in a farmer's field, but you could read the circle imprinted in ecuna. I gazed for at least an hour from the fence by the side of the road, thinking about how this sacred ground connected my oldest known relative, Tustennuck Hajo, Osceola, the Trail of Tears, my home ground of Gar Creek in Oklahoma, my father, John Fixico, my younger brother, Ron, my youngest brother, Gerald, and my son, Keytha. As I left the ancient Seminole ceremonial ground, I picked up four small white stones, one each for my dad, Gerald, Keytha, and me. I had no idea that two of the stones would be returned so soon. On February 4, 2010, my father passed away from a heart attack following years of heart problems. When we buried him, I placed one of the white stones in his hand and closed his fingers around it. On a Sunday afternoon, December 18, 2011, Gerald was watching the Green Bay Packers play football against the Kansas City Chiefs on television at home in Broken Arrow, Oklahoma. At the same time in Arizona, I was watching the same football game. Gerald went to the garage to check on his clothes in the dryer. His chest pounded with pain as he leaned on the dryer and my hero passed away immediately from a massive

Gerald Fixico.
Author's collection.

heart attack. In Mesa, at the same time, I was thinking how my younger big
brother was a fearless linebacker, wearing 66 for the Will Rogers Ropers in high
school, like Green Bay's Clay Matthews that day, and then my phone rang. As
customary, we buried Gerald four days later and now he rests facing West in the
Wakolee Cemetery near Stroud, Oklahoma. At his funeral, I placed one of the
small white stones in his hand. Tears welled in my eyes. In my heart, I could feel
that my dad's and my brother's spirits were singing and dancing at our original
ceremonial ground in central Florida. My tears were of happiness for their spirits joined together with the spirits of my mother and my brother Ron who were
already there.

FOUR

Indian Oratory

A welcome greeting to all people at a stomp dance: "You are welcomed tonight. We all come here to give thanks to what the Master of Breath has given to us. We are glad that you made it here safe. Be respectful of our men in charge. Be respectful of the ceremonial fire. We respect all of you and you are our guests tonight. We come at this time now, men, women and children from all grounds and sister grounds to eat, sing, and dance. Our people have been doing this for many years and this is what we know and it is good."[1]

A town *mekko* (leader) instructs the town speaker about midnight or shortly thereafter to give the speech just before the Green Corn Dance begins as he introduces the first dance to begin. The above words in Mvskoke, roughly translated into English, are an example of a welcome speech lasting two to three minutes about the protocol for the dancing. The Mvskokes celebrate the annual harvest of corn to start their new year as all Indian towns did, following up with similar dances until late fall. I grew up hearing these words or similar ones in the Native language, which a town speaker would deliver as he invited all of those attending to participate in the dances that would last throughout the night. To me, the melody of the welcome speech and the rolling sound of the Mvskoke language was a meaningful part because everyone was invited to participate—all tribes, all people, Indian and non-Indian.

When my parents were still alive, I lived in Kansas and would drive with my son, Keytha, to visit them in Sapulpa, Oklahoma. Kellyville was several miles away and it was the home of a Euchee stomp ground where Green Corn

Dances were held. When we visited during the summer, we would go to two or three dances. Sapulpa was where my son was born. Sapulpa and Kellyville have become suburbs of southern Tulsa as it has grown along old Route 66 and the turnpike toward Oklahoma City. My dad used to call Route 66 "the old mother road." The Euchees are a proud group who have always been allies with the Mvskoke Creeks and are considered to be a part of the Creek Confederacy. The Kellyville stomp ground is hard to find at night and easier to find if you go there often. Kellyville is one of several stomp grounds I visited as a child and it is certainly an impressive one. Not for anything colorful, or its site, but because the dancers consist of a community of both working-class and professional people and of both Euchees and part-Euchees, including Mvskokes. Lawyers, judges, carpenters, schoolteachers, counselors, and others belong to the community. During any song, you might see two or three or four blonde women shaking shells, wearing turtle shells or tomato soup cans filled with river gravel tied to each lower calf. You can tell they probably learned to shake shells when they were little girls because they are very good.[2]

Once my dad and I were sitting in lawn chairs watching the dancing and Keytha, who was about six years old at the time, went missing. My dad asked people if they had seen Keytha since my dad knew most of them. Finally, we found him. Keytha was sitting under the main arbor with the mekko and the heles hayv (medicine maker) of the stomp ground, where he was not supposed to be. But they let him sit with them because he enjoyed the singing and dancing so much. He told them who my dad was, a Baptist minister in the Sapulpa area, and of course they knew him from his earlier stomp dance days and knew his dad, Jonas Fixico, and our relatives from the Gar Creek ground near Seminole.

Keytha's appreciation for the Green Corn Dance convinced me to share more of our heritage with him. His mother, Sharon O'Brien, and I adopted him in 1995 when he was a day and a half old; his birth parents were Mvskoke Creek. During December 2007, Keytha and I made the long trek to the Ocmulgee Mounds near Macon, Georgia. Our Mvskoke ancestors were mound builders, and their origin is near Macon and Ocmulgee was the principal town. We arrived at the Atlanta airport and rented a car to begin the long drive to where our people originated. We arrived at the entrance of the park mounds and walked down, then up toward the complex of mounds. Here is where our people first began to hold the Green Corn Dances. Centuries ago, the town mekko would have given a welcome speech like the one above. Called Creeks by early European traders, our true name is Mvskoke, "people of kind of swampland." The Ocmulgee Mounds complex is impressively large with several mounds focusing on a tall ceremonial mound that is flat on top, like a temple. Another focal point is the council mound where you can actually go inside and where the same feeling of inside the lodge surrealism is present. The past and the present become one feeling. I felt a spiritual connection with being Mvskoke and being raised as a child in the Mvskoke-Seminole tradition. Some people may doubt this, but if you are Mvskoke, you will feel connected to the mounds. Long ago, town mekkos and their second-in-command officials gathered at Ocmulgee for the annual Green Corn Ceremony. Purifications had to be made before any business could be conducted to make sure that everything was clean and fair and that only good spirituality was present.

My earliest memory of purification is going through the ceremony as a child—being given instructions, washing with the black drink, drinking it, and spitting it out. The whole idea is to purge your body of anything bad in a good way to withstand any physical test that you might face during the coming year. Naturally, there is a spiritual dimension to it as well. And an elder carried out his role of the *sapke* (scratching) of arm and leg muscles, too. This is the part that kids were afraid of, and we cried, but in retrospect I understand the purpose and logic of it.[3] All of it was amplified by the oratory and telling of the past and importance of cleansing, which meant there was a lot of speechmaking.

But Native eloquence also emerged during times of duress and urgency, when Native leaders spoke effectively to help their people. Some of the most eloquent oratory has been given by American Indian leaders: Chitto Harjo of the Mvskoke Creeks, Richard Pickup of the Cherokees, Ada Deer of the Menominees, Dennis Banks of the Ojibwes, and Wilma Mankiller of the Cherokees. Each of the speeches was delivered by an articulate Native man or woman. From these oratories, you can recognize the dignity, eloquence, emotions, power, persuasion, and visions described by the speakers.

The place and circumstances of oratory are important, as is the audience. Some of the following speeches were delivered within tribal communities before an Indian audience; thus, metaphorically, they were presented inside the lodge to encourage a community feeling. Internally, the power of oratory manifested within an Indian reality. Other speeches were given to a mixed Indian and white audience. The third circumstance is when the Native speaker gave a speech outside of his or her Native element to a non-Indian audience. Outside of the lodge, Native orators labored twice as much to be effective in their words in order to make their points understood and persuasive to a non-Indian audience, especially when they were opposing the allotment of tribal lands.

The Dawes Act of 1887 forced land allotment that resulted in tribal land reduction; many people resisted, such as Chitto Harjo, who spoke adamantly against the wrongs of allotting tribal lands and breaking treaties. He spoke for the old ways, and Richard Pickup, a Cherokee minister, spoke for the new ways of Indians accepting Christianity. In the late 1960s and early 1970s, Dennis Banks spoke numerous times for Indian rights as a leader of the American Indian Movement. In 1993, Ada Deer gave a significant speech as assistant secretary of the interior about tribes working in partnership to establish a different kind of political relationship with the federal government. In the same year, Wilma Mankiller, the principal chief of the Cherokee tribe in Oklahoma, gave an inspiring speech about the progress and future of her people.

These Indian orators, and other Indian orators of the past, were articulate, combining politics with philosophy as they elaborately described how the advancing white race intruded into their ways of life. In modern times, Indian oratory and speeches still have special tribal emphasis, such as the Lakota Way or the Cherokee Way. Among the Cherokees, orators held speaking beads to empower the speaker to find the right words and tone needed to persuade listeners to take the words to heart. Sometimes, speakers from other tribes held a feather or staff that had been treated with personal medicine to make the person find the right words and gestures. These oratories constituted speech events, which sociolinguist Dell Hymes defines as an activity governed by particular rules or norms of speech within larger speech situations.[4] Such a moment became an oral historical event among Native people that many would remember.

Oratory represents power and elevates one's status among one's people. Lewis Henry Morgan, early ethnologist among the Iroquois, observed the significance of oratory among these people. He wrote, "The Indian has a quick and enthusiastic appreciation of eloquence. Highly impulsive in his nature, and with passions untaught of restraint, he is strongly susceptible of its influence."[5] Morgan offers us insight into the importance of oratory even as he adopts a condescending attitude toward Natives in his description of them as highly susceptible. Many listeners fell under the spell of a Native orator and the power of the spoken word. The power of the oratory was regarded as a special talent. Morgan noted, "The chief or warrior gifted with its magical [oratory] power could elevate himself as rapidly as he gained renown upon the war-path."[6] Effective oratory gained notice and elevated orators above everyone, as they possessed the articulate gift of persuading their listeners.

Among the Lakotas, medicine maker Severt Young Bear emphasized that some of his people were especially good speakers. He said, "There are proud parts to a good speaker's skills. First, is the ability to speak with a strong voice and change his volume at each given point to suit the point he wants to get across to people. The next is the ability to blend humor in so he can have a little smile or nod of the head back from the people in the audience, which, in our way, means they agree. The third is to have the knowledge of different areas or different topics that he talks about.... The fourth area is what I would call his public image. Many of our gifted speakers can really use their body language. They might have a special way of getting up to speak."[7] The ability to communicate effectively in Native oral traditions is a power that is personal to only a few speakers in a community. Having found their voices with authority, such individuals are leaders because of their oratorical talent.

Chitto Harjo against Allotment

Chitto Harjo of the Mvskoke Creeks spoke firmly on the issue of allotment. His calculated oratory combined his powerful intellect and personal experiences with his passionate feelings about the injustice of the tribal situation. Undoubtedly, he waited for the right time to speak against the individual allotment of tribal lands and broken treaties. He likely rehearsed his thoughts, mapping out what he wanted to say as he used geographical references and political events. Harjo had assessed the history of treaty negotiations and what had been promised. In his words, he addressed the wrongs done to his people.

The organization of the Oklahoma Territory and the growing statehood movement in 1906 convinced Chitto Harjo and several of his followers called Snakes to plan a delegation to Washington. Harjo and the Snakes referred to the Treaty of 1832 made in Washington, which provided a new homeland in the West and did not mention allotment. Harjo argued that other Creek treaties did not include allotment and needed to be upheld to protect tribal land from being allotted. Federal officials refused to recognize the Snakes, and the Indians' efforts failed.[8]

The federal government remained convinced of the righteousness of its overall plan to allot lands to individual Indians in order to civilize them.

Chitto Harjo (Crazy Snake).
Courtesy Oklahoma
Historical Society.

However, many Mvskokes opposed allotment, causing the government officials to listen to the Indians. A special Senate Investigating Committee surveyed the old Indian Territory to evaluate Indian progress, and the committee agreed to hear the dissident Mvskokes. On November 23, 1906, the Senate committee held a hearing at the Elks Lodge Hall in Tulsa. A large number of people gathered at the hearing, many of whom supported Harjo and his Snakes.

Chitto Harjo spoke against the allotment program. With his hat in his hands, his face full of despair, he stood before the committee and spoke about the treaties and his beliefs. Harjo said that he had heard a rumor that the U.S. government was surveying his tribe's land and giving it away to other people. He said that this was not possible for it was not a part of the removal treaty that his people had agreed to in coming to Indian Territory. Furthermore, Harjo wanted to know who the people were to whom the land was being given. "They have no right to this land," said Harjo. He reiterated that it was assigned to him and his Mvskoke people as payment for their original homeland in Alabama. Neither black nor white people had any right to the Mvskokes' new homelands. He asked again in this speech before the crowd of people in Tulsa, how could it be happening. It was injustice and he knew that "some citizens of the United States have title to land that was given to my fathers and my people by the government. If it was given to me, what right has the United States to take it from me without first asking my consent?"[9] Chitto Harjo's words described the feelings of many traditional members of the Five Civilized Tribes.

Many full-blood Cherokees joined a secret society called the "Pin Indians" because of the insignia they wore expressing their opposition to allotment. The membership of the Pins reached approximately five thousand full-bloods under Cherokee leader Red Bird Smith, and they officially called themselves the Keetoowah Society. Eufaula Harjo, another Mvskoke traditionalist, helped Smith to organize other Mvskokes, Cherokees, and supporters from the Chickasaws and Choctaws to join them. With members from all four tribes, they changed their name to the Four Mothers Society. Trying to find a solution to get out of their allotments and return to traditional ways, the Four Mothers Society sent a delegation to Washington to try to convince the federal officials to change government plans to allot the lands of the four tribes. Federal officials refused the delegation's request.[10] Harjo's efforts had led to a growing anti-allotment movement among the traditional Indians of the Five Civilized Tribes.

Chitto Harjo's death in 1909 did not end the traditionalist movement. His belief, like that of his ancestors, urged Mvskoke poet Alexander Posey to write, "Such will! Such courage to defy the powerful makers of his fate! Condemn him and his kind to shame! I bow to him, exalt his name!" Posey's words spoke the sentiment of many Creeks and many Indians whose lands were allotted and lost. By 1934, Indian land holdings had declined sharply from 138 million acres to 48 million due to allotment, affecting an estimated 135 tribes, confederated tribal groups, rancherias, pueblos, and nations recognized by the federal government.

Harjo's position, like that of Black Hawk and Tecumseh, fell on federal officials' deaf ears. He was one of many opposing allotment and his ringing words were not forgotten. The Mvskokes remember allotment and Chitto Harjo very well because he represented the resilient spirit of his people. In a larger conversation, his words are about injustice, rights, and mistreatment. His words and actions did not stop the allotment momentum, but Chitto Harjo's oratory addressed the injustice of how Native people felt about the Dawes Act of 1887. Over a hundred years later, I had my turn to speak about it.

On May 29, 1993, my dad drove the two of us in his old Silverado pickup from my parents' house in Sapulpa to Okmulgee, a little over thirty miles away. I had the honor of speaking at the rededication of the Creek Council House built in 1878, located at 106 W. 6th Street in the heart of the downtown. On that special day, I was among other speakers and my assignment was to talk about the history of allotment as a general federal-Indian policy and how the amendment to the Dawes Act impacted the Mvskoke Creeks by allowing the U.S. government to distribute allotments of the Creek reservation to tribal members. That day was especially warm and anyone knowing Oklahoma weather likened it to Coyote, the trickster of many tribes who plays tricks on people. It was a Coyote day; cold one hour, hot the next. You cannot trust the weather. The celebrated Cherokee Will Rogers said once, "If you don't like the weather in Oklahoma, then wait a few minutes and it will change." But it remained warm in the afternoon as I began my speech. Sweat poured off my forehead as I mopped it with my handkerchief. The organizers had asked us to speak from the roof of the back porch. At the back and off to the right stood a tall old oak, which still stands, and it provided magnificent shade that I longed for. But what I remember most that day was six original Mvskoke Creek allottees who sat in lawn chairs like my dad or who stood in the shade among the many people. The allottees listened and nodded in agreement to what I had to say. I spoke about Chitto Harjo and how he disagreed with allotment and how he voiced his views against it. He was right because allotment brought so much destruction to our people and other tribes, too.

As I addressed the audience that day, I sensed the troubled history of Indian-white relations and the trauma that the Mvskokes felt. A long feeling of hurt and injustice has colored the Mvskoke past and it hung in the air. That feeling has always been there, starting with the removal of our people from the East to Indian Territory, and then allotment. As I spoke, I stopped looking at my notes and my words came from my heart. I could feel the injustice that Chitto Harjo spoke about and felt a tribal despair. The old ones under the shade of the tree nodded in agreement. I realized that oratory is not always powerful and enthralling, but urges acceptance of the present conditions and deciding to move forward with life. To try to make things better and move forward were my thoughts and my words. Oratory is a shared feeling as much as a shared experience.

Richard Pickup

Richard "Duke" Pickup is a Cherokee preacher of the Baptist denomination from eastern Oklahoma. He was born in Salina, Oklahoma, in 1947 and has five brothers and three sisters. On a Sunday morning in 1973, Pickup's five-year-old son invited him to go to church and after listening to the sermon, he converted to Christianity. Three and a half years later, he felt the call to become a preacher. In 1982, Reverend Pickup answered the call again and this time he became a full-time evangelist. Reverend Pickup is also a missionary, minister, zealot, and traveling evangelist. While Chitto Harjo spoke for the old ways, Reverend Pickup spoke about Indian people finding God and becoming Christians. The old dilemma of Indians believing in the old ways or making a life decision and adopting Christianity might be what most people would think in this situation. But I have seen Indians adopting both belief systems.

I first learned about Reverend Pickup when I was a teenager and forced to go to church. The reverend spoke at a revival at the First Indian Baptist Church in Muskogee, Oklahoma. The church invited him and was lucky to get him because he was booked months in advance. I had become a Christian at age sixteen after my dad had a terrible auto accident that hurt him pretty badly—broken ribs, broken arm, and a couple of teeth knocked out. A teenage girl came speeding over a hill as my dad made a left turn onto Old Bacone Road; she hit him broadside on the passenger's side. It was winter, we did not have a telephone, and my dad was coming to pick me up after basketball practice at the high school located on the edge of Muskogee. Usually, I walked four to five miles home with wet hair after taking a shower, and sometimes I asked friends for a ride. That evening changed my dad's life and ours, too. While he was recovering in the hospital, my dad became a Christian, and in a few months he became a minister. Some people might see a conflict of interest because my father believed in the traditional ways of the Mvskoke-Seminoles, and he would have to forego the old ways to embrace Christianity. And he did until the last few years of his life.

Christianity and Indian beliefs have been at odds in Oklahoma for a long time, even when the state was Indian Territory in the early nineteenth century. Traditional beliefs continued and persisted into the twentieth and twenty-first centuries. Baptists, Methodists, Presbyterians, and other religious groups preached among the Indians and throughout the West and no fewer than twenty-two denominations have sent missionaries among the tribes. In Oklahoma, many Indians embraced Christianity, and so did my family. As the days drew closer to when Reverend Pickup would preach, church members were eager to hear him.

Richard Pickup is a fireball preacher. I have heard him on two or three occasions and he shook the rafters, as they say. He started his sermon thanking those who invited him, then led the audience in a prayer. He pulled his white folded handkerchief from his back pocket and laid it carefully on top of the pulpit; on a side table was a pitcher of water and a glass. Reverend Pickup led a second prayer before he began to preach, and one thing was certain: he prayed a lot, although sometimes not very long because Indian prayers can be dreadfully long. Then he would go to parts of the Bible and relate them to experiences in life and to his own personal experiences. He described his early reckless life when he drank alcohol, felt broken, and how Jesus came into his life and he felt the call to preach. He had a certain melodic tone in his deep rolling voice, and he would gesticulate, raising his hands at the right time to punctuate his points. He hit the emotional raw nerves of his listeners; people began to cry, wiping their tears. He preached harder until sweat ran down the sides of his face. He patted his forehead with the handkerchief, took off his suit jacket and rolled up his sleeves, and kept preaching. The audience would yell, "Amen!" and when they agreed with him, he shouted, "Praise the Lord." Others would nod their head, yes. And as he ended his sermon, you felt like he had taken you to the brink of Hell, showed you the fire and brimstone, and brought you back. If you were not a Christian, the invitation of the preacher was the deciding moment. Some decided to accept the invitation—to accept Christ as their Savior. Some decided to rededicate their lives to being better Christians. Others wanted a special prayer with the preacher for him- or herself or for someone ill or in trouble. As the invitation started, Reverend Pickup stepped from behind the pulpit and disappeared into a backroom as the song leader took over to lead the songs inviting people to come forward and give their lives to Christ. Reverend Pickup returned from the backroom and you could tell he had changed his shirt and toweled off from preaching so hard.

Richard Pickup is a legend, a well-known evangelist among Indian communities. There were and are others like him, such as Johnny Lay and John Douglas Bemo Sr. but when you heard Richard Pickup it was an experience you would never forget. He is in a genre of Indian preachers that dates back to early years of the nineteenth century when missionaries converted Indians to Christianity and allowed them to preach. The old Indian ministers preached in their Native languages, like my grandfather Jonas Fixico, who was also the medicine keeper of our dance ground at Gar Creek near Seminole before he became a

Christian. The dynamic Indian preachers that I know about gave their rous-ing sermons in English. Like Tecumseh, Chitto Harjo, and others before them, they stirred the emotions of their listeners, even those who did not understand the Native language, because in the end the emotional understanding is more powerful than language.

Dennis Banks and Wounded Knee in 1973

During the late 1800s, the Ghost Dance spread among Plains tribes and other tribes on reservations in about a half dozen states. Panic among whites com-pelled the Seventh Cavalry to round up the Minniconjou Lakotas under Big Foot's leadership and ordered his people to camp at Wounded Knee Creek in South Dakota. Two searches for weapons among the Indians and pushing the Indians around escalated to the military firing upon the defenseless Indians when they pushed back. In 1890, the last significant battle was waged between the United States and American Indians, although it was actually a massacre of a group of Lakotas. The last Indian war many say was in 1890, and with-out doubt a lot of people connect it to the takeover of Wounded Knee in 1973 because Indian activists recalled the massacre.

In the early 1970s, the American Indian Movement rose to protest for Indian rights. AIM activism turned into militancy, especially when called on by Lakota elders for protection against the corrupt Lakota government on Pine Ridge Res-ervation. AIM seized the small town of Wounded Knee as a point of operation against the Lakota government led by Dick Wilson, who was supported with weapons by the U.S. government. The event included many Native people and it captured headlines across the country. Many stories and books have chron-icled the takeover of the small white town in South Dakota called Wounded Knee. The Indians pushed back with activist orators like Russell Means, Clyde Bellecourt, and Dennis Banks. When this did not work, AIM activism became militant.

The story of Dennis Banks, Ojibwe—an important leader in this last great conflict—provides powerful insights into the struggles of fighting for Indian rights on a national stage. His story is one of achieving a national role in fight-ing for Indian rights and upholding U.S. treaty responsibilities.[11] In the spring of 2003, then-acquisition editor Nancy Scott Jackson of the University Press of Kansas, some university staff, and I organized a conference of 1960s Red Power activists at the University of Kansas. At the time, I was the founding director of the Indigenous Studies graduate program. We invited Dennis Banks, Clyde Bellecourt, and other activists, and it was a great conference for our new program. Dennis Banks is an incredible person of more than one persona. I sat next to him as we ate box lunches on the day that he spoke in the Kansas Room in the Student Union on campus to a crowd of over two hundred people. He seemed mild-mannered and kind of quiet, and I wondered if this was the real strong outspoken activist who led the American Indian Movement. I asked him if he still wrote poetry after moving back to his reservation at Leech Lake in Minnesota. Dennis studied the pattern of the wooden floor as he ate, and he would look up periodically at the people. The former AIM leader replied that he spent most of his time organizing spiritual long-distance runs throughout Indian Country. The depth of his seriousness about life struck me: he had risked his own life for the United States in the Korean War when he served in the Air Force and more than once when AIM confronted injustice, primarily at Wounded Knee. That afternoon Clyde Bellecourt spoke first, and Dennis Banks joked that Clyde had stolen his speech and he did not have much to say. In the following minutes, we learned his statement was very far from the truth. As Dennis began to reminisce about the founding of AIM, he talked about the police brutality that he and other Indians faced in the streets of the Twin Cities. His gentle soul became aflame with bitterness toward injustice and mistreatment of Indians. In the overflowing crowd in the room, an electrical power could be felt emanating from the charismatic Banks. His emotional energy captivated the entire room of people. Some people had to stand and others waited in the hallways to get in as his provocative words convinced all to agree with him. He vilified the United States for historical wrongs committed against Indians. I will never forget that day and listening to the AIM warrior.

Dennis Banks grew up in Minnesota on Leech Lake Reservation and he went to Pipestone Boarding School, two hundred miles from home. It was his belief in justice that motivated him to help Indians and to make the United States understand how badly it had mistreated them. Banks was a warrior in more than one way. AIM political prisoner Leonard Peltier stated, "We found our inspiration and our strategy in the example and message of AIM leaders such as Dennis Banks, John Trudell, Russell Means, Eddie Benton-Banai, and Clyde and Vernon Bellecourt, and all imperfect men, no doubt, yet men whose vision and bravery and fiery, even incendiary, words gave voice to a whole generation of Indian activists, myself included."[12] Russell Means described Banks as impressive, stating, "Dennis practically glows with charisma. . . . A week in Detroit with AIM [in December 1969] had changed my whole outlook. It had crystallized thoughts and feelings and desires long buried within my psyche. . . . Never again would I seek personal approval from white society on white terms. Instead, like Clyde [Bellecourt] and Dennis and the others in AIM, I would get in the white man's face until he gave me and my people our just due. With that decision, my whole existence suddenly came into focus. For the first time, I knew the purpose of my life and the path I must follow to fulfill it. At the age of thirty I became a full-time Indian."[13]

After its formation in 1968, AIM quickly grew in membership across Indian Country in both the United States and Canada. Various protest activities led to the Trail of Broken Treaties march in 1972, resulting in the takeover of the Bureau of Indian Affairs building in Washington, D.C. The following year, Dennis Banks and AIM took over the small town of Wounded Knee, South Dakota. The Indians occupied the town for seventy-one days, and when they learned that local authorities and the National Guard had been called in to restore order, they armed themselves with hunting rifles and small firearms. More than three hundred U.S. marshals were sent to Wounded Knee, including their Special Operations Group. The government sent over one hundred FBI agents to set up roadblocks on two of the highways going to the takeover site. The Central Intelligence Agency also was involved. Weapons used by this collective force included M-16 automatic rifles, M-79 grenade launchers, and .30 and .50 caliber machine guns. In addition, these forces used various lighting equipment and nighttime-sensing devices. The U.S. army delivered eighteen armored personnel carriers, and rented three private helicopters.[14]

Finally on May 8, the two sides laid down their weapons after the Oglala chiefs and federal government signed an agreement. The two sides agreed that the government would investigate charges against tribal chairman Dick Wilson and hold treaty meetings with the Oglalas in order to review the 1868 Fort Laramie Treaty. The intensity of Wounded Knee carried over to a shoot-out in 1975 between AIM members and two FBI agents, who were killed. In the end, Leonard Peltier was arrested and sentenced to two consecutive life terms for the deaths of the two FBI men, Jack Coler and Ron Williams.[15]

The occupation of Wounded Knee was the high point of Indian resistance in the twentieth century. It repeated the old theme of Indians versus whites in the battles of the so-called Indian wars. The takeover added a second chapter to the history of Wounded Knee. Some of the inspiration for the takeover resulted from AIM talking about the Wounded Knee massacre of 1890. Some AIM leaders like Banks, Bellecourt, Trudell, and Means became powerful political speakers. Their oratories connected the militant present to past violence. They used their oratories as tools and used the persuasion of rhetoric and history to remind all Americans of the past injustice committed by whites against Indians.

No one at that time had forgotten what happed at Wounded Knee in 1890, especially the Lakotas. Yet Dennis Banks and other AIM members proved themselves to be modern warriors. Banks was twice a warrior, having served in the Air Force in the Korean War and as a leader of AIM during its activist protests. But as a leader, Banks proved pivotal in helping to change the course of modern Indian history. He helped to instill pride among Native people in the 1960s and 1970s. In 1973, I was in my junior year at the University of Oklahoma and it was the ending of the Vietnam War. Civil rights was still a huge issue that we saw on television almost every night. What I remember most about those volatile times was that something important happened every day practically and the norm was change—change affecting people's lives and the future of America.

Indian leaders have learned to use oratory most effectively during times of conflict and war. Just as Dennis Banks used oratory, Black Hawk, Osceola, and other warriors used the power of the spoken word to garner support for their causes. Their objectives were for the good of their people, whether for political rights or defending tribal homelands. Difficult times called these individuals to leadership and they found they were endowed with oratorical abilities that made indelible impressions on their audiences. Oratory has been a long-held tradition among American Indians, and certain Indian orators are very impressive.

Ada Deer before the Senate Committee on Indian Affairs, July 15, 1993

Exciting energy describes Ada Deer, a Menominee of Wisconsin. Blessed with oratory skills, Ada Deer also possesses a wide range of knowledge about federal-Indian relations. Ada Deer is a tall woman who speaks impressively with decisive objectives in mind. Her oratorical motive is to get things done. Her cause in life began with the injustice done to her people in being terminated of trust status, ending all treaty obligations to the Menominees. After her resignation from her position as assistant secretary of the Interior in 1997, Ada Deer returned to her home state of Wisconsin and became a senior lecturer and chairperson of the American Indian Studies program at the University of Wisconsin at Madison. This is when I met Ada, when I was a new faculty member in the history department at the University of Wisconsin at Milwaukee. She was tall, wore glasses, and had short black hair. She came to our campus with a couple of colleagues and spoke to our American Indian Studies staff and faculty. No doubt, she was a woman of action.

The Menominee of Wisconsin was a timber-rich tribe whose reservation was blessed with abundant stands of tree types—pine, white pine, red oak, hemlock, beech, maple, white cedar, and Canadian yew. Of the several tribes scheduled for immediate termination according to a new federal policy in 1952, the BIA and Congress selected the Menominee to be first. The Menominee tribe was the first tribe to have its "trust" status terminated by the federal government. Congress did this in 1954 in an act, Public Law 399, which fulfilled that promise in 1961.[16] Afterwards, other tribes saw their federal trust status terminated with the U.S. government until the total came to 109 termination cases by the early 1970s. The ultimate purpose of the termination policy was for tribal communities to be integrated into the other communities within their states, but the policy failed miserably.

Ada Deer along with other Menominees and with help from Joseph Preloznik, a lawyer, set out to reverse the termination of the Menominee tribe. In starting an organization called Determination of Rights and Unity of Menominee Shareholders (DRUMS), Deer led a grassroots movement to pressure Congress into introducing a bill to restore her people to federal recognition as a tribe in 1973. Their success ended the termination policy and began a restoration policy that restored over a dozen terminated tribes to their original status.[17] Deer's deliberate lobbying efforts convinced many bureaucrats that her tribe needed to be restored. I have heard her tell the story more than once about how she would get a congressman's undivided attention to listen to her idea for restoring the Menominee tribe via legislation. When Ada would take a flight leaving Washington, she would deliberately be one of the last passengers to board. She would look at the other passengers and yell, "Senator?" Often two or three would look up, and she had them captive for twenty or twenty-five seconds, and she encouraged each one to sponsor her Menominee restoration bill. Strapped in their seats with their seat belts, they had to listen to her!

Deer's oratory enabled a pivotal change in modern Indian history. In 1993 President Bill Clinton appointed Deer as the first Indian woman to be assistant secretary of the Interior. Ada Deer articulated her plan for a new kind of federal-Indian relationship founded upon partnership. She stated in a speech before the Senate Committee on Indian Affairs that her vision for the Bureau of Indian Affairs was to create a "progressive federal/tribal partnership." She stressed that the government's Indian policy must maintain and sustain "effective tribal sovereignty." Assistant Secretary Deer believed there was no reason for anyone to be reluctant in supporting the permanency of tribal sovereignty any more than they would be reluctant to support the permanency of federal or state sovereignty. Deer emphasized that it was the moral obligation of people to support the rights of American Indians. Specifically, she stressed that the federal government should support and implement "tribally inspired solutions to tribally defined problems." Lastly, Deer argued that the days of federal paternalism were over. In her final statement of this speech, she reiterated the position of Secretary of Interior Bruce Babbitt, "We must accelerate the trend toward self-governance so that we can reshape our role from paternal guardians to active engaged partners."[18]

The Clinton administration strove for government-to-government relationships between tribes and the United States. This partnership is what Ada Deer tried to build as a new kind of federal-Indian policy that emphasized tribal self-government. Deer followed in the footsteps of Sarah Winnemucca, a strong, impressive Paiute woman, and others as she represented the modern Native woman leader who actively accomplished things that seemed impossible. She combines energy, power, and words to accomplish her deeds as a role model to young Native women and men. An analysis of the actions and oratory of Deer shows that she established a lexicon arising from her objective of restoring her tribe to federal recognition and while she held the office of assistant secretary of the Interior. Deer used oratory to establish a new language. For example, she used words like "termination," "restoration," "tribal sovereignty," and "self-determination" that other Indian orators began to adopt as a part of their political rhetoric to be used as tools in their own oratory to speak about the past and the future.

Ada Deer's oratory intersected with past traditions and it did not. Typically, Indian orators were men, although Sarah Winnemucca, a Paiute woman in the late 1800s, was another powerful speaker. Like Native orators of the past, Ada Deer addressed the future. Winnemucca talked about the conditions of her people at the time. Both envisioned the big picture of U.S.-tribal relations and emphasized the significance of political rights and the formation of federal Indian policy that would benefit Indian people. Simultaneously, Ada Deer challenged the U.S. government and her own people to strive for a better understanding of sovereignty and to protect it. Sovereignty means the freedom to live as you wish, but it is not free.

Wilma Mankiller, Rebuilding the Cherokee Nation, 1993

The oratory of Wilma Mankiller combines the past with the present. She also pulls together Cherokee heritage and mainstream history. Like Sitting Bull, Mankiller's wisdom and broad knowledge served her speaking ability. She orated with vision like Ada Deer because she had goals to achieve; yet she could also reflect impressively on the past, sometimes in the Cherokee language.

In 1945, Wilma Mankiller was born at the Indian hospital in Tahlequah, Oklahoma. Her family lived in rural poverty in Adair County. She was one of eleven children. Her father's limited employment forced the family to move to California via the federal relocation program for Indians from 1952 to 1972.[19]

The year of 1992 represented five hundred years of Indian-white relations, starting when Columbus found himself mistakenly on the shore of North America instead of India. Since that time, Indian nations have prospered, declined and only in the last part of the twentieth century did many of the 567 federally recognized tribes begin to establish self-governance. Mankiller said she had learned from living in an almost entirely African American community and from living in her own Oklahoma community that the federal government underestimates the great capacity of poor people for solving their own problems. When Mankiller was a part of the tribal government in 1977, she learned that the Cherokees could solve their own problems. By 1982, Mankiller was founding director of the Community Development department of the tribe. She had conceptualized the idea with her husband of how to rebuild a community. The Cherokee government did not look like the U.S. government in Mankiller's opinion, but it was a functional government and she saw leadership in the tribal communities that also may not have looked like leadership in the rest of the world. But leadership among the Cherokees existed. Mankiller stated that if she was asked what was the most important issue among her tribe, she would respond that it was "development" and that leaders needed to make that happen.

Other people, according to Mankiller, might respond specifically by building a clinic or doing something in the community. But, she said, "I think the most important issue we have as a people is what we started, and that is to begin to trust our own thinking again and believe in ourselves enough to think that we can articulate our own vision of the future and then work to make sure that that vision becomes a reality."[20] In this way, Mankiller described key characteristics of leadership that were needed to run tribal governments and communities.

With eloquence, Mankiller combined history and present conditions to make her points in her speeches like the one above. Her oratory drew upon world examples as well as Cherokee experiences to address a global future for all people predicated on the need to acknowledge others. With stories in the oral tradition of the Cherokees, Mankiller touched the minds of her listeners, appealing to their intellect. Not a leader by personal choice, Mankiller felt that circumstances forced her into the position. Mankiller said that she served her people and that including being the principal chief of the Cherokees in Oklahoma. In this sense, when she ran for office, she was her people's choice to be leader and was elected to this position in 1984 as the first woman chief.

Mankiller spoke of tribal sovereignty as the Cherokee people and other Indian nations entered a second five-hundred-year existence with the white man. Determined and dedicated to helping her people, she became one of the most celebrated Indian women leaders in modern times. Besides being reelected chief of the Cherokees, Mankiller won several distinguished awards, including *Ms.* magazine's Woman of the Year in 1987 and the Presidential Medal of Freedom. A lecturer in great demand, Mankiller wove tribal eloquence with modern ideas for a better future for her people.

On October 2, 2008, Wilma Mankiller visited Arizona State University and that night I went to hear her speak at the Heard Museum in downtown Phoenix. Her topic was "Challenges Facing 21st Century Indigenous People." She emphasized the resilience of Indian people and stressed the importance of preparedness. Wearing blue earrings and glasses, she spoke with dignity from a basis of history and being Cherokee, but she heavily stressed Indian people telling their own stories. She spoke about Indian legal rights and building tribal communities, but she stressed that this could not be done in a vacuum and that Indians needed to connect with non-Indian communities, tribal communities, and other Indigenous people around the world. She talked about the earth, as our mother who needed to be respected and how people needed to fill their obligations in restoring the balance with nature. Like Indian orators of the past, Wilma Mankiller described the big picture for Indians. The audience applauded with great respect for Wilma. I made my way in line to congratulate her on her presentation. As we shook hands, I said, "It's good to see someone from Oklahoma." She responded with a question, "When are you coming home?" During the last several years of her life, Wilma suffered from a series of health issues. This was the last time that I saw Wilma alive; she died from cancer in her rural Cherokee homeland on April 6, 2010.

Like all societies, American Indian communities had impressive leaders who were also impressive speakers. Eloquence was a leadership quality. To be eloquent was not enough, however, as an effective speaker needed to relate his or her message to the people. Specific causes inspired them because they believed something had to be done to help their people. In each situation, the Native leader responded, but also believed in the need to be pro-active to change the conditions.

Historical and modern Indian speakers have also impressed white officials and the American public. They were broad-thinking and had visions of promise. Their speeches have been recorded in the long chronicles of American Indian history. In the minds of their peoples, they are heroes and heroines. They are role models to their youth and to other young people as well. There are many other noted leaders of nearly six hundred Indian groups and the several discussed here are only a sample of the most famous Indian leaders in American Indian history. Such leaders sometimes gave their lives for their communities; above all, they served their people, placing this role before their personal needs. This unselfish way is how American Indian leaders in most cases prioritize what is best for their people ahead of their personal needs and ambitions.

Native oratory is beyond an art, as Indian leaders have used their rhetorical skills to convince their listeners to join them in war or to convince officials to give them what they desired. Oratory in war, even in surrender, was a necessity of effective leaders like Chief Joseph, Sitting Bull, and Tecumseh. To be an effective speaker to more than one kind of audience and across language barriers was to be great in oratory. Eloquent, but with firm words, Native leaders orated with conviction to convince people to see things from their perspective. They invited listeners to see the big picture and not just to listen but to become participants in a cause. These Native orators invited others to envision what they saw and convinced them of what needed to be done for a better future. Indian orators inspire people.

FIVE

Ghost Stories and Little People

Many years ago, I was raised in the country outside of Shawnee, Oklahoma. We lived next to a white family of six kids and it was a lot of fun playing with them. My father and their dad were young men and they enjoyed hunting and fishing. Carl was a bricklayer and the out-of-doors type. One summer day after they got home from work, the two fathers went fishing and planned to spend the night at the nearby lake. After casting their fishing lines into the water, they talked and talked as the sun began to go down. Dusk approached first with pink, orange and red rays as the last one slipped away in the West—a pivotal portal where day and night intersect twice: at sunrise and sunset. These are powerful moments for Indians. In this twilight, the two young men were silent for a while as they watched the red and white floats on their fishing lines. Then suddenly, Carl looked at my dad, and then looked back at the water. My dad noticed Carl looking at him oddly and at the same moment, my father heard Indians singing and dancing. Both men studied their fishing lines in silence for a moment. Carl felt uneasy, then he turned toward my dad again, and this time, he said, 'Did you hear that?' My father was much surprised because white men are not supposed to hear Indian spirits, much less see them. Carl then said, 'There must be Indians nearby.' My father shook his head slowly that there were none. My dad was still puzzled that Carl heard the singing and dancing again. Furthermore, my father knew all of the stomp grounds in the area and none were nearby. Indeed, this was stomp dance country long, long ago when the tribes practiced the Green Corn Ceremony after removal to Indian Territory. Suddenly, Carl suggested that they not spend the night at the lake. He wanted to get out of there and he was in such a hurry that he left his rod and reel and my dad left his, too! Carl had driven them to the lake, so my dad had to run to catch up with him or walk home in the dark.

Spirits have been known to exist in societies around the world. Among Indians, spirits and spirituality play an important part of life, and they appear in stories as a part of oral traditions. Most of the time these stories are simply referred to as ghost stories. Spirits are a part of the Other Side of the physical life with which Indian people try to interact. And the attempt to interact has been a continual effort. The Other Side is a dimension that includes harmless spirits and bad ones, such as witches, antagonistic supernatural beings, and the dead. While many people in the American mainstream may dismiss the Other Side, there is enough evidence that speaks to the presence of spirituality among them, such as Christians believing in the Holy Spirit and feeling a metaphysical presence. Many non-Indians of all ethnicities will admit that they have experienced, heard, or seen ghosts. Most of the members of the American mainstream are nonbelievers and are quick to say they do not believe in ghosts. I differ. The Other Side of ghosts and spirituality is something that at present we do not fully comprehend. Yet there are stories in all cultures around the world about ghosts and spirits.[1]

Spirituality

Spirituality among Native people is an energy that is abstract and intangible. It does not always reveal itself to people and sometimes only some people experience it in the presence of others. Spirituality can also exist outside of an individual person and can be transitory, so it is synonymous with spiritual energy rather than a system of beliefs. Once this encounter happens to you, you never forget it. Spiritual energy has the power to create vivid memories for us.

Spirituality among American Indians is a combined human-metaphysical feeling that touches the soul of people and their community. It is what bonds Indian people together in the same way as a shared experience. This commonality of knowing when the metaphysical is present exists within tribes, yet is powerful enough to cross over to other tribal communities and to embrace outsiders. For example, when Jesus rose from the tomb after his death, most everyone was astonished and believed that he had risen from the dead.[2]

Spirituality is like an invisible smoke that engulfs one person among many at a gathering and gives each person a sense of belonging. Being connected to one's family, clan or society, and community or town is most important. Spirituality manifests its presence when ceremonies are held, dances occur, or when a song is sung, seemingly coming from nowhere as if it was always there and has been awakened. Spirituality makes you feel different, light; it makes you forget momentarily about everything.

What has been described thus far is spirituality "within." That is, spirituality emerges and permeates a group of people and has the same effect on all of them. This experience is as if they all share the same feeling and thoughts; it is as if they are one live being. Such spirituality within is also momentary; it may last only until a song ends or a dance comes to a stop, or the people disperse. The spiritual momentum comes and goes, and the longer it lingers, the closer the people feel connected to each other in a sacred way.

For Native people, there are at least four primary manifestations of spirituality or spiritual energy. One is the spirit of a person. In fact, the spirit after a person dies is an extension of this type of spirituality. Such spiritual energy is within us all of the time and sometimes outside of us. Much of our lives are spent trying to connect with the spirit inside of us.[3] The second type is similar to the first, but it is the spirituality of another person or being, which includes nonhuman things such as rivers, meadows, canyons, mountains, stars, and other sacred places. The third type is the spirituality of community. Within a family, clan, village, town, or tribe, spirituality occurs often at special occasions like celebrations, dances, or ceremonies. It is the feeling of group happiness or community sadness. For example, those who remember the assassination of President John F. Kennedy can tell you exactly where they were and what they were doing when they heard of his death, and the same is true for 9/11, when foreign terrorists flew two airliners into the twin towers of the World Trade Center in New York and another into the Pentagon in Washington. The fourth type is that of the unexplained or the supernatural. This spiritual energy comes from the Other Side of Life where spirituality dwells in a continuum where time does not exist. Time is less important due to the fact that spirits seem to live on.

Spirits are forms of energy. Spirits manifest themselves in two different forms and a third one that combines the two. Sometimes, they can be heard but not seen as told in the above story about Carl and my dad: they heard the dancers, but could have seen them only if the ancient fire allowed it. At other times spiritual beings can be seen but usually not heard. Yet it is not always one or the other. It is indeed a "power being" of spiritual existence that can be heard and seen simultaneously.

The second category of manifestation is when people hear a noise or someone's voice humming or singing, even whistling. This is not hearing one's own spirit but that of another spiritual being. It is usually clear that a person is certain when he or she has heard something or someone, perhaps someone calling his or her name, like when my mother heard her young dead brother call to her. "Seeing" is less certain. Seeing ghosts and spirits is not always obvious to the Western mind. Although Western beliefs and their reliance on empirical science often follow the adage "seeing is believing," many Americans are eager to discredit visual manifestations of ghosts and spirits as illusions, or some form of energy that exists at that moment but is not of the supernatural realm. Yet nonbelievers will often tell a story of an experience that happened to them and it is not a story based on evidence of the rational mind.

Their undeterred belief is that nothing exists if it cannot be proven to exist. This is when uncertainty enters, for example, in the minds of Carl and all people who are western-minded. The mind's eye is not sure what it has seen when something goes against all scientific logic. But in the mind of the Indian person, it is logical to "see" and accept what one has experienced as being real because it is not inconsistent with their understanding of the world and spirituality.

The realities of traditional Indians and mainstream America are culturally incongruent and arise from different mindsets. The logic of Indian people who believe in their old ways and tribal values is a continuation of their tribe's past. The same basic ethos guides a person's life and the community's belief system for as long as the individual believes in the ways of his or her people. This is Indian reality. Such a life for Indian people true to their beliefs is a tandem of the physical and metaphysical realities. The connection between the physical and metaphysical is not always constant and this is why "place" and "power" are so important in comprehending the Other Side.

This connection of power and place leads to the question of where do ghosts and spirits come from? What is their source? Since this answer comes from beyond the reality of this world, speculation suggests that such beings are energies of expression to the physical world. Furthermore, we ourselves are forms of energy as our bodies consist of a mixture of elements and are 55 to 78 percent water while exuding heat at 98.6 degrees Fahrenheit when healthy. Analogous to leaving footprints in the sand, spirits leave traces of their energy that can be heard or seen. Human beings can sense these traces of energy, from tiny to large in size, and individuals who are more sensitive to such evidence can interact with spirits. Yet this opportunity raises further questions.

What is the purpose of ghosts and spirits? Ghosts appear for a purpose mostly unknown to people, but in the process they provide some clues "about something that they had left undone during their lives, or to warn loved ones of impending danger."[4] Certain people are more prone to hearing sprits and seeing them than other people. Why would this be?

While such intuitive people are often ridiculed, they can also be identified as being gifted for having the ability to hear or see spirits. This is an Indian and non-Indian commonality. Again, Carl is an example of the nonbeliever hearing spirits, but in his situation he was able to hear Native spirits. In fact, he did not hear just one; he heard several men and women. The story proves the sacred power of an ancient fire that rekindles itself, and the Native people's traditional belief in it connects with the earth at this particular place. The ancient fire at this place where Carl heard the spirits allows us to assume other people have heard the same thing at the lake, but at times when light and dark intersect, and only when the ancient fire wants it to happen. In analyzing the situation through the lens of Indigenous logic, it seems that the powers of the elements of earth and water had been brought together by Native people long ago. And at this site the two powers still intersect, most likely when the Green Corn Dance, a common ceremony of many eastern tribes, is held in midsummer.

For Those Who Doubt

For anyone who might doubt what has been discussed up to this point, the Indian understanding of spirituality shares many commonalities with that of Christians. The Bible is full of accounts about spirits, ghosts, angels, the Devil, and the Holy Spirit itself. Angels in particular played an integral part in the Bible, carrying messages from God to people. They are spiritual and are among us, according to Christian believers.

Moses and the burning bush revealing God is a prime example of spirituality in Exodus 3:2–6. Furthermore, the account about God talking to Moses through the burning bush involved a holy or sacred place on Mount Horeb, according to the Bible. Then, God instructed Moses to remove his sandals, for he was treading upon sacred ground, before He presented Moses with the Ten Commandments.

The Holy Ghost is mentioned in the Bible in the Gospels of Matthew 1:18 and 3:11, Luke 3:22, John 14:26 and 20:22, and Acts 1:8 roughly fifty times. Christians believe in the Trinity of the Father, Son, and the Holy Ghost. Hence, much of the Old and New Testaments are about the presence of God and that of Jesus Christ.

The Devil is also spiritual and said to be a great power of evil, according to Christianity. Christians have condemned the Devil to be the opposite of God. But believing in God also means believing in the Devil, for both exist based on the fundamental tenets of Christianity.

The Devil is first mentioned in the Bible in Deuteronomy 32:17: "They sacrifice unto the Devil and not to God." In total, the Devil is mentioned thirty-five times in the Bible. The idea that the opposite of God is in the like of the Devil or evil is not uncommon to Indian beliefs. Among the Mvskoke Creeks, the excess that is available to people represents the potential to become evil by using more than what is needed, such as eating more food or acquiring more possessions than are needed. Enjoying and desiring the excess is the beginning of evil that leads to a life of wrongdoing as one strives to obtain more than what is needed in order to live.

Many people have had premonitions and even been warned by a voice or a spirit or ghost. In one incident, the actor James Cagney and his wife were speeding along one night on a California highway. The deceased father of Cagney spoke to them, saying slow down. Cagney slowed the car and at that second they came upon a wrecked trailer in the middle of the highway, which they would have hit.[5] The ghost of Cagney's father saved their lives.

Beverly Hungry Wolf, a Blackfoot woman, described her grandmother and her special power. She recalled her grandmother having the power to call and talk to ghosts. Undoubtedly the grandmother was ultrasensitive as a receptor to the energies of the spirits, which enabled her to interact with ghosts. Hungry Wolf stated, "She was a very powerful person. . . . She had the Power to communicate with ghosts, and I once saw her do this."[6] Hungry Wolf's admission that she saw the interaction with ghosts echoes Cagney and his wife's experience of seeing Cagney's father. This exchange is also an example of physical reality intersecting with the Other Side as two types of energy come into contact.

Other Cultures with Spirits

In the Bible, God has been described as a light, and early artists have painted a halo on Jesus or even the face of Jesus as if a light were shining on it. Such light represents the radiation of energy and some kind of metaphysical power that we have yet to fully understand. In a similar way, ghosts and spirits appear because they exist in the form of an outlined light, a shadow, or even a colored light, such as green or red. Such ghosts and spirits are greater than ghosts or spirits who cannot be seen. It requires greater energy to manifest into a visible form than into a sound or sounds like my father and Carl heard many years ago. Furthermore, if the light is bright, a lot of energy is being emitted from its source.

One might first question the possibility of seeing ghosts, but seeing ghosts is not unlike characters in the Old Testament of the Bible who saw angels. And many people are reported to have seen Jesus more than ten times in spiritual form in the New Testament. Angels are apparitions that appeared in the Old Testament. It is certain that people need to believe in apparitions like angels to have hope and belief in a greater power than themselves, especially when they are in despair.

In some situations, visits by an angel to human beings occurred on a regular basis. In Italy in the case of Saint Gemma Galgani (1878–1903), the young woman conversed with her guardian angel almost daily in her young adult life. At the age of twenty, she developed meningitis. She prayed to Saint Gabriel of Our Lady of Sorrows and miraculously recovered. One year later, she had stigmata, wounds of crucifixion like Christ. Her guardian angel became a friend, stayed with her upon her request, and stood guard when she slept until she died.[7]

In the Bible, there are other accounts of angels visiting men and women. Some angels are known by names, such as Gabriel. Raphael and Michael are also good angels and both are archangels, or leader angels. In the Bible, Michael is mentioned by name in the books of Daniel, Jude, and Revelations. Gabriel is mentioned in the book of Daniel and in the Gospel of Luke. The Bible also mentions that Apollyon and Satan are bad angels.

Throughout the world, other cultures have and continue to believe in spirits as do Native people in the Western hemisphere. Older religions of the world in particular believe in animism and that animals and nonliving things host spirits. This was a part of the historical druid belief in England during the Iron Age.

Places of Power

The point of interaction or connection between the physical and metaphysical realities of spirits creates a "sense of place." Place is the point of intersection of the two realities, and many stories have been told about place via the oral tradition. This point of intersection of Native people and the spiritual dimension are extraordinary. Typically, the Indigenous regard these intersections as sacred spaces and they are certainly places of power.

Indian elders say spiritual powers guard sacred places and render illnesses to those who do not adhere to the observances of respect. Local information is relevant. It is important to know the rituals for behavior with respect to such areas.[8] Such places where spirits are more commonly encountered are roads, meadows, mountains, houses, rivers, and almost any kind of environment where energies of various sorts converge. There are likely many more places of power on earth, but humans only know of those that radiate energy in some form.

Ghosts haunt places where they were happiest or where they were involved in a tragedy. The psychical researcher Frederic W. H. Myers explains this as being like seeing a picture; he calls this a "vertical afterimage," which is an impression of the ghost when he or she was alive and experiencing "great emotional stress."[9] Among Mvskokes and Seminoles, it is best to avoid haunted places and places where bad things have happened, hvmakimata. And if it has to be, elders advise going through shadows on the land or negative places where evil dwells to avoid any possible danger. This is when personal protective medicine is of the utmost importance to Indians.

The story about Carl and my father is one that involved an important place that some people might call sacred. Such places are empowered by some force of energy that Indians call spiritual. For Carl, a white man, to hear the stomp dancing is indicative of the power of the place that yielded itself at dusk. This happening was like a time portal and similar to other thresholds at many such sacred places. The opportune times are when day and night interact like they also do just before sunrise when they look almost the same. Their polarized entities come together, joining together the powers of both light and dark. Such an interaction of double powers can sometimes be dangerous and should always be respected. When this door to spirituality is momentarily opened, sounds and sights can occur and may even be powerful enough to be seen by more than one person or even a crowd of people. Does this seem unbelievable? After his death, Jesus appeared to Mary Magdalene, and four other significant occasions occurred in which his disciples and others saw him in spirit.

This shared experience might be called a phenomenon. Carl and my father heard the same stomp dancing, but this is not always the case. Both men could have heard something different, or perhaps my father could even have seen Indians stomp dancing, but in this shared experience, he did not. Because traditional Indians tend to humanize everything, including beings and other things that are nonhuman, such places like the one above would be given a name, if the experience happened repeatedly. In this case, such regularity would have earned the place a name due to the growing respect for its supernatural power, if other people experienced the same ancient sound.

The Other Side

All tribes have stories about the supernatural world on the Other Side of this life. Some people suggest that it is a better world where everyone of the past is alive and life is much better. Sometimes spirits visit people in the world on earth and their manifestations offer clues to be understood. Their arrival to our physical world engenders caution, fear, superstition, and considerable respect from the living. This is the way that it is and the way that it has always been. The Other Side of Life manifests itself in the form of ghosts, spirits, and visions called apparitions, which are defined as unusual or unexpected sights, like a ghostly figure.

Native groups have their own explanation for the appearance of spirits in our physical world, such as the Shoshones of Wyoming who say the spirit is the soul itself. Other tribes have a different conception of the relationship between spirits and souls, and they are not always understood as the same thing. The

Shoshones believe in the "transmigration of the soul" to another world and the journey is important for the continuance of the soul.[10] The Seminoles believe that the dead make a journey across the Milky Way in the night's sky. Other tribes, like the Sac and Fox, believe that the dead travel westward at the end of life just as the sun travels westward at the end of each day.

The Choctaws believe in the Death Trail. The Choctaws say that after a man (meaning men and women) dies, he must travel on the Death Trail. This is a journey that goes to the dark land where the Sun slips over the edge of the plain of the earth. The spirit of the man approaches a deep, flowing stream. On each side are steep, rugged hills so that no one can follow on land. The trail leads over the stream, according to the legend, and there is a pine log that serves as a bridge. The log is slippery and the bark has peeled away over the years. On the Other Side of the pine bridge are six people waiting, holding rocks in their hands. They throw them at the spirit when it reaches the middle of the log. If the spirit of the deceased is evil and he is on the bridge and sees the stone coming at him, he tries to dodge the stones. This makes the evil one slip off the log. He falls into the stream where evil creatures exist. The water swirls around in a whirlpool, bringing the evil one back to the evil creatures. Sometimes the evil one climbs up on the rocks and looks over at the distant country of the good spirits, but he is not permitted to go there.[11]

The Choctaw legend states that the good spirit walks over the bridge safely. He does not dodge the stones and successfully crosses the stream. He makes it to the good hunting land. The land is more beautiful than on the earth plain. In this land, there are no storms and the sky is always blue. The grass is green and many buffalo roam there. This enables much feasting and dancing for the spirits.[12]

The Other Side intersects with our physical reality in more than one way, but for how long? The presence of spirits in our physical reality is revealed in a movement of energy that lasts from a few seconds to two or three minutes. But in a spiritual reality, time is less relevant and a single moment could be an hour or lifetime. Or time does not even exist at all.

Traveling to the Other Side

Sometimes a person who has had a vision—a very ill person or an individual who had a vivid dream—travels to the Other Side and likely does not know that he or she has entered another dimension of existence. The Other Side is a reality where all physical laws break down and an experience happens, or multiple experiences combine into one. These experiences become stories that are told in the Indian oral tradition.

Spiritual beings frequently visit Native physical reality, but on an irregular basis medicine people and sometimes individuals experience the Other Side. Medicine makers who possess enough power can visit the Other Side, but they must possess sufficient knowledge of how to return to this side of life. In Native myths, medicine makers are asked to search for the souls of those who are sick or those who are near death. Often three medicine makers act as a team to return the sick person's soul or spiritual form to the Other Side. They act in concert, according to their own spiritual strengths or powers, to help navigate the vulnerable spirit back to its body.[13] Frequently, it is too late and the spirit has left the body permanently.

In the above Choctaw story, a young warrior meets a very old man along the way, who in fact was the guardian of the path or way to the Other Side, called the land of the spirits. The age of the guardian indicates his position is one for all time in spirituality where time does not exist. The guardian is an interceptor and he decides whom he will and will not assist. Those whom he does not help, he allows to go on to make mistakes, even with the possibility of losing their souls and being lost forever.

Other stories about the journey to the spirit land have a similar host, like a guardian or keeper of the way. Among the Teton Lakotas, an old woman sits alongside the road to the ghost world. Her responsibility is examining all travelers, mostly spirits, to see if they have the proper tattoo. If they do not, she pushes them over a cliff and they fall back to earth where they will wander forever.[14] That is why their friends and loved ones can hear them.

Native Belief and Ethos

American Indian reality is a tandem of the physical and metaphysical worlds. Indian people who are close to their traditions believe in the subconscious of their minds as well as their conscious being. To understand this point even further, one must accept that such a reality is not limited to the human dimension of life. Native reality extends to the nonhuman presences of the animal and plant worlds, including the earth itself and the cosmos.

Black Elk, the holy man of the Oglala Lakotas, explained "that all things are the works of the Great Spirit. We should know that He is within all things: the trees, the grasses, the rivers, the mountains, and all the four-legged animals, and the winged peoples; and even more important, we should understand that He is also above all things and peoples. When we do understand all this deeply in our hearts, then we will fear, and love, and know the Great Spirit, and then we will be and act and live as He intends."[15]

To see is to believe in the Native way and those people who are close to their tribal ways "see" things in a certain manner. Even more, they think and view the world and universe in a Native ethos based on certain tribal ways. Generally, these people have been raised since childhood with this ethos and in a manner of philosophical circularity and visioning instead of the linear perspective of the Western world.

To understand this particular Native ethos, it is important to realize the significance of relationships. Among the Mvskoke Creeks in Oklahoma, relations include the known and the unknown because all things are a part of the universe. It is believed that there is a continuum of energy at the heart of the universe and this exists everywhere in a spiritual energy called *boea fikcha* or *puyvfekcv*. All things should be respected for all things possess this energy. With such potential, all things are capable of releasing spiritual energy, hvmakimata.

By attempting to understand relationships between all things, an Indian way of "seeing" has developed according to different tribal beliefs. It is the connections that are important as Indians believe that being connected to one's people and homeland is essential. In the traditional Indian world, it is important to realize and respect one's surroundings, whether they are good, bad, or both. This is Indian thinking and the basis of the tribal ethos for the many Native groups.

Native peoples have always sought visions as a means to see the Other Side of Life, if given the opportunity. In a humble way, Plains tribal members typically go to a chosen hill where they chant, pray, plea, or sing for a vision so that they may be blessed with this gift of insight that will help them in a particular way. The vision is an experience in which the human body experiences the metaphysics of another kind of existence. These visions are a part of the broader Native ethos and how one understands within one's worldview.[16]

Spirits

Whether it is a momentary or extended existence, spirituality is the state of being in which the nonliving dwell and it often involves the physically living. This has happened to practically everyone, even to people who will deny that they have experienced something spiritual. For those who will say they have experienced the spiritual, they may describe the experience as it happened to them through a story. That they had no control over what happened is also characteristic of the Other Side intervening into people's lives.

Native people tell stories many times about spirits and ghosts. Spirits exist among the Indigenous and this belief in spirits continues into the twenty-first century. Basically, the many Ojibwe groups throughout Michigan, Wisconsin, and Minnesota believe in spirits called "manitous." Each tribe has its own names for spirits. The Lakotas refer to the spirit as *wakan*, which is most easily translated as "holy." For example, to say that someone is wakan is to mean that they are spiritual.

The spiritual "other" is that which is within a metaphysical being. The metaphysical is always spiritual and the sacredness exists always, not fleetingly like spirituality, which can leave a human body at death. The Other Side is always of this metaphysical nature and it lives forever. If a medicine person becomes of such spirituality from the Other Side, then he or she becomes spiritual forever. The name of this medicine person exudes this manner, and memories about them are sacred because they are powerful in a good way and have lived a metaphysical existence for a good part of their lives. These people are few. They are gifted and have been directed to live a certain kind of life with special routines and responsibilities. Spirituality is stored metaphysical energy, and these special people are able to tap into this energy to help others and perform medicinal tasks beyond the abilities of normal individuals.

In Native reality, many people see visions, ghosts, and spirits. Telling ghost stories, especially at night, reminds one of the Indian physical and metaphysical realities. In the dichotomy of the universe of light and dark, as the latter meets any light when the two come together, spiritual interaction with people occurs most often at night. It is a case of a person encountering a spirit. For example, at night when a person enters a dark, strange room, he or she turns on a light. Instantly, light and dark come together, allowing one to see new things in the room for the first time. The first time you hear or see a ghost, you will never forget it. Ghosts and spirits are told of in many tribes' stories and are a part of many oral traditions, including many non-Indian oral traditions.

Little People

Little People are small spiritual beings about as tall as a man's knee or not much taller. They live in wooded areas or tall grass areas so that they cannot be seen. Their small voices sound like those of children, so they often sound like they are playing. They prefer to avoid humans and live their own way of life.

Societal beliefs in Little People are not unique among American Indians. The Irish believe in leprechauns and early Britons had their druids living in trees as a part of their religion. In the Black Forest in Germany, Little People live and play tricks on visitors to the area. Europeans of the Renaissance believed that gnomes were dwarflike people with deformities who lived in the earth and avoided sunlight. In most instances, the small people live in their own communities and often act as tricksters to the physically larger human societies. For example, soldiers during World War II often said that gremlins were playing tricks when people misplaced something. Other cultures have been known to have trolls, fairies, and elves, mostly in folklore, but many people believe that they exist and have actually seen them.

Little People are among the Mvskoke Creeks, Seminoles, Cherokees, Choctaws, Klamaths, Catawbas, Arapahos, Lakotas, Cheyennes, Poncas, Crows, Delawares, Senecas, Southern Paiutes and Chemehuevis, and many other tribes.[17] They are analogous to the gremlins American servicemen spoke of during World War II and the leprechauns of the Irish. They are magical, keepers of medicinal knowledge, and sometimes they are tricksters. Little People are feared, for sometimes they seduce children into following them away to play. Often, the children are returned to their parents. Native people say the returned children are different after having been among the Little People. They are more open to magic, have vivid memories of their experience among the Little People, or have no memory of being away.

Mvskoke people fear and respect the Little People, who they believe live in hollow trees or under rocks or elsewhere where woods are dense. The Mvskokes also believe that the Little People have the power to drive a person insane.[18] According to the Mvskokes, it is best to not have contact with the

Little People. If a person hears them, he or she acknowledges them to show respect, for ignoring them provokes an encounter that could be dangerous.[19] These Little People are nocturnal and mischievous, playing tricks on people, especially at night. Hvmakimata.

Among the Cherokees, a pair of twin deities is called "Little Men" or "Thunder-boys."[20] In addition to the Little Men, the Cherokees believe there are Little People who are spiritual beings who are usually invisible but can sometimes be heard. They live in rock shelters or thickets in the woods and sometimes allow themselves to be seen by people. They dress in historic Cherokee clothes, but they are small in every manner. It has been said there is a race of spirits called the Little People. The Cherokees say they live in rock caves and in the mountainside. They are as tall as a man's knee. They are said to be not very handsome and have long hair hanging to the ground. Very fond of music, they spend half of their time drumming and dancing. The Cherokees say that sometimes in lonely places in the mountains, the drumming of the Little People can be heard and it is not safe to follow the sound. The Little People do not like to be disturbed and they cast a spell over people who bother them. When this happens, a person feels drugged until he or she gets home. At night, sometimes the Little People approach a house, but if the people inside hear them talking, the people should not go outside. In the morning, for example, they may find that the corn has been gathered or the field has been cleared, as if many people had worked all night. The Cherokees also say that when a hunter finds a knife in the woods, he must say the words "Little People, I want to take this" because it may belong to them. If he does not say these words, they may throw rocks at him as he goes home.[21] They also may cast a spell on him, bringing him bad luck or making him temporarily forget where he is.[22]

Tribes like the Crows believe there are Little People. The Crows have a story of the "Lost Boy and the Little People" in their oral tradition. On a certain hill in their homeland, there was "the Medicine-rock of the Crows, sacred as the home of the Little-people, the Dwarfs, who made stone arrow-points. Each year, following tribal custom, the old men shoot arrows into crevices of this rock, and the women leave offerings of beads and other finery."[23] The Little People lived in the large rock where they took in a lost baby who had fallen from a travois when a dog pulling it raced with other dogs after a deer into the woods. The mother and father looked for four days for their baby while the band of Crows moved on. Finally, the parents returned to the band's camp to get help and the whole village searched for the child, but the Little People had taken him. The War-eagle had told them that they would find a boy on the mountain alone and to carry him into the Rock to live with them. When he was nearly grown, the Little-man made him a strong bow out of two mountain-sheep horns. The boy could not even bend it until the Little-man poured water upon his wrists and arms, singing as he poured. The boy could feel the strength flowing through his muscles. He felt them grow until his muscles were like ropes of sinew, hard and ready for work. The sheep-horn bow was easy to bend now, and any weight that the boy lifted was light as feathers. In return, he began to hunt for the Little People. He was their provider of meat. None of his arrows ever missed their mark.[24]

Over the years, the Little People raised the child into a tall young warrior who hunted elk for them to eat with sacred arrow points. And the Little People gave the warrior super strength so that he would not tire in bringing home the elk that he killed. Each time the warrior returned with elk, he disappeared into the Rock to join his Little People parents. Finally, it was time for the young warrior to return to his original people.

The Lost Boy, now a grown young warrior, joined his real parents and the rest of the band. He told his story about the Little People in the Rock. He could not remember when he went there to live with them. For a long time, he believed that the Little-man and the Little-woman were his father and mother. They told him that they found him on the mountain and they carried him into the Rock where they lived.

Like the Crows, the Senecas have a story of Little People living in a rock. The Little People were powerful medicine makers. The Senecas tell a story about when their people were starving. They hunted along a long trail and found a place where deer came to a salt lick. The Seneca hunters waited in the trees and they killed many deer. They killed so many that they had to throw away the meat in order to save the skins for leather. The story continues, "There was more meat than the wolves could eat, but the hunters shot many deer every day, until no more came. The hunters went on carrying great rolls of deerskins, which were very heavy and they believed that they would never see home again. The hunters became convinced that they would starve and that the deerskins would never be used. Fatigued, they sat down by a large rock. One of the hunters accidently hit the great rock with a stick, according to the story, and a little man appeared. The small man told the hunters that they were starving because they had killed and did not eat the meat. The little man said, "You fed the wolves and now they will eat you."[25]

The little man also told the hunters that they had driven the deer to another forest where they now lived and could be found by other hunters. He told them that they were selfish and wanted all of the deerskins in the forest. He said that they were not wise. According to the story, the little man told the hunters that they would have meat if they were willing to give up all of their deerskins. The little man sent the hunters away. He told the hunters to hit on the rock again when they wanted to talk to him. The hunters returned and rapped on the rock when the sun was setting. The little man appeared and led the way to a great cave filled with food and furs. The hunters ate and slept deeply. Then, at midnight the hunters were awakened by many of the Little People. They informed the hunters that they might take their packs of skins and all the food they wished from the cave, if they would never again shoot the deer to feed the wolves. The hunters promised the Little People and the hunters fell asleep again. When the hunters awoke they were near their homes.[26]

Little People know the earth and learned its secrets about herbs and passageways. Sometimes they reveal this knowledge to human beings, if they so choose. You should avoid thinking about them, because then their presence enters your mind, hvmakimata. Little people cause confusion; they are spiritual beings and are of the spiritual world. At this point, all of your thoughts are about them and in this sense your mind is controlled by them, especially if you are talking about them. And this is a form of ehosa that was mentioned in the beginning of these pages of this book—a state of confusion.

Medicine Makers

Medicine makers are special individuals who have been given talents from a greater power than humankind. Some individuals possessed power and the gift of healing. Black Elk of the Lakotas was such a person. Born around 1863, he lived into the twentieth century and died in 1950. Phillip Deere, a Mvskoke Creek, was a spiritual leader for the American Indian Movement during the late 1960s and 1970s. Sanapia, a Comanche eagle doctor, was another gifted person who helped to heal the sick among her people during the post–World War II years. Severt Young Bear of the Lakotas and Left Handed of the Navajos are among the many notable medicine makers of the twentieth century. Early medicine makers include Handsome Lake of the Senecas; Neolin of the Delawares; and Tenskwatawa, the Shawnee Prophet. Some medicine people prefer not to be recognized because their numerous responsibilities for helping others consume much of their energy. Yet they are well known among their people and stories are told about their feats of using medicine.

These special people have certain kinds of powers and these powers exist at various levels. Definitely, they are not the same. Some are curers of simple illnesses, others are more powerful healers, some are visionaries, and some are prophets. But it is known that the Creator gave them certain powers and these gifts can be taken away. The powers and gifts were given to serve their community and take care of others who need help in illness, direction in life, and protection from evil. These individuals are in contact with the Other Side on a much more frequent basis than other people, although a metaphysical presence can make itself known to anyone.

Fred McTaggart, an English professor, studied the Mesquakies of Iowa and tried to collect their stories. He began to feel the spiritual environment of the Indians, who were also known as the Fox. He recalled that on their reservation during the winter, he was shivering but he continued to stand in the wind, listening carefully and looking across the clearing to his left. Behind McTaggart stood timber and he could feel a definite presence. By now, a sound had caught his attention and he was transfixed by what was behind him. As anxious as he was to leave to get inside the warm house, he felt compelled to listen and turned around to look. McTaggart believed that spirits permeated the land and he was later told that they were spirits of people, animals, plants, dreams, and stories that belonged to the earth. McTaggart had wanted to believe what he been told and to believe in the mysticism of the Mesquakies, but now it became real to him.[27] Rather than McTaggart coming into the realm of Indigenous, it came to him to experience something he had not known before—the ethos and reality of the Mesquakies.

What Can We Mortals Do?

Spiritual energy can even convince nonbelievers that spirits and ghosts are real. If this is so, how does a person confront or interact with the spiritual world? The first step is trying not to be afraid. The next step is to try to understand what has happened within a spiritual context.

Comanche eagle doctor Sanapia advised people how to confront a ghost, especially if a person thought it was going to harm him or her. She described how if you are walking along somewhere, you might hear a sound moving along behind you. It might be a spirit or ghost. If it is the latter, it is not good. To protect yourself, Sanapia said, "If you are going to turn around, you got to turn all around, turn your whole body around, and look right at it. See what it is. But if you just turn your head, take a peek, that's when they twist your face. Turn all the way around and look at it and say, 'What do you want? Come here, let me see you,' or 'Go away. You're dead.'" She added that you have to stand up to the ghost and show it that you are not afraid of it. If you do not, she warned that the ghost would harm you and perhaps deform you until a medicine maker could cure you.[28] When I was growing up, my mother told us kids not to look in the direction of the spirit because it might be bad. It could harm you by making you ill. This is something that stays with you; such a warning is a lesson in life. It is a belief that is a part of me and I have learned to live with it, similar to a Christian believing in the Devil.

Ghosts, spirits, and witches have influenced the lives of Oklahoma Indians who are close to their traditional beliefs. Indian traditionalists believe that these spiritual powers have control over people's lives, and they use protective medicines and take precautions to keep themselves safe. It is a life in which the metaphysical world is more powerful than the physical world. Certain ceremonies and important rites need to be performed for protection or blessing by those powers that are greater than all human beings. As a precaution, my mother also used to tell us kids not to eat late at night. But if you did, put a pinch of the food outside for the spirits, or else you might wake up sick in the middle of the night or in the morning a part of your face might be twisted.

Sanapia described when ghosts visit most often. She said they are jealous of the living and they come to do harm and give a person ghost sickness. In her words, sometimes people get scared when they are lying in bed at night, especially after a family member has died. Her story continued, as she said that the dead family member may become jealous of a person who is living in the house, like a sister or an aunt. And that is why they bother you. You can hear them walking across the floor. They may open a door and come into your room and even jerk the covers off of you or pull your hair or even hold your hand. There is also the chance that they might deform your face because they are jealous.[29]

Often, the presence of elements of the metaphysical world such as spirits is not good. Evil comes in the form of witches as N. Scott Momaday, Kiowa Pulitzer Prize–winning author, described in his autobiography, *The Names*, about his young life in Jemez, New Mexico. He remembered one night when he saw witches. The night began in Momaday's story when some children came and told him and his family that the witches were about. The children said to follow them. The children led Momaday and the others outside and pointed with their chins in a certain direction. Momaday saw lights at ground level far off in the distance. There were three or four of them, moving back and forth and darting here and there. Momaday recalled that the children watched seriously, but they were not afraid. He understood immediately that the children were not playing tricks and they did not care one way or another what he thought about what he saw. They only thought that he might be interested in seeing witches. He believed at first that some men with flashlights deceived the children and were running around in the distance. That was all there was to it. But one of the lights flew higher into the night sky very fast like a shooting star moving with great speed.[30]

In another story, a young Pueblo boy, Patrick Quirk, had a sick cousin, Cheeway. Elders were attending to Cheeway in the house. Patrick sat outside and it became dark. His grandfather and elderly friend Two Bears went outside to check on the young boy. Patrick said, "Keeping my eyes on Grandfather and Two Bears, I could see that their faces went completely void of expression and were being lit by a blue glowing light that seemed to be coming from behind me." All three of them realized at that moment that something powerful was present. Patrick said, "I turned my head to see where it was coming from. When I did, I saw that there was a small circle of light that had formed just above the large stone that was behind me. As the light became brighter, it began to circle all three of us then it went into the house where Cheeway and the others of our village were." The small light was the spiritual energy of a spiritual presence and medicine making was needed to help Cheeway. Patrick continued, "As the glowing circle of light went into the house, we all followed it with our eyes and could see that it placed itself just above Cheeway, who was lying on the floor. There was a glowing that seemed to surround Cheeway from the light that was above him. Then, as quickly as it had appeared, it disappeared and left the sight of all who had seen it."[31] The small blue light was known among the Pueblo medicine makers as the Old Woman who healed people and was a good spirit.

In a similar way, Peter MacDonald described the metaphysical world of the Navajos. In this story, MacDonald recalled that there was a link or connection between all living things and the Navajo people. He said that some spirits were good and some were bad. In his story, he used the example of the snake, which can be protective but can also be vicious, thus, it has to be approached with great care. In the same way, a spider can be both protective and deadly. The positive qualities of the spider derive from the legend about the construction of the web. When an enemy approached the spider, the web could be woven very quickly to stop the aggressor like a fence. MacDonald described a Navajo warrior going into battle who might pray to the spirit of the spider for the ability to spin a web to stop his enemy. With such power called upon, the attacking enemy would instantly find himself helpless, as though he were tied up. The Navajo person would not expect to actually see the web, but the proactive power of the spirit of the spider would be evident. In the same way, a Navajo might take some corn pollen to sacrifice to the spider. He might say a prayer, too, like "I pray to you, spider spirit, that you will accept this sacrifice. And in return, I want your spirit to protect me from my enemy by the use of your web."[32] This state of helplessness is similar to the state of confusion I introduced in the first story of this book. It is a medicine power to make others helpless so they will not hurt you. At the same time, it is knowing how nature works.

In other situations, Native people have become fond of talking to plants and animals. While people use language to speak to a dog, it is really understanding on a basic level that is communicated back and forth. So rather than talking, it is communicating understanding between people and animals. Navajo surgeon Lori Alvord described the dogs that ran everywhere on the reservation. But they were used to watch the sheep or guard the hogan. And when people arrived, the dogs appeared magically like annoying friends who appear just at mealtime.[33]

While skeptics will naturally doubt the validity of conversations with animals, consider how often we catch ourselves talking to our pets, to our horses, or even to our car. We even give names to nonhuman beings, like an automobile or truck. In this way, we are anthropomorphizing or humanizing other beings by giving them names and talking to them in conversations. To Indianize is to humanize all things so that they are understood in a human context, such as Father Sun, Mother Earth, and so forth. Sometimes these important beings include great powers and they are given titles. For example, the wind is controlled by the deity, Hesaketvmese (Master of Breath) among the Seminoles and Mvskoke Creeks. Wakan Tankan is the term for the Great Spirit among the Lakota people. Pet owners will concur that their animals understand them.

In a similar way, it is possible to communicate with spirits, but this communication needs to be taken seriously if one wants to truly understand the Other Side of Life. Some of the individuals mentioned above and many others not mentioned have this ability. Their communication is not necessarily a means of holding a conversation but a way of understanding the significance of actions of spirits. Such individuals are typically medicine makers and they interpret experiences, dreams, and visions for themselves and for anyone who has requested their help. Such gifted individuals are very good observers and listeners. Their role is to serve and help their relatives and friends in their communities. In this way, they share their gift as it is meant to be among their people. But in order to do so, they likely require certain conditions or even a favorable place that becomes something of a key to the door to the Other Side of Life. Hence, ritual and responsibility are critically important for the medicine person who may be a healer, curer, or even a prophet.

Spirits have been and are a part of Indian reality and they are a part of oral tradition. Their existence should not be denied and should be simply accepted as a part of the Indian world, especially by those people who are close to their tribal traditions and values. Furthermore, spirits should not necessarily be feared but instead should be respected. We should look upon spirits as opportunities to learn more because Indian reality is the physical and the metaphysical combined in the tandem of life. In order to take relevant steps toward learning more about spirits, it is advised that we learn more about ourselves and personal values. Knowing who we are and most importantly what we believe establishes the core of reference because spirits offer a very different way of "seeing" and understanding the Native universe. Perhaps the spirits exist in another state of energy. According to one story, on the Other Side where this state exists, "the sky is much more blue, the prairie is more fertile, the scenery more gloriously beautiful."[34]

So what can be said as a final word about Carl, the now retired bricklayer, who heard the singing of Indians and dancing at sunset? For such an incident to happen, some force of considerable energy exuded enough power to cross cultural and racial barriers. As mentioned, non-Indians are not supposed to hear Indian things like this. Furthermore, this incident crossed a greater barrier by making a believer out of someone who had no clue that something like this could happen. Weeks later, Carl was working on a building site and my father happened to be working there, too, for a few days on the roof of the new building. Carl told his fellow workers as he pointed at my dad, "If you don't believe me [about the Indians singing], ask that guy." This incident of power was not to be denied. Both men had been allowed to cross the threshold of the Other Side, or more accurately the door had been brought to them so that both could hear and realize that something spiritual had happened to them. The spirituality of a presence was so powerful that they would never forget this experience as it connected the past, present, and the future in that single moment.

SIX

Moccasin Trail

In 1989 my mother told me about her childhood. She said:

> The Moccasin Trail is long and has many stories as people long ago
> traveled it by wagon, horseback, on foot, and in later times by automobile.
> Much of my childhood is associated with the trail, and as I grew up
> with the stories resulting from incidents along the trail, or in the area
> of the Sac and Fox, increased during my early lifetime. At that time, my
> grandmother had passed away in 1945, and we lived in the same old
> two-story with my grandfather. By that time, I remember the Old House
> needed painting I thought many times as I walked along that gravel road,
> which many parts of it was sandy dirt, called the Moccasin Trail.

Moccasin Trail meanders in Sac and Fox Country, coursing from where it crosses
Oklahoma State Highway 18 to State Highway 99 and beyond, going farther
east. Today a modern sign posted at one intersection along the trail marks a
point exactly eight miles north of Shawnee. Two generations ago, Moccasin
Trail was very different. At the time, my mother lived with her parents near
Shawnee, and they all lived with her grandparents, Jackson and Ester Wakolee.
Most people would not likely have heard of Wakolee as a last name, but it is
common among the Sac and Fox. They lived during difficult times of the Great
Depression when the economy of the nation collapsed and other nations suffered too. This was a time when Franklin Roosevelt suggested if you are at the
end of your rope, tie a knot in it and hang on. The outbreak of World War II

Moccasin Trail, Shawnee to Stroud, Oklahoma. Courtesy Michelle M. Martin.

ended the Depression, as the United States and allied countries struggled to win the war. A postwar boom changed things, modernizing society as communities in Indian Country tried to keep up. For them, life was still a struggle as my relatives and other Indians held on to the old ways and beliefs in traditions.

The Old House

Many Indians, like other people, lived with their parents during the Depression just before the United States entered World War II. My mother's grandparents had a large two-story they called the Old House. The aged two-story white house stood two miles from the corner on the north side of the road, the last house on the left for a distance. From that point going east, there were not that many houses. My mother and her parents often went into town; they usually walked two miles to catch a bus at the corner of Highway 18 and Moccasin Trail since most people did not have an automobile during those *Grapes of Wrath* years. A lot of working people did not have jobs, and even if they did, they could not afford a car that cost over $600 with gasoline to run it costing ten cents a gallon. Even if you could afford an automobile, four new tires cost a lot of money when they needed replacing. During those hard-pressed days, it cost about seventeen cents to ride the bus. About a year later the fare went up to twenty-five cents, finally increasing to seventy-five cents after the Depression. My mother was a young girl at the time; she was born in 1934 on the second to the last day of the year.

During the rest of her adolescent years, my mother lived in various apartments in the small town of Shawnee, which began to thrive after World War II. Shawnee began as a settlement resulting from one of six land runs held when Indian Territory opened up to white settlement at noon on April 22, 1889. My mother's family moved around the young town quite a bit, and when her father ran out of work, they moved back to the country on the Moccasin Trail. They moved in with my grandfather's parents and lived in the same old two-story. By that time, the Old House needed painting, which my mother often thought about as she walked along the road that resembled a wide trail in some places. Much of the way was nothing more than sandy dirt. Blackjack oaks, cedars, elms, and cottonwoods lined both sides of the Moccasin Trail, a crude road that had received its name because it had been well traveled by hunters in the nineteenth century.

The stories here are written as remembered by Sac and Fox Indians, naturally reflecting the background and upbringing of my mother, Virginia Lee Wakolee, as a young Sac and Fox and Shawnee girl. She was raised the first six years of her life along the trail with her parents, grandparents, uncles, aunts, and cousins. They had a bountiful life of family, much conversation, and many activities around the Old House.

With space to roam, the two-story homestead had blackjack trees with a large elm tree in the front yard. In the spring, my mother's extended family planted a vegetable garden and a patch of blackberries to pick and can for food needed during the wintertime. These were the difficult years of the Depression and World War II when President Franklin Roosevelt called upon all

Americans, including Indians, to sacrifice. Roosevelt declared meatless Tuesdays, and rationed gasoline and rubber so that American soldiers, including my uncle Telmond in the army, might have enough food and supplies to help the Allies win the war against Germany, Italy, and Japan.

The Indian families helped each other and shared their food. My mother recalled attending some of the tribal feasts with her grandmother Ester McClellan Wakolee. She remembered hearing her grandmother Ester tell a woman that she, Virginia, was Glade Wakolee's daughter. She would hear her father's Indian name and she knew by sound what they were saying although she did not speak the Sac and Fox language.

Moccasin Trail

Much of my mother's childhood was associated with stories shared along the trail. As she grew up, the tales resulting from incidents along the trail or in the area of the Sac and Fox became a part of local gossip and history. The Moccasin Trail meandered up and down hills, and it contains many stories as people traveled it by wagon, horseback, on foot, and in later times by automobile. The trail started just north of Shawnee. Originally, the new settlement called Shawnee was on the former Indian lands of the Shawnees, Pottawatomis, and Kickapoos in the immediate area.

There were and are other trails in the Indian Territory and in Oklahoma following statehood in 1907. In fact, there is another Moccasin Trail located in Kickapoo Country. This trail is said to be located in Pottawatomie County and was the path that Indians traveled many years ago. Eventually, this trail became County Road 109 and intersected with what became known as U.S. Highway 177. Winding to many Indian settlements, the homes of Indian families, the trail hosted historic places, like Smith's general store and blacksmith shop in Kickapoo Country, Abram's log house, and Abram's cemetery. Since then, many of these places, like Smith's, have passed on with time. This Moccasin Trail continued west from Kickapoo Village across the North Canadian in McLoud, passing the Bizzles' two-story white house and the McLoud School. This was the route until about sixty years ago when a heavy wagonload of cotton pulled by a team of horses caused the North Canadian Bridge to collapse in about 1928, and now the trail bends around the river to County Road 108 before entering McLoud.

But within my own family, my mother's Moccasin Trail became a worn pathway as people carried stories, gossip, and the latest news in Sac and Fox Country. Travelers talked about what was going on in Shawnee, and bits of news about FDR's government relief programs and later any information about the war was welcomed. During World War II, Shawnee in landlocked Oklahoma became a site for a naval base to train air navigators and pilots.[1] The war also enabled the construction of Tinker Field east of Oklahoma City and many people from Shawnee commuted about forty-five minutes to work there; others worked in town at the new Jonco Company making aviation parts, or at Sylvania making tubes and electrical parts. Some worked at the Shawnee Milling Company once it was rebuilt after a fire in the 1930s.[2]

The old two-story had a screened-in porch on the south side, but mostly my mother recalled sitting on the porch on the east side during the warm Oklahoma evenings with the grownups talking while she listened. In fact, my grandmother Rachel gave my mother the nickname "Ears" because my mother wanted to stay up late to listen to stories. My mother's grandparents did not have a radio. No one played a musical instrument, so conversations and telling stories passed the time until it was time to go to bed. Many years later, my mother said how she missed her grandparents' homestead where she had spent so much of her childhood living out in the country in that Old House.

During the summer evenings with no air conditioning, the family often sat on the front porch hoping to catch a cool breeze, talking, and looking to the clouds for any sign of rain. From the porch, they could watch the road for travelers, who sometimes would come up to the house to ask for a drink of water. Many of the people who passed were friends, or at least my mother's parents and grandparents knew who they were. So there was a lot to talk about, new stories and old ones. Many of these stories were about strange happenings associated with Indians traveling the trail, particularly at night.

The Traveler

One of my mother's favorite uncles was Guy Wakolee. Uncle Guy would visit Indian families for a couple or few days at a time. This was his practice and the custom in those times. Upon his return, he would have new tales to tell, and they were fun to hear, mostly because Uncle Guy had an animated way of telling stories. In my mother's mind as a young girl, she could see the people

Uncle Guy talked about, and she wondered if she would ever meet them. Uncle Guy's stories captured the attention of the entire family because he was a fantastic storyteller. He had an infectious smile and he loved to laugh and make others laugh.

One of my mother's favorite stories involved her uncle. Many times Uncle Guy walked all the way to town, which was about nine miles or a little more. Uncle Guy told of coming home over the hill west of the house late one night about eleven o'clock. He was getting close to the house, west of the mailbox that stood at the road's edge. He was coming down a hill and met a stranger approaching him on the other side of the road. Over the hill coming in his direction was a man walking. It was dark, so Uncle Guy could not see very well, but by the moon's light, he could tell that someone else was on the road coming toward him on the other side. The trees shaded much of the moonlight, which only made the night even darker. When they were about even on opposites of the road, Uncle Guy said, "Ho," an Indian way of saying hello many years ago. The stranger said nothing; he did not utter a sound. Uncle Guy thought that this was unusual, or perhaps the stranger did not hear him. Always, people returned greetings when meeting others on the trail, even strangers. Most of the time, you never met anyone else, so meeting someone coming the other way was something that happened only sometimes and they might tell you about something useful ahead of you, like if they had seen a snake, especially a copperhead or rattlesnake. At that instant, the stranger nodded his head once in reply. It was almost not even a nod. Still, he said nothing. Uncle Guy noticed that the man was wearing a hat that seemed to be black, but he was not sure because it was so dark. He could not tell who it was. Just a man, an Indian man most likely, but he wondered, "Who was he?"

Uncle Guy kept walking and began to slow down, but the stranger puzzled him; it felt almost as if he knew him or maybe had seen him before somewhere. In an odd way, the outline of the stranger seemed familiar, but Uncle Guy could not place him. He decided to turn and look back at the stranger, thinking this might jog his memory. Uncle Guy stopped. He wondered again who the stranger might be. When he looked back, the stranger wearing the hat was already going west over the next long hill.

"How could he cover ground so fast?" Uncle Guy wondered. This surprised him. No one covers ground that fast, even running. The stranger was already out of sight, almost as if he did not want to be seen. No doubt, he was in a big hurry to go somewhere, or he had left from somewhere in a hurry.

Some people thought that my mother's uncle saw someone's spirit who might have passed away in the area. Sometimes spirits are restless, and they frequent the same places they used to frequent when they were humans. Other relatives thought the uncle might have seen a witch. A lot of medicine was practiced in that area of old Moccasin Trail. Some relatives thought that Uncle Guy was trying to be clever and made the story up. Maybe he was trying to impress everyone, especially the kids. But my mother knew better. The way he told it, the story had to be true. The way Uncle Guy talked about the stranger with the black hat, or what he thought was a black hat. He did see someone, or something. It was nothing unusual for something like that to happen along Moccasin Trail, especially late at night. Many things happened at night along the trail, hvmakimata.

There are other accounts of a mysterious traveler, and the local belief is that it is always the same spirit. He travels Moccasin Trail and is a kind of guardian or keeper of the trail. Some people have said that the Traveler is a large person; others have said he is normal size like what Uncle Guy had encountered. But, there is a possibility of their being more than one Traveler. Perhaps, it was a one-time spirit that Uncle Guy had met, like seeing someone only once and you never see him or her again.

Other strange stories involved the community building where members of the Sac and Fox tribe would meet for social gatherings. Many years have passed, and the building is no longer there. But during those years long ago, it was important for dances, pie suppers, and box suppers to raise funds for various activities. At one time, my mother's family had a box supper where people made bids on boxes of cooked food. My mother remembered eating a box meal with her parents at the community building like everyone else. On another occasion, the children in the area received their vaccination shots. A government nurse from the Indian Health Service administered the inoculations. Like any children, they were afraid of needles and did not want to get the shots. They were scared but had to get the shots anyway. In the end, my mother and all the children were rewarded with ice cream.

One year, a first aid class was taught with several men attending a night class. One of the members' wives decided to remain in the car while her husband attended class. After a time, the woman fell asleep. She awoke suddenly when she heard someone tapping on the window of the car. She looked around and saw nothing. But one thing was for sure; she did not feel alone and felt as though someone or something like a spirit was in the dark playing tricks on her. After a few minutes of feeling nervous and afraid, she decided to go inside to join the others. She jumped out of the car and ran inside, but she felt that whatever it was, it was still out there.

The Old Woman in the Window

In another instance, a small boy — my mother's cousin — was in the community building's kitchen area on a rainy night while the others were in the main part of the building. It was during one of those heavy rains when lightning flashed and thunder made a rolling sound. It was a sweeping rain with the wind blowing, the kind of rain people try to run from to find shelter. The storm thundered again and the cousin walked toward the window. At that moment, lightning flashed, and he saw an old Indian woman looking through the window at him. My mother's cousin had a good look at the old Indian woman but did not recognize her. She had a black handkerchief wrapped around her head. There was nothing unusual about the handkerchief because many elderly Indian women wore their hair wrapped this way.

The people wondered who it might have been that he saw. Women wore handkerchiefs, especially when it was windy, and do so even to this day. The young boy was told that he probably saw someone's grandmother. What they actually meant was that he saw someone's grandmother who had passed away, or walked west, as the Mvskoke Creeks would say, "That's what they used to say." Perhaps the spirit of the grandmother had returned just to see if things were okay. Maybe the spirit was looking for someone, like a grandchild, to see if the child was all right. Among the Sac and Fox, we have a tradition in that we believe the dead walk toward the West. In fact, in Wakolee Cemetery, most of the dead are buried facing west. West is where the sun goes to sleep, the end of the day's light ends, and the spirit land comes to life at night.

Indian people believe that they can hear the spirit or see a spirit of a loved one after the loved one's death. This is a common occurrence, especially where the dead person used to live. It is not haunting, but a peaceful way of the dead just seeing if things are okay. And in this way, they are letting you know that they are still there, and have not forgotten you, hvmakimata.

A Visitor on the Fourth of July

One Fourth of July, my grandparents and my mother were sitting outdoors. They talked about the heat of the night and the conversation shifted to concerns about a young friend who was very sick and going to die. They were trying to see the fireworks from town, but it was too far away. All of a sudden, they heard someone in the house lapping one door over the other, like closing one cupboard door and the next one that meets it. They heard it again—one door closing and the opposite cupboard door closing, like someone was looking for something. My grandfather Glade looked at my grandmother Rachel and she in turn looked at him. My mother could tell they were both startled, yet they both knew who it was.

The next day, my mother said they heard that a young Indian woman had passed away. She had been a friend and her spirit had stopped by the house to let them know that she had died. My mother's parents talked about what they heard. It was common to offer a visitor a glass of water or cup of coffee, so maybe the spirit was looking for a glass or cup.

The family of the young woman who passed away probably partook in a kind of adoption ceremony after her passing—a ceremony that was common among the Sac and Fox. A few families still practice the adoption ceremony. When a family member dies, the adults decide whom they might consider symbolically adopting to substitute for the person who passed away. The idea was to adopt someone who looked somewhat like the deceased person. The family would treat the adopted person just like the loved one. This allows the spirit of the deceased to continue his or her journey toward the West where the sun passes into darkness at the end of each day. If the chosen person accepted the invitation, then in a ceremony the adopted person walked west at sunset and then returned to a new set of clothes and a favorite meal of the deceased. The purpose was to allow the spirit of the dead to realize that all was fine and it was all right to begin the journey to the Other Side of Life. The spirit would know that his or her role and responsibilities would be assumed by the adopted person and the family would not be burdened for having lost its loved one. Symbolically, this made perfect sense to the Sac and Fox after having been removed three times, then building new homes in Indian Territory, followed by the Great Depression.

Another incident that my mother remembered involved a family friend who was visiting for a few days. After supper, the women washed the dishes as usual. The friend decided that she would empty the dishwater outdoors. It was rainy, misty, and foggy that evening. She looked down the old driveway and she saw a man wearing an army coat approaching. She announced to the others in the house, "We are going to have a visitor. Someone is coming." My mother said they all waited and waited. "But the stranger never arrived. In fact, no one came to the door, and none of us heard a knock."

After a few minutes they all wondered who she might have seen. The family friend was positive she had seen someone coming toward the house. The next day, we heard that one particular old man had died. So maybe it was him, and his spirit was making his rounds to let people know that he was going to the Other Side. Perhaps the image with the army coat was the Traveler, but no one was sure.

Not What Happened; Who Did It?

One day my grandfather Glade was going to the water well just as it was getting dark. The well was located in the opposite direction from the kitchen. He walked around the north side of the house toward the east as he had many times before. All of a sudden, he said that someone threw a ball of dirt at him. It came from the roof of the house, and the dirt hit him directly on his head. Who threw it? No one was there. He was not imagining anything because he felt the ball of dirt hit him. And who would be on top of the house? According to tradition, the proper question was not how did it happen, but who did it? Because the Sac and Fox and Indians in eastern Oklahoma believed in spirits and greater powers, they humanized everything, including the nonliving, like valleys, rivers, and mountains. By humanizing everything, all things could be more easily understood in human terms. It was just one of those things; he never found out who did it.

Another strange occurrence happened one night when my grandfather had to use the outhouse, a common fixture for those living in the country. No one really wanted to walk outside at night, especially on a moonless night when it was pitch black. My grandfather was sitting in the outdoor john in the dark. Someone knocked really hard on the backside of the john. He thought it was his wife playing tricks on him. He said, "Aw, Rachel! I know it's you!" There was no response. As he sat there tending to his personal business, another knock hit the backside of the outhouse. Real loud. Then, silence.

When he returned to the house, Rachel stood next to his mother, Ester, helping to wash the dishes. He asked if Rachel had been outside. Ester replied, "No, she's been here all the time." Someone was playing tricks. Spirits usually played tricks at night. A lot of times these tricks happened at dusk or just before dawn, when spiritual energy acts as light and dark meet. Among the Sac and Fox, you just have to accept it and try not to be afraid. If you show that you are afraid, more tricks might be played on you.

Whistling in the Dark

The Sac and Fox people believe in a spirit world. A person does not decide to be a part of the spirit world; the spirit world is a part of his or her life. But many people, including some Indians, refuse to believe in spirits. Whether people do believe or not, almost all religions have spirits of some kind in their histories.

It is unsurprising then that spirits play such a big role in my family's stories. One of these stories was created when tragedy struck the youngest son of my maternal great-grandparents' neighbors. One year at Christmas time, a drunk driver ran over their youngest son, Richard. He was a young boy who loved to whistle and he was good at it. He whistled tunes and mimicked birdcalls. My mother's grandmother Ester buried his blood-stained clothing north of the Old House near the timber. My mother's grandmother and one of her uncles at times heard whistling coming from that direction, usually at night.

My mother heard the family say it was little Richard's spirit that they heard. Because so many people heard it, it could not be denied that Richard's spirit lingered. It was one of Richard's favorite tunes that he liked to whistle. Weeks later the whistling was not so regular; then my mother said they did not hear it anymore. Richard's spirit had found his way to the Other Side and all was fine.

When I was growing up with my brothers and sister, our mother used to tell us, hvmakimata, don't whistle at night! If you did, they said someone might whistle back; someone like a spirit would play tricks on you. The same goes for singing at night by yourself or even with someone because spirits are awake and they might sing with you. Hvmakimata.

Hearing the Dead

An older uncle of my mother and his wife had a baby boy. Unfortunately, during winter one night the baby died from illness, most likely pneumonia. It was a cold winter, and my mother's uncle and his wife slept in the upper south bedroom of the old two-story house that was poorly heated.

Afterwards, the family heard a baby crying from upstairs. They said that the sound came from the south bedroom where the baby had been. The couple grieved for their baby, especially the mother. Their love for their child was so great that they did not want to be disconnected from their baby. The lack of closure in saying goodbye to the child allowed its spirit to linger because he wanted to be with his parents.

The Old House had many memories and new ones occurred as the years passed by along Moccasin Trail. At the family home, my mother's grandmother Ester passed away after a long illness. My mother's two uncles heard their grandmother's spirit in the kitchen putting away the dishes late one night like she used to do after washing them. They told their grandfather Jackson about the sounds coming from the kitchen. He replied that her spirit must be hungry.

After dinner one evening, he put a small portion of food into the fire of the kitchen woodstove. The Sac and Fox believed that this would feed the dead and the dead would remain connected to the family. Their sounds of movement reminded the family to always remember their dead. Feeding the dead is also a common belief among the Mvskoke Creeks and Seminoles. After dinner, a tiny portion of food is put on a plate or saucer and left at a distance from the house. This offering lets the spirits of your loved ones know you have not forgotten them and they will likely leave you alone.

When people are sick and near death, strange things are known to happen, especially along the Moccasin Trail. People were too poor to go to the doctor—that is, a physician trained in Western medicine. The distance was too far to travel, making it difficult, especially during bad weather. And some believed in the old Sac and Fox ways of curing. Families believed in curing themselves, using herbs, and someone usually knew what to do about an illness. In fact, almost two hundred Indian medicines are known to exist that Western medicine has adopted. However, an old person who was ill was not expected to last long. Old Indians usually did not live into their sixties. And it was rare for a person to have such a long life, especially in that part of Oklahoma. Things were tough and life was hard. Especially during winter with the cold, death visited many families; most often either the very young or the very old were called away.

Tales were often told about the times when my mother's grandmother Ester was ill. Nothing seemed right. Sounds could be heard. It seemed as if someone or something was outside, always waiting, always watching. Perhaps it seemed that way because so many people traveled on Moccasin Trail, although houses in those days were far apart.

Family members noticed an owl would come to the elm tree in front of the Old House. The great horned owl always came at night, and one of my mother's uncles took a shot at the owl but missed it. The family believed that the owl was a witch. Maybe the witch came to visit my mother's grandmother. When witches came like this, it was not good. They came to gain any part of anyone else's life energy to add to their own. My mother's grandmother Ester Wakolee died on October 5, 1945, about a month after World War II officially ended. Among many Indians, when an owl calls your name it is a bad omen.

The Blind Witch

My mother's grandfather Jackson told a story about a certain old blind man. A ceremonial event was held and all the men slept in one area. Grandfather Jackson decided to attend while an aunt stayed with my mother's grandmother. The old blind man asked about my mother's grandmother. After midnight, grandfather Jackson watched this man leave to go to outside and he walked like he could see in the dark. After a time, he heard a large bird, like a great horned owl, flapping its wings to fly away. Undoubtedly, the owl was going to hunt its prey.

Grandfather Jackson waited and waited for the blind man to return. Finally he heard the man breathing as if the man was tired. He had been somewhere, and if he had become an owl, he had traveled far away. Grandfather Jackson kept out of sight, just in case the blind man could actually see at night.

The Indian way was to say, "The man knew something." It is wise to not be too friendly with such people. Among Mvskokes and Seminoles, such individuals are called *estekene* (a witch in animal form).

Red and Green Lights

One time my mother and her twin cousins asked if all three of them could sleep together. My mother's parents agreed. They slept in the upper north bedroom. This was the same room where my mother's baby sister had passed away in grandmother Ester's arms.

My mother said that as they opened the door to the dark bedroom, they saw a small green light. The greenish spot was in a corner and it flickered slowly like it was alive. One of the cousins screamed and all three girls grabbed each other's hands. They ran and jumped in the bed, covering their heads with blankets for the rest of the night.

Green and red lights are important to old Sac and Fox beliefs. The Sac and Fox believe that a green light represents a spirit and a red light represents a witch. Both lights are known to be bad omens and to be avoided, if at all possible.

My grandmother Rachel (my mother's mother) was returning home after a long day of visiting with her sister Florine. As it was said, in those days, traveling took a long time, even during good weather. A lot of people walked, and traveling normally consisted of going several miles or less. Mostly people walked in those days.

When grandmother Rachel got near the house leaving the crossroads and about a quarter of a mile from the house, something began to happen. Rachel felt like she was being followed. But no one was there, at least as best she could tell. At that instant, a long green light passed over her head, like a bird flying on a path.

On her return, my grandmother Rachel learned that an Indian man, a neighbor of theirs, had passed away. Rachel had passed his house when she walked west to go home to the Old House, expecting she might see the old Indian.

I Hear My Name Being Called

It was dusk when this event occurred, and at the end of the day spiritual energy seemed to awake. The last rays of twilight are when light and dark come together, when those of the night awaken. Spirits begin to stir and take advantage of this opportunity when light and dark momentarily share the same space.

One evening before dark, my grandmother Rachel and my mother were going to the outdoor john. My mother was six years old. My mother remembered they had to open a small gate to the barnyard. At this point, my mother heard her brother call her name three times, seemingly like he was running to catch up with them.

My mother told my grandmother Rachel, "I can hear Delaine calling me." My grandmother Rachel held my mother's hand firmly, forcing her to keep walking faster. Grandmother Rachel told my mother, "Don't look back!" Later my mother asked her why she was told to not look. She answered, "It might bring you bad luck."

That happened after my mother's three-year-old brother had died from pneumonia on April 25, 1941. The family members believe that my mother heard Delaine's spirit. Spirits came in various forms, even unexpected ones, like animals.

When my mother was about six years old, she recalled hearing a hog coming to their house before midnight. That night her parents decided to sleep in the bark house as the night was warm during this summer. The bark house was the old Sac and Fox house type. The Sac (Sauk) and Fox peoples lived originally in the western Illinois area of the Lower Great Lakes. The people of the two communities learned to make their houses from the birch trees in the region with strips of wood tying the bark to a wooden round fame. Her mother recalled wanting to sleep in the bark house because she was curious about it and people had talked about it.

Before midnight my mother's parents heard a hog coming from the direction of the road. And it kept coming closer. My mother's father, Glade, ran to get his youngest brother, who was her uncle Walter, to help. Uncle Walter had just arrived, riding on his horse, earlier that night. They were not sure what to do, but they felt threatened by the hog. While Glade went to get his rifle, Walter's horse began to act up. The horse was tied and it knew something was not right and tried to get away.

My grandmother Rachel recalled being very afraid, feeling that the hog was now so close she could hear it snorting like it was hungry. They decided to catch the hog because my mother's grandfather Jackson believed it was a witch. If the animal could be caught and be held captive for four days, they could find out who the witch was. At the end of the fourth day, the animal would lose its power from weakness and would transform back into a person and the people would discover who it was. They were not successful in catching the hog and it escaped into the night, squealing and snorting as it ran among the blackjacks into the woods.

Don't Look in the Rearview Mirror at Night

Another story along the Moccasin Trail was about a shadow man. He was seen standing on the northeast corner of the second mile east from Highway 18. Different stories were told about people seeing things along the Moccasin Trail. People did not actually see a shadow; rather they saw the outline of a man. He was an Indian man wearing white man's clothes, but that was all that anyone knew about the shadow man. He did not appear all of the time, but it was always at night. Some people said maybe it was the Traveler who walked Moccasin Trail.

Some folks believe if a person was killed on a road, their spirit might be seen. When someone, like a young person, dies before their time, then the spiritual energy of that person lingers on that particular spot until time passes, and no one really knows why. Some sites remain active with spiritual energy and people say such sites are haunted, but Indians believe it is the spirit of the people who were killed before they were meant to die.

The most memorable story was when my grandfather Glade was cleaning his .22 rifle late one night at the kitchen table. He and my grandmother Rachel and my mother heard someone scratch on the window screen. Grandfather Glade blew out the old kerosene lamp. He ushered his wife, Rachel, and my mother up the stairs for the night. But nothing happened. Sometimes the spirits of the dead play tricks on people to let them know they are still around. In this way, this story is connected to the next one.

After World War II ended, some young sailors who were discharged from the navy and their duties at Shawnee's naval base remained in the Shawnee area. Many others, like my uncle Telmond, came back to the Shawnee area after being discharged from the army. These were still the days when not many people in the area had automobiles. Most Indian people, especially among the Sac and Fox, were still poor after the war and had to walk along Moccasin Trail, so anyone who had a car was special.

My mother's cousin had been in the army during the war, and when he returned, like many returning GIs, he bought a car. He spent a lot of time in town and usually stayed too long, causing him to drive after dark. One night late, he was driving back from Shawnee along the Moccasin Trail to return home. He was by himself. He turned onto the trail from Highway 18. As he was driving, he looked into the rearview mirror. At that moment, he saw a man sitting in the backseat, and he was shocked with fear. He did not know what to do. He kept driving, but he was afraid to look into the mirror again until he reached home.

Everyone warned everyone else after that incident to be careful. People were told to be sure to lock their car doors. And everyone hoped that the same thing would not happen to him or her.

Hey, boy!

My mother's uncle's wife and her children used to visit her sister-in-law near the Moccasin Trail. The sister-in-law welcomed them, fed them, and told the visitors to make themselves at home. She had to go and get her husband who was working in a field nearby. It was about noon, and it was lunchtime.

One of the children decided to take his fishing gear to a nearby pond. He liked to fish, and he was just dropping his line in the water. But the fish were not biting.

At that moment, my mother's uncle's son heard someone say, "Hey boy, Hey boy, Hey boy! What are you doing?" Three times, he heard someone say, "Hey boy!" At about the second or third time, he turned to see who it was. The boy looked around, but no one was there.

Frightened, he ran to the house and told his story to his family. After he told his story, the sister-in-law said that six months earlier two women were killed in an auto accident close to a bridge not too far from the fishing pond. Maybe the spirits of the two women were calling for help.

How do you explain this?

My mother's cousin, her mother, and my grandmother, Rachel, were driving in their car on Moccasin Trail one cold wintery evening in the fall. It was dusk. As they drove slowly due to the weather, they passed a young girl with long, dark hair. My mother's cousin was driving. She asked her mother, "Did you notice the girl had no jacket and no shoes on?"

When the mother looked back over her shoulder, the dark-haired girl was gone. They shuddered, and wondered if the young girl was real, or had they seen a ghost girl. Some people believe that your mind plays tricks on you. But a spirit has to be real when at least two people see it at the same time or about the same time.

After all, this was the Moccasin Trail where many things had happened in the past. It may seem that things happened all of the time, but they happened often enough and they were things that you did not want to hear or see.

My mother's aunt by marriage told a story about two of my mother's uncles, Edgar and Guy. One night the two brothers sat on the porch. A small white light appeared that mesmerized them. About the size of a flashlight, the light flickered like it was dancing. It would appear frequently, and then disappear in the same spot in the weeds. Edgar and Guy decided to try to catch the light. It did not seem hard because the light did not move, and they caught it. As they held it in their hands, the light turned into dirt. Startled, they did not know what to do, or what they had done.

Then, the two uncles threw away the dirt, and it started to sparkle until each particle died out. This took Edgar and Guy by surprise and they looked at each other, bewildered.

At my mother's grandparents' house, she heard of such things happening. My mother said they did not have a television or a radio. Yet they were entertained with stories about things that happened to relatives and friends in the area. The two-story house is long gone, but the memories are there and so is Moccasin Trail. Once an old dirt road, it is now paved and a travel way for many more neighbors who live along the historic famed route.

Located east of Moccasin Trail on Brangus Road and east on a dirt and gravel driveway lies Wakolee Cemetery. Many Wakolees and other relatives of mine are buried at Wakolee Cemetery: my great-grandparents Jackson and Ester Wakolee, great-uncles Edgar, Guy, and Walter, my grandfather Glade Wakolee, uncle Dwayne Wakolee, who served in Vietnam, and my youngest brother, Gerald Fixico.

On a Friday afternoon on November 7, 2014, Michelle and I drove a rental car to travel the length of Moccasin Trail, starting near Prague. A detour sign blocking the road frustrated our effort, so we drove to Highway 40 to Shawnee and started at the other end like when my mother as a child used to walk with her parents from town heading back home. Highway 99 is now a busy four lane and the turn on Moccasin Trail going east yielded an upscale housing addition, so very different from the trail my mother knew as a young girl. Going east, there are two hills within the two miles where my mother's grandparents' house once stood on the north side. We pulled the rental car over to the side of the road and got out to take photographs of the trail, which did not seem very impressive. As we looked west, the sky was getting dark and the trees cast their shadows across the road. Evening was approaching and my thoughts shifted to the Old House and the trail where we stood. The grand old two-story was torn down long ago, but the trail going uphill is still there where the Traveler used to travel and maybe still does.

SEVEN

Indian Humor

"Did you hear the story about the relocated Indian who had never used an elevator?" That question introduces the urban Indian story told about a young Indian man going on relocation to a big city during the 1960s. He applied for the relocation program, left his reservation for the first time, and arriving in the big city, he did not know the name of the building where he needed to go. He asked around, found out where to go and how to get there, and went to the building. Once there, he asked where he could find the relocation office. He was told it was in a certain room on the third floor. He asked how to get there and was told to take the elevator, but he did not know what an elevator was. The helpful office attendant told him to go to the end of the hall where he would find a small room. He should enter the room and push the button he would find on the right side of the door. As the young Indian walked cautiously down the hall, a young white man wearing business clothes rushed past him, brushing him with a briefcase. The businessman stood in front of the small room and hurriedly pushed the button three or four times. The door opened, and the businessman jumped in, the door closing after him. The young Indian man studied the door and waited for his turn to go into the small room. In a few seconds, the door opened and a woman walked out. The young Indian man stared at her as she walked by, looked at the empty room, then backed away, saying he was not going into the small room![1]

Almost all Indians who moved to urban areas have a story about themselves making dumb mistakes while learning to live in the city and laughing about it later. For example, the above story demonstrates how humor is used when there is nothing else left to combat the ills of urbanization. Yet humor is the most natural part of Indian oral traditions. As a result, Native people carried their oral traditions with them to the cities and shared stories about their new experiences and about how things were back home on the reservations. Living in a strange environment called for making critical adjustments, and urban Indians found each other in the same general situation. Full of frustration, they told stories about their experiences in the big cities and laughed at themselves and other Indians as a way of adjusting to a new, foreign life. Then, they brought the relocation stories back to relatives and friends on the reservations and rural home areas.

In the midst of difficult adjustments, the Indians who relocated found new urban identities as city Indians. For comradeship, they teased each other and depended upon each other to urge one another not to give up. The next generation of urban Indians would have fewer obstacles to face, and the following one would have even better lives. By the mid-1970s, urbanization and modernity impacted Native people heavily, thereby creating a new phase of modern Indian history called self-determination. The way of self-determination has been beneficial, giving back to Indians even the freedom to laugh out loud about whatever. In humor is irony and it is ironic that Indians can say "I told you so." Federal Indian policy after federal Indian policy tried to change Indians, and many of them changed on the outside. But on the inside, Indians were still Indians as they reinvented themselves and Indian humor has been a part of this transition of changes.[2] Being yourself is self-determination and humor is a big part of being Indian.

When meeting someone for the first time, it is good to start the conversation with a good joke. Laughing is good for the soul, especially when a big belly laugh cannot be held back. It is spontaneous and the timing is right. Indian jokes may seem to others to be a bit strange, but it is important to keep in mind that they are embedded in a cultural context and that is what makes them funny to Indians. Laughter is a part of being human and being alive, so Indian humor is important in this way.

Humor becomes particularly important in groups or populations that have undergone repeated trauma, and the long white mistreatment of Indians has made laughter essential for survival. Coping in a situation where you are not in control becomes a learned condition, almost like a tradition.[3] But Indian humor has always been a part of being Indian, and laughter lightens bonds of control. Being Indian and knowing other Indians is a particular life context to be celebrated. We celebrate life when we have a good hearty laugh. If a person laughs seventeen times every day on the average, that is over six thousand times a year.

So, why the math? Well, we laugh much more than we think we do. And since all that laughter is good for us, it seems appropriate to have begun this chapter with a joke. So here is one about my relatives. Families have nice relatives and not so nice ones. When I was a child, I had an uncle whom all of my cousins respected out of fear. He had an ornery personality and was mean to all of us kids. In fact, no one really liked him very much. He was that mean, kind of a nasty mean. He never smiled, except when he was teasing us at our expense. He was the type who you sometimes wished something bad would happen to him. Well, one day he was out hunting in the woods by himself. Eastern Oklahoma has thick woods of pecan trees, oaks, and blackjacks—and snakes. Rattlesnakes! Chittos! Yes, rattlesnakes! As my mean uncle walked in the woods that memorable day, he did not see the chitto lying on a log. A rattlesnake, enormous and five feet long, bit him. He was a goner! For two days, the pain and agony were too much to bear! So much suffering occurred, hour after hour. Then, finally, the snake died![4]

Indian Stereotypes

Supposedly Indians are stoic and never smile, but like all people, once you get to know them they are just the opposite of the stereotype. I am sure that you have seen that type in a store or while buying gas traveling in the West—the cigar store Indian standing like a statue. The wooden Indian, so to speak—or not speak. One time, I actually ran into one. You have seen him, the Plains Indian standing tall, leaning forward just a little bit with one hand shading his eyes looking at the horizon because he has an eagle eye for seeing things far away. Well, one sunny day when I lived in rural Michigan, I walked into an Ace Hardware store, looking for something. I thought about how cloudy Michigan was most of the time, as I looked up at the bright sun and walked blindly into the store. The store was sort of dark inside, so I shaded my eyes to see better. When I could see, I was standing face to face with the Plains Indian shading his eyes. You might say this was two Indians seeing eye to eye. I tried hard

Statue and Donald Fixico. Courtesy Michelle M. Martin.

not to laugh at myself and hoped no one saw me looking face to face at the wooden Indian with our hands raised trying to see better. But I suppose it is how you look at things, and at other people. Like Robert Berkhofer, who wrote *The White Man's Indian: Images of the American Indian from Columbus to the Present* in 1978, perspective is important, even when looking at other people and othering them.[5]

For some unexplainable reason, most people of mainstream America are not familiar with Indians. Therefore, most Americans are left believing the many stereotypes about Indians. This is a mistake; the "othering" process of making assumptions about and foisting opinions on Indians results in negative understandings about America's first peoples. To learn about Indians can occur from first reading about them in a book like this, but the real important step is meeting them and hanging out with them.

The majority of non-Indians simply do not know any Indians. Literary expert Kenneth Lincoln noted that "Indian humor remains a mystery, if not an oxymoron to many" Americans.[6] The following stories offer insights into

Indian reality on the fun side. But first we must get past the barriers of stereotypes and simple ignorance about American Indians.

Almost all stereotypes about Indians are pejorative. I have counted them
myself and there are some thirty-eight that are negative. Some examples of
negative terms or phrases are "red devil," "savage," "drunken Indian," "dirty savage," and "wagon burner." About eight stereotypes are positive, such as being
stewards of nature, natural man, and environmentalists or ecologists. The most
common positive stereotype is "warrior"; it is interesting that of the many warrior cultures around the world, the Indian warrior best captures the image of
warrior and this has great appeal to mainstream Americans, who want to be
warriors in competitive sports.

The origin of stereotypes about Indians dates back to the earliest so-called
Indian Wars during the late 1600s. When Indians fought Indians, they naturally saw the other tribes as the enemy to be destroyed, which resulted in mis-
representations and misunderstandings.[7] As the fighting continued each new
generation of whites learned to dislike Indians, although it would be fair to say
not all whites hated Indians. Some befriended Indians and even married them.
Unfortunately, the stereotypes caused a barrier to be constructed, creating a
knowledge gap between Indians and whites. A lack of familiarity with and
ignorance of Indians led to early white Americans vilifying them and the following generations continued to suppress the Indigenous peoples.

Inside Indian Humor

Hence, an important step in overcoming these barriers is learning about Indian
people. The late Lakota activist scholar Vine Deloria Jr. once said, "One of the
best ways to understand a people is to know what makes them laugh."[8] Getting
people to laugh, especially by surprise, tells a lot about the inner perspective
of what people really value, their politics, and outlook on life. What we laugh
about reveals our honesty and our true feelings. At the same time, it is notice-
able when everyone in a group is laughing, and one person is not. Then, why
is that person not laughing? What we laugh about and what we do not laugh
about reveals who we really are.

Fake laughing is maybe even worse than not laughing at all. It hides or
disguises what we really think or feel about another person or circumstances.

These shallow laughs mask the true personality, and humor is likely less important to a person who fakes laughter.

Like laughing, smiling exposes much about our sense of humor. Many people smile naturally, saying to the public that I am an open person and I am an ambassador of good will. But an insincere smile can mask a person's true feelings, like my favorite uncle who killed the snake that bit him. For most of us, despite whatever mask we wear, a hearty laugh shows who we really are. And then the honest smile appears.

To know Indians, it is a good idea to learn about their many cultures and not presume there is a general "Indian" culture. Each tribe has its own culture and its own worldview. However, some tribal communities from the same region may share a worldview, like the Mvskokes and Seminoles mentioned earlier. The same worldview sharing can be said of the Sac and Fox, Cheyennes and Arapahos, and other groups that live in the same area of Indian Country. Environments have shaped the cultures and worldviews of tribal groups in their areas and made Native groups very different when they live at the other end of Indian County. Thus, the humor will be different. Indians of different tribes from the Great Lakes might laugh at something different than Indian tribes of the Southwest.

For example, an Ojibwe from Minnesota might say that his brother-in-law caught a walleye that was a couple feet long, and this would likely impress a Navajo. The joke is this would be a small fish in the Great Lakes region. On the other hand, a Navajo might boast about his brother-in-law having a handful of sheep, and the joke is that five sheep would be a tiny number for most Navajos.[9]

Everyone loves a funny story, especially when it is about someone else. Tribal differences from different parts of Indian Country show that Indians laugh at different things. I have seen Hopi cartoons, and I just did not understand the humor because I am not from the Southwest, though I now live in Arizona. To give you some idea for a big comparison of differences, which includes humor in various cultures, there are 196 countries in the world at this date and there are 567 federally recognized tribes in Indian Country. This means that there are more differences among tribes than among countries in the world, although the word "Indian" lumps all Indigenous Americans together as one people.

Humor in Stories

Indeed, stories are a main source of Indian humor. Funny stories about life experiences involving friends and relatives offer the greatest evidence of Indian humor. Indians are expert storytellers and it is via stories that Indians relive the past. Humorous stories can be about foolish things and silly experiences, like a haunted bridge deep in Mvskoke Creek Country in eastern Oklahoma in the late 1800s. On unpredictable moonless nights, when a rider crossed the bridge, a ghost rider would jump on the back of the horse. Of course, this would startle both the rider and the horse.

One brave Mvskoke man, Asa Harjo, boasted that he was not afraid of the ghost rider and that he would take care of it once and for all. No one questioned his bravery, only his sanity. During the moonless part of one month, Asa went into town night after night and crossed the bridge coming home each time. Nothing! Finally, he went to town as it got dark, had too many drinks, and started on his way home. Fortunately, his horse knew the way home. The brave Asa hid his shotgun under his coat as he rode his horse toward the haunted bridge. As Asa and his horse crossed the bridge, he suddenly felt something strange. At the same moment, the horse whinnied in fear. Old Asa got excited and pointed his shotgun behind him and fired with both barrels. The scared horse reared and threw off Asa. The horse galloped away as fast as it could, leaving Asa sitting in the middle of the bridge. He got up quickly and started chasing his horse, which was galloping toward the barn. Hearing a commotion, Asa's wife rushed out of the house to the barn with a lantern to see what was happening. In the next few minutes, Asa came running into the barn, huffing and puffing. The wife consoled the frightened horse, rubbing its back. At that moment, a proud Asa ran to the barn and said he had shot the ghost rider. His wife replied, "You also shot off the tail of your horse!"[10]

If you are not laughing, then maybe you missed the Indian point here. Indians are superstitious, and many of us have heard and probably know of a haunted bridge. The story about the ghost rider highlights a dark theme of fear and death among the Mvskoke Creeks. Because the story is placed in the context of a haunted bridge, it immediately captures listeners. The involvement of a ghost adds to its appeal, pulling listeners into the story about the dark and mysterious. Then the story becomes a joke about being afraid of the dead and what could happen because you really cannot kill a ghost. The irony is that it is already dead. So now you might be smiling about the story at this moment. And if you are not, then sigh and keep reading.

External Humor

Facing prejudice, discrimination, and racism from non-Indians has been a part of the living experience of American Indians. Much of this racist treatment is learned from prejudiced parents, grandparents, and society in general. Being Indian means knowing what racism is, and unfortunately jokes and poking fun at Indians has been a common practice of non-Indians.

A kind of cultural gap has and continues to exist between Indians and non-Indians, but most of it comes from a lack of knowing Indian people. To really understand American Indians requires embracing the concept of cultural relativism, as Franz Boas described it.[11] Cultural relativism means understanding Indians according to their distinct cultures and realities. An Indian reality really means a collective of tribal realities and each one has its own kind of humor.

The United States' blind Americentrism has made the rest of the world criticize its mistreatment of its Indigenous Americans. Yet American exceptionalism does not excuse mainstream ignorance or apologize for the mainstream's disrespect of Indians and most other people of color. Most Americans choose to know only things that pertain to their lives. Thus, learning about other people is not relevant in their views.

These two barriers—ignoring Native people and disrespecting them—have maintained the cultural gap between Indians and whites. Yet Indians can laugh at themselves for not knowing about the unfamiliar white ways. Those Indians who are too proud often find themselves the target of teasing. Indians have found that one has to be able to take a joke. The cultural gap between Indians and non-Indians has been filled with misunderstandings, but sometimes we can laugh at them. One interracial joke involves a white woman in a fancy new car who is just leaving the store and decides to drive across a nearby Indian reservation to return to her home. She sees an elderly Indian woman walking along the highway. So, the white woman stops and offers the Native woman a ride. The Indian woman gets into the car and thinks what a new shiny car it is. She then looks at the expensive bottle of wine lying next to the white woman on the seat of the car. The white woman sees the Indian woman noticing the bottle of wine and she says, "I got this for my husband." The Indian woman nods approvingly a couple of times and says, "Good trade!"

Indians and non-Indians can laugh at themselves if both have a sense of humor. To laugh is healthy, releasing energy, perhaps lessening tension. Lowering the blood pressure, as they say. Dealing with stress, which Indians call "ethnostress." But laughing about someone else is not always funny. Hopefully, such jokes as the one above can provoke both Indians and non-Indians to laugh at the same story, thereby breaking down prejudiced views.

Humorous Indian Characters

The old television series *F Troop*, the old Sunday newspaper comic strip *Tumbleweeds* with the Poohawks, and other remnants of pop culture included humorous Indian characters. These portrayals poked fun at the old "cowboy and Indian" cliché, using comedy teams somewhat like Amos and Andy, Abbott and Costello, or Rowan and Martin.

In the *F Troop* series, which ran for two seasons from 1965 to 1967, the comedy was a satire about a bizarre U.S. cavalry unit at Fort Courage in the Wild West. F Troop formed a social relationship with make-believe Hekawi Indians, who were equal misfits led by Chief Wild Eagle and his leading warrior, Crazy Cat. The Indians' weird behavior was the same theme as found with *Tumbleweeds'* Poohawks, a mythical Indian tribe getting along with comical citizens of Grimy Gulch and the 6 and 7/8 Cavalry at Fort Ridiculous, running for forty-two years as a comic strip. In *F Troop* and *Tumbleweeds* (1965), both Indians and whites are the victims of stereotypes for the enjoyment of all viewers and readers.

Some people may not realize it, but it is hard for Indians to laugh when external humor makes fun of Indians. In this type of comedy, there is a funny man and a straight man. One does not have to guess which role the Indian plays. Indians find humor in telling jokes to other Indians; they get them, but for an Indian to share jokes with people of other ethnic, racial, and cultural groups and make them laugh is challenging. In the case of Indians meeting non-Indians for the first time, it is easier for the Native person to break the ice. Many non-Indians do not know how to approach an Indian person, much less a group of American Indians. Yet they can laugh together. Humorous stories where Native people are not the butt of the joke enable both Indians and non-Indians to enjoy each other's company.

It can be awkward, but Indian-white relations can be worked out, as happened with the Lone Ranger and Tonto when jokes are told from both perspectives. And so much has been said about the Lone Ranger and Tonto since they were introduced on radio in 1933. Tonto is the Indian sidekick the Lone Ranger needed to elevate himself to a superior status over Indians while Tonto struggled to express himself in English. This popular radio show and later television series of the 1960s finally went off the air, but the two characters became legends. They are also legends in Indian joking. When the Lone Ranger found himself surrounded by Indians threatening to kill him, he said to Tonto: "Tonto, we're surrounded by Indians." Tonto responded with an ironic grin, "What do you mean 'we,' white man?"

In another Lone Ranger and Tonto joke, the hero cowboy finally asks, "Just what does 'kimosabe' mean?" "Hmm, kimosabe, Lone Ranger," says Tonto. "'Kimosabe' means, if you ask that dumb question again, I'm going to kick your butt!"

Jay Silverheels, a Mohawk from Canada who played Tonto on television for a long time, was interviewed by Johnny Carson on *The Tonight Show*. In a skit in 1969, Carson pretended to be a personnel director interviewing Tonto for a new job. Carson asked Tonto a series of questions after the loyal Indian had been a longtime sidekick for the Lone Ranger. Carson asked how Tonto felt working with the Lone Ranger. Silverheels replied in character, "Tonto hunt for Kimosabe. Fish for Kimosabe. Sew clothes. Sweep up. Stay up all night for Kimosabe. Risk life for Kimosabe." At this point, Silverheels looked deadpan at the audience, paused, and said, "Thirty lousy years!" The audience roared with laughter. Carson reacted to Silverheels's punch line in his silent fidgeting style to the delight of the crowd.[12]

The comedy plays off Silverheels's sidekick role with the Lone Ranger. Carson and Silverheels work together as a team to exploit the paternalism of the Lone Ranger and his central role as the hero. It is the underside of any relationship where one person's status is higher than the other person, and Silverheels and Carson bring this out to the delight of the television audience.

Indian Comedians

While Indians had long been the objects of humor, during the 1980s a new generation of Native comedians gained prominence. They became the front men of modern Indian humor. Such Native comedians as Charlie Hill (Oneida) and Vincent Craig (Navajo) have become popular throughout Indian Country. Originally from Detroit, Michigan, Charlie Hill has performed in tribal communities and in major cities like Los Angeles. Hill has been around for a while and has shared the stage with well-known entertainers like Steve Allen, Johnny Carson, and Richard Pryor. He is well known in Indian Country and the documentary *On and Off the Res'* has been produced about his life.[13]

Vincent Craig is another multitalented Indian. He is most known for creating the cartoon strip called *Muttonman*. He has been called a singer, humorist, and storyteller, and he has sung on soundtracks for "Jerry's Song" and *The Awakening*.[14]

Hill and Craig used short humorous stories to entertain audiences. At the same time, they demonstrated Indian humor by using the full range of Native cultures from historical times to the present. Indians were the focus of their humor and they included Indian-white relations as a part of their trade as comedians in telling funny stories.

Hill and Craig are more recent examples of the long legacy of Indians in entertainment. From among their predecessors, Will Rogers is perhaps the most well-known Indian entertainer. He was known internationally during the years of the Great Depression. Born a mixed-blood Cherokee in Cherokee Country, Rogers was a humorist, storyteller, commentator, and radio personality. A proud New Englander, whose ancestors came over on the Mayflower, once asked Will Rogers about his heritage. He replied, "Well, I am not sure if I had any ancestors coming over on the Mayflower, but I know that I have some who met the boat."[15]

Rogers was born in 1879 near Oologah, and lived a dynamic life until his sudden death in a small-plane crash in 1935. His parents raised him on a ranch in northeastern Indian Territory before Oklahoma statehood in 1907. He grew up wild and reckless, and was willing to try anything that interested him. Unable to focus in school, he dropped out of high school in the tenth grade. He learned about ranching, and a freed slave named Uncle Dan Walker showed him roping tricks. Rogers became a cowboy and exhibited his roping tricks at rodeos. He enjoyed entertaining people and his outgoing personality propelled him to stardom with the Ziegfeld Follies as a comedian and trick roper.

As he became more popular, Rogers practiced his humor as a syndicated newspaper columnist in the 1920s. With the radio becoming a part of family households, Rogers made the radio a source of news and entertainment. His infectious smile and outgoing personality led to many invitations, including to the White House, and he befriended celebrities of his time. The adventurous Rogers traveled around the world three times. He wrote six books and starred in seventy-one motion pictures, becoming the highest paid actor in his day.

His humor combined rural country satire about society and politics with input from his Indian heritage. In history, Rogers has been described as a cowboy, comedian, national icon, and legend. He is famous for his one-line signature, "I never met a man I didn't like."[16] Will Rogers's personality and stories dissolved many racial, religious, and political barriers in society.

Places of Humor

Indian humor stretches far beyond the bright lights of the entertainment world. Indian humor can be found at various places where Indian people gather on a regular basis. Similar to a barbershop or beauty salon, Indian bars, front porches of homes, or the kitchen were and remain places of much humor. My mother recalled that her family's front porch was such a place where she heard numerous stories about Indians around Shawnee, Oklahoma, in the evenings in the years before the development of air conditioning. To keep cool during the summer, my mother and her parents sat on the front porch of the Old House in the evenings after the sun went down. At times, my mother's uncle Guy would visit, always bringing new stories to tell and make everyone laugh. My mother recalled that he was just funny and fun to be around.

Some Indian bars became famous as gathering places and were where a lot of humorous stories were exchanged. Much socialization typically occurred in Indian bars and this continues to be the case. Some of these legendary places, however, have been closed for many years. Red Race in Oklahoma City was one popular bar. Others were in the San Francisco Bay area, the Twin Cities, Gallup, New Mexico, and other urban areas, like Los Angeles, which boasted the Shrimp Boat. One time an Indian walked into a bar just as happy hour started. He went up to the bartender and ordered a pitcher of beer for a dollar. He saw another Indian sitting by himself drinking a pitcher of beer. He did not want to drink by himself, so he took his pitcher over to the table where the other Indian was sitting. He sat down and enjoyed the suds, saying, "I like this brand of beer." The second Indian said, "I like it too," as he poured the first

Indian another round; then they drank another round and started on the second pitcher. The first Indian said, "I miss home." The second one asked, "Where are you from?" "Oklahoma!" "Me, too," said the second Indian. Then he asked, "What tribe are you?" The first Indian said, "Mvskoke Creek." "So am I," said the second one as the bartender brought them another pitcher. Then the first one asked, "Where did you go to high school?" "Muskogee," said the second Indian. "So did I," said the first Indian. Then he said, "You look kind of familiar." The other Indian replied, "I think I have seen you before." A young attractive woman walked into the bar, went up to the bartender, and ordered a beer. She asked, "Well, Sam, anything exciting happening?" Sam said as he wiped the bar counter clean, "Nope, just the Fixico twins getting drunk again."

Any Indian family name can be put in place of Fixico. It is a joke about missing home and being glad to see another Indian face when Indians find themselves lost in the mainstream, since they are only about 2 percent of the nation's population. The real point here is that Indians enjoy the company of other Indians, most of the time. It is possible to become intoxicated with the camaraderie of friendship by itself. The Indians are friends joking, teasing, and laughing. This is Indian humor. Laughing in a group, with one funny story leading to another one until tears come to your eyes and your belly shakes.

When a person might ask where to find Indian humor, the most likely place is on the reservation. Follies about misunderstanding about Indians have set scenes that seem to naturally involve Indian Country, on the 326 federally Indian reserved lands throughout the United States. Reservation humor involves funny stories that occur on the reservations. Yet reservation humor is generalized, meaning that tribal lands are the background to the funny stories such as the urban Indian jokes mentioned earlier. Tribal lands are the setting of many funny stories, but the act of *leaving* tribal lands provides the background for other funny stories, such as the urban Indian jokes. But to understand the jokes, you have to understand Indians and their lives on reservations, what they enjoy, and their pastimes. One joke that my friend Peter Iverson, who has studied Navajos much of his life, likes to tell is the following: "What are the five favorite sports among the Navajos? Basketball, basketball, basketball, basketball, and rodeo!" You do not get the joke unless you know that Navajos really love their basketball, like certain other tribes on reservations that relish the sport and drive for miles on weekends to watch their young relatives play.

Tricksters and Coyote

Stories involving tricksters have been told during wintertime in living rooms and on front porches of Indian homes during summers. Such trickster tales have been passed down through the generations across Indian Country. The younger generation may not always understand them, but they listen out of respect for their elders who use Coyote, Hare, and Raven, and other animal characters to show the humor of earlier times. Coyote, who sometimes chases his tail, is like a lot of us in mainstream America, so busy that we do not know what is going on around us.[17] So we need Coyote to provide a kind of irony in life and as an example to learn from.

Coyote is widely known throughout Indian Country. He is the most popular trickster and appears as the buffoon in many jokes. He is supernatural or humanlike and often the object of blame. He is like Wile E. Coyote in television cartoons, with many things happening to him. Created by Chuck Jones, Wile E. Coyote made his first appearance on September 7, 1949.[18] In the television cartoon, Coyote is a buffoon and exemplifies slapstick comedy for children and adults. Wile E. Coyote is always paired against the Road Runner, an exaggerated tall blue and purple bird whose legs move so fast that they look like wheels producing a lot of smoke as he zips ahead out of the reach of Coyote. In one cartoon, Coyote ties a large rocket to his back so he can run faster than Road Runner. He begins to catch him, but Road Runner makes a turn and Coyote with the rocket on his back can only go straight. You see the look of panic on Coyote's face just before he hits a canyon wall. At this point, you might be smiling. For those not smiling, in real life a coyote can run as fast as forty to forty-five miles per hour and a roadrunner can only run up to twenty miles per hour—food for thought.

In the Pueblo Southwest, the clown is another being of much mischief and a focal point of humor. Similar to Coyote, the clown represents both truth and irony in daily life. In this light, the Pueblo people see themselves, relatives, or people they know when the clown acts like the perpetrator. For example, in a dance, a clown may act egotistical or greedy. This puts things in perspective for the Pueblo people, and teaches them social norms. The clown acts out social and cultural behavior that is not acceptable as an example to the community. A clown might be dressed in a heavy costume and perform a dance acting out the role of eating too much corn and not being able tie his shoes. He would not look like Bozo the Clown; instead, his costume would be Pueblo style.

On the northern plains, the Heyoka is like a clown, but he is an abnormal person. He brings laugher from the people at a dance; for example, because he is dancing the wrong way as the others dance around the circle. Heyoka is like Coyote, and he always represents the "opposite" or the "contrary" in life. He is a village jester and a sacred-like clown as his role has been defined by Lakota culture. In an ironic way, Heyoka heals people through laughter. For a moment every time they tell the story of seeing the dancing Heyoka, they forget their concerns and personal problems. Some people are even relieved of depression. You might call this serious humor. Heyoka stories are a part of the Lakota tradition and reminders of the virtues and norms in life and that there are some people who go against those virtues and norms. But you do not have to be a Heyoka among the Lakotas for people to laugh. One story describes an incident that happened long ago. Rattling Blanket Woman told about a herd of buffalo running into camp early one morning. Every man immediately grabbed his bow and arrows, except for one who was known as a late sleeper. He quickly put on some clothes, grabbed his bow and arrows, and jumped on his horse to join the hunt. He noticed his sleeves kept getting caught in his bowstring, which made people laugh at him. Then he realized that in his haste he had put on his wife's dress.[19]

Need for Laughter

A lot of people make fun of themselves in order to get by in life. This is particularly true for American Indians. Difficult situations often leave us no choice but to cope. These can be low times when Native people recognize that enough is enough and that something has to be done about getting out of the bad situation. First, one recognizes the irony of a situation like being poor and laughs at it.

Being poor among tribal communities is so common that the condition has become a part of Indian humor. In this case, humor provides a form of escape from the mainstream, reminding you that you are a person of color and existing at the poverty level. It may not be the best answer to poverty, but joking about being poor is a way of coping. Among themselves, Indians laugh much more because they can be themselves.

When you are poor, you probably do not drive a new car, but instead one that has to be repaired on a regular basis. This is an Indian car, which breaks down and becomes the object of many comments and jokes. Ironically, every Indian driving a car on the reservation has an Indian car—the type where some duct tape holds a signal light in its place and wire holds up part of the bumper or fender. There is some rust on the body, and there are other distinctive characteristics, but most of all, the car keeps going. People joke about cars and pickups. Trucks are very common on the reservation because of the not-so-great roads. And, Indians find all of this is good stuff to joke about. Since the Crows and Dakotas have been enemies for many years, a Crow Indian might laugh and say to other Indians that he got into his Dakota pickup and it let him down because it would not start. On the other hand, I have had a Dakota pickup and found it very reliable.

But the true Indian car never dies. Its spirit is kept alive in this world with more duct tape and baling wire like the Energizer Bunny. The American Indian Movement, more commonly called AIM, seized the Bureau of Indian Affairs building in Washington, D.C., in 1972. News reporters interviewed Floyd Young Horse, a Minneconjou from Eagle Butte, South Dakota, because he represented the real-looking Plains Indian with his braids wrapped in red cloth and his sense of humor appealed to them. Having come to Washington as a part of the Trail of Broken Treaties caravan, he had fun with the reporters. He said that "he had come in [to Washington] in an 'Indian car' with so many things wrong with it that it shouldn't be up and running at all, but somehow 'its spirit was keeping it going.'"[20]

In the movie *Smoke Signals* (1998), two teenage Native women hang out together and one of them has a car with a bad transmission. The car can only be driven in reverse. So the two Indian girls hang out and occasionally give a ride to the main characters, Thomas and Victor, driving the car backwards. This scene is a modern Indianness genre from the "rez," suggesting that it is like this all of the time in tribal communities. The movie is a spoof on rez life; it is not like this in the twenty-first century on reservations, although some people might disagree. But now you know the story, and you can imagine seeing a cloud of dust on a reservation road and a car driving backwards very fast toward you. And you know it is Lucy and Velma coming to see you.

Name-Brand Humor

At the same time, it is interesting that automobile companies have produced a lot of models of cars that they have chosen to name after Indians. Look on any high road or street and you will see a GM Pontiac, Jeep Grand Cherokee, Mazda Navajo, or Dodge Dakota. You may even own one.[21] In addition to the Indian-named cars, a very large recreational vehicle called Winnebago is named after an Indian tribe that has changed its name to Ho-Chunk. In the air, several military attack helicopters have been in operation, such as the Chinook, Huey (Iroquois), Comanche, Kiowa Warrior, Apache Longbow, and Black Hawk. The last two are well known on the battlefield and have a "don't mess with me" presence. In Mesa, Arizona, my family and I live several miles from a Boeing helicopter production company. As my then wife and I drove near the company to get to the Red Mountain Highway, she said, "Look at that Apache." As I looked on the sidewalk for an Apache Indian, she pointed to the sky where an Apache Longbow helicopter hovered in the air in an eerie way facing us.[22]

In American society, the theme of Native people using or interacting with things named after Indians has become itself a joke. On the Fourth of July, an Indian decides to put on his Arrow brand shirt, stuffs his Red Man chewing tobacco in his pocket, goes out to get in his Dakota pickup to drive to the ballpark, puts down a couple of Andrew Jacksons for a baseball game to watch the Cleveland Indians play the Atlanta Braves in an exhibition game in Sioux City, Iowa.[23]

Indian cars may sometimes be painted like war ponies or even have expressive bumper stickers like "Custer had it coming!" Bumper stickers are one-line takeaways and a part of Indian humor. In the 1960s and 1970s, "Red Power" was a common phrase making the political statement that Indians were tired of government paternalism. Indians wanted control over their lives. "Fry Bread Power" is a classic bumper sticker that serves as a reminder of daily life on the rez.

Fry bread is well named for how to make it. Flour and some baking powder are mixed together with water to make a soft dough that is fried in oil or lard. The origin of fry bread was a matter of survival when the federal government forced Indians to reservations in the late 1800s, giving them supplies of flour, lard, salt, coffee, and sometimes powdered milk. In the twentieth century, grocery stores were too far away to buy bread or when light bread was not available, making fry bread got the job done and fed the family. Who makes the best fry bread has always been contentious and Indians will even joke about it. Getting back to the brother-in-law, a person might say when eating fry bread, "Why, my brother-in-law can make better fry bread than this!" Fry bread has become almost a universal food for many rural and urban Indian families, and women may tease each other about their fry bread. One retort a woman may come back with is that her fry bread is so good it can make a freight train take a dirt road to come and get it.

Indian Time

Another Indian universal originating from the mainstream view of Indians is the idea of Indian time. Often an Indian who procrastinates becomes the butt of jokes. When people make fun of Indians in this way, it is not Indian humor. Teasing a person about being late and operating according to Indian time is a worn-out putdown of Indians. The insinuation is that Indians are always late; they are never on time because they do not own watches, and even when wearing watches, they are still late.[24]

Clock time causes stress, trying to meet deadlines, and it is less important to traditional Indians. They told time by looking at the sun to find its position in the sky. At night, Indians could tell time by observing the positions of stars or cycle of the moon. A Comanche friend of mine liked to play a joke when he was asked what time it was. He would locate a window, look out to check the sun by shading his eyes, and with his arm stretched he would tease that Mickey's big hand was holding the sun's nose, so it was about 12:15 after noon.[25] This was an Indian Rolex sundial.

The response to the Indian time joke is that whites invented flextime, which allows the procrastinator to be late. Such individuals are not on time, but the common belief is that Indians operate on Indian time.

The cultural gap between Indians and whites continues because the latter do not know enough about the former. In many cases, Indian-white situations become uneasy, awkward, and even lead to paranoia.

Paranoia giving rise to fear might explain joking to ridicule Indians, including a person putting a hand to his or her mouth and chanting "Woo woo woo!" But whites do not mock Indians when they see two Indians, especially Indian men, standing together. The white American becomes a bit uneasy when the Indian men have long black hair, perhaps in braids, with a reddish brown complexion. They really look like Indians, but what else would they look like? The white person really becomes nervous when three or four Indians are gathered on a street corner. The white may even begin feel like Custer just before the Indian attack. But history tells us that Custer attacked first. Perhaps Custer thought he would defeat the Indians, but he should have started counting, "One little, two little, three little Indians," and so forth. He did not and his surprise backfired.

This story brings to mind the "two greenhorn soldiers in the Cavalry who were thinking about the government's posting that stated $2 would be paid for every pair of Apache ears brought in. As they were riding, not paying attention, and talking about this possible windfall, they suddenly found themselves surrounded by Apaches! One soldier says to the other, 'Hey Jake, look! We're going to be rich!'"[26] This brings to mind Vine Deloria's most important book, *Custer Died for Your Sins*, which makes a lot of sense to Indians and can be funny, but it is an angry book full of sarcasm aimed at non-Indians.

Old Indian Tricks

An old Indian saying is that if you ever get lost, remember that west is always to your back. Indians never get lost; if it looks like we do, we are just scouting around. You can start a fire with two small sticks, put some dry leaves under them, and then flick your Bic lighter. When you are out hunting or on a long hike with the sun beating down, and you need to look for water, ask your partner for his or her water bottle. These are OITs, also known as Old Indian Tricks. And the Irish have their own version of OITs, Old Irish Tricks.

Indian Teasing

In Indian teasing, the general rule is that only Indians can make fun of other Indians, and even this might go too far. Indians teasing each other strengthens the Indian-to-Indian bond just like the storytelling creates the inside the lodge feeling. Togetherness in a brotherhood, sisterhood, or peoplehood is perpetuated by teasing each other in a healthy way, but only if the other person can take a good joke. Being Indian also means feeling what it is like to be Indian when othered by non-Indians. This creates an automatic bond because we have been through the same thing, being Indian. In this teasing way, it is identifying an Indian's Indianness.

A long time ago, an Ojibwe friend of mine and I were leaving the University of Wisconsin campus and we were talking about Indians and leadership. We were so immersed in our conversation that we forgot where we parked the car. So we scouted around until we found it and declared that we were really great Indian leaders trying to lead our way out of the parking lot.

At the same time, many members of other ethnic groups will feel the same intergroup connection via humor. African Americans, Irish Americans, and other ethnic groups understand this intergroup teasing. Being a part of the group renders membership like being in a club. This kind of teasing can test relationships among relatives and best friends. The harmless putdowns are humorous but are not meant to do harm to relationships. Sometimes the teasing involves stories about another person making a blunder and the funny story is a joke about an experience that ended in a funny way.

In Indian teasing, men and women have jokes that are gendered. There is the one about "Indian women where the Navajo woman walks several paces behind her man. The mixed-blood Cherokee woman will walk beside her husband, feeling equal to him. But the Sioux woman will walk right over her man!"[27] The joke is set up so that any three tribes could be put in the roles.

One-Liners! Tribe versus Tribe

Some Indian humor borrows from mainstream American jokes, mostly one-liners levied at particular tribes based on old rivalries. The jokes have been borrowed and then modified: "A Hopi asking, 'How many Navajos does it take to screw in a light bulb?' A Navajo might ask, 'What is three feet tall and a mile long? A Pueblo Grand Entry.'[28] Generally certain tribes like the Pueblos are not on average tall people, and this is a putdown joke about them. One-liners also include brother-in-law jokes, meaning a guy who might not be too smart that your sister married—someone from a different tribe and the family jokes about him. After he does something dumb, someone in the family might say, "He could mess up a two-person grand entry."

These tribe versus tribe one-liners include a Crow teasing the Lakota, and the latter tribe uses the same joke against the former by changing the tribes.

So Lakotas also have Crow jokes. Other tribal rivals like Cherokees and Creeks have their mutual jokes. The list of tribal-rival jokes goes on. They are most fun when a Cherokee tells another Cherokee a joke about Creeks. The caveat here is that any tribe can be substituted as the tribe that is the butt of the joke.

In the case of the Lakota-Crow, a Lakota friend tells a story about some Crow Indians who are not too smart. The Lakota joke teller explains, "One day the leader of a group of Crow saw a one-eyed dog walking across their path behind them. He said to his Crow friends, 'Look at that dog behind us with one eye!' At that exact moment, every Crow covered up their left eye with their other hand and looked at the dog!"[29]

In addition, one-line quips, quick shots, or potshots are a kind of mainstream humor and this one-liner kind of joke has been borrowed by Indians and incorporated into their humor. "She is a Cherokee princess," or "He is as poor as an Osage," are one-liners. People with maybe some Indian blood, especially women who think they are of Indian ancestry, sometimes claim to be Cherokee with an ancestor who was a princess. But the Cherokees did not traditionally have princesses. The standard joke is a white blonde with blue eyes saying with sincerity that one of her grandmothers was part Cherokee and she believes she was a Cherokee princess. Osages became wealthy in the early twentieth century due to oil royalties paid to them, so a poor Osage is really a joke because the "poor" Osage actually has money. This modern Indian practice is post-1960s with mostly mixed-bloods using this kind of humor. This joking is borrowing from the mainstream style of humor.

Us and Them

Just as non-Indians have made jokes about Indians, Indians have made jokes about whites. This "us and them" rivalry dates back to the earliest Indian wars in the 1600s, as both sides have othered the other. The added problem has been considerable cultural and racial differences that have caused hostilities between Indians and whites. This negative history has ebbed and flowed like a tide as Indian-white relations have improved and then changed, most of the time following the lead of federal-tribal relations. What is interesting is that some white Americans have crossed the line to identify with the Indian cause. Indeed, Indians have been the underdog in the long history of Indian-white relations, but some non-Indians want to be a part of the experience of oppression at the hands of whites. These people are Indian wannabes because they desire to be like American Indians. Some wannabes are less sincere and claim Indian heritage and more. The standard Indian joke is that a person of little Indian ancestry, or claiming to be Indian, had better not cut his or her finger or that person might lose all of their Indian blood.

For whatever reason, the wannabe lacks something in his or her own society. The wannabe is seeking something that Indians have, perhaps the inside the lodge experience, but Indians know this feeling. Perhaps it is wanting a connection with the natural world. "I want to experience being Indian" is what the wannabe seems to be saying, including the trauma, second-class citizenship, and mainstream discrimination.

Over the years, Indians have taken many captives, and trappers have lived with tribal communities, but there is a type of person Indians are plagued by. This is the anthropologist who has chosen an Indian community to study and has attached himself or herself to the tribe. The old joke is that the Indian extended family consists of the mother, father, children, a grandparent, and an anthropologist. This means that at Christmas time, "the Indian family gets presents for everyone in the family, including the anthropologist who hangs out nearby."[30]

Indians feel that anthropologists have exploited them, advancing their careers, extracting cultural knowledge from Indians to write their books to make themselves important at the expense of Indian people. Maybe this is why there are few Indian anthropologists, even today. Vine Deloria Jr. writes that "some people have bad horoscopes; others take tips on the stock market. . . . But Indians have been cursed above all other people in history. Indians have anthropologists."[31] But what does one look like? Deloria says that "anthropologists can readily be identified on the reservations. Go into any crowd of people. Pick out a tall gaunt white man wearing Bermuda shorts, a World War II Army Air Force flying jacket, an Australian bush hat, tennis shoes, packing a large knapsack incorrectly strapped on his back. He will invariably have a thin sexy wife with stringy hair, an IQ of 191, and a vocabulary in which even the prepositions have eleven syllables. . . . This creature is an anthropologist."[32]

Besides anthropologists, in alphabetical order, the BIA, Columbus, and Custer are favorite targets of Indian jokes.[33] They are in the Coyote sense of being inept, incompetent, and acting stupid. The BIA really stands for Boss Indians Around, Columbus by confusion thought he had landed in India in

1492, and at West Point, Custer was not a math major, resulting in his being badly outnumbered at the Little Bighorn. Indians have said they are grateful that Columbus was not searching for Turkey or the Virgin Islands.

Charlie Hill's standup comedy routines often include one-liners about Christopher Columbus, no holds barred, and barbed sarcasm. Keeping in mind that white Americans have occupied 98 percent of the North American continent for hundreds of years, Hill "quips about Columbus, 'Goin' Stay Long?' And 'Well, there goes the neighborhood!' reminds us that this was only the beginning of the taking of Indian lands by whites. When asked, 'What did Indians call America before Columbus arrived?' Charley Hill replied, 'Ours!'"[34] Hill's jokes are in reference to the shifting of political power from Indians to whites as a part of the process of colonialism and bureaucracy in the BIA. So, what did Custer tell the Indian agent of the Bureau of Indian Affairs before he left to fight the Sioux and Cheyenne at the Little Bighorn? "Don't do anything until I get back!" And the BIA has not done anything since then.

Pushing back against white oppression has been a regular target for Indians joking about the past. Using puns and jokes, Indians remind mainstream Americans about the truth of colonization and or trying to vanquish the Indian race. The idea of America being virgin land for the taking has entered Indian humor. One example is "The white man arrived with the good book and Indians had the land, now Indians have the book and the white man has the land."[35]

The Western Apaches find the white man to be an "abstraction" of complicated ideas and values that has caused great confusion.[36] To them, the white man is everything that is not Indian. Like the Heyoka "contrary" among the Blackfeet and Lakotas of the Plains tribes, the white man is not what he appears to be. Like Coyote, who says many things, his sole objective is to gain what he desires for himself. "One time a white rancher and an Indian stood side by side on the rancher's huge spread of hundreds of thousands of acres. The white rancher said proudly, 'I have a pickup and I can drive on my ranch for an entire day in one direction and finally reach the end of my land.' The Indian looking in the same westerly direction as the sun was going down said, 'You know, I used to have a pickup like that too!'"[37]

Indians will likely laugh at this joke, or just nod their heads. Whites may not think it is funny. This is ironic Indian humor where Indians have learned to laugh at their own situation. The point here is the long history of losing all of their land, yet Indians shrugged their shoulders as if to say c'est la vie.

Finally, Indians are the way they are because they are politically power-less and the media does not listen to them. Ironically, the trite phrase of being surrounded by Indians is actually, in reverse, the reality for Indians, who are surrounded by non-Indians. When former Navajo tribal chairman Peter Mac-Donald was forming the Council of Energy Resources Tribes in 1975, he recommended that the twenty-five energy tribes whose reservations contained oil, coal, water, and other resources should circle their tribal wagons against the energy companies.

Indian humor is trying to hang on to being flexible while feeling power-less against the federal government and the cultural mainstream that controls daily life, or even worse neglects Indians as if they do not exist. Every so often, Indian humor is not funny at all. It is a way of coping. But funny Indian humor is beyond hilarious, like when you hear a funny story that is so funny that someone snorts, and someone else is drinking coffee and laughs so hard that the person shoots coffee through his or her nose. Indian humor is being among Indians who are having fun laughing and it is a sharing experience where past trauma and present happiness release spiritual energy.

This very humanness—using humor in this way and its commonality—occurs among other groups of people, too. Such humor told in jokes are like stories creating an inside the lodge experience of fun. Certainly, its manifestation and the exact role it plays among Native people is specific to their experience as Indians, but the impulse to laugh at oneself and one's own situation is something that connects us as all human beings. At the same time, humor can pave the way to bridge a cultural gap between Indians and white mainstream when they laugh together. The expression of humor is universal, but two very different cultural sides need to find something in common in order to laugh together. Not always, but a good joke teller is a good storyteller in the oral tradition. And the next time that you hear an Indian joke and do not get it, it might be good to take an introduction course to Indian studies or online course and enroll in NDN 101.

EIGHT

Prophecies and Visions

The Lakotas tell the story of White Buffalo Calf Woman's prophecy. According to the story, ages before the coming of the white man, the Lakotas suffered from starvation due to being unable to find food in the cold of winter. This human suffering lasted until community elders summoned two warriors. The two warriors set out to hunt for food. During their exhausting but fruitless pursuit, a White Buffalo appeared in the distance. As the White Buffalo approached them, it turned into a beautiful maiden dressed in white. One warrior desired to be with the maiden and made his intention known. The other warrior grew cautious as the transformation of the buffalo into a woman had frightened him. The first warrior left with the maiden, and an overpowering fog shrouded them. When the fog cleared, the second warrior found his friend being eaten by worms. The beautiful young woman told the second warrior to return to his people and announce that she would come to see them. The people waited, still in hunger. The White Buffalo Calf Woman arrived and gave the Lakotas the sacred pipe for spiritual strength. Next, she told them where to find food and said that she would return as a White Buffalo six hundred years later. She warned them that as long as the people lived the right way, they would prosper, but if not, then all life would suffer and come to an end. The White Buffalo Calf Woman said that she had been sent to help them learn to survive, and now they were on their own.[1]

No one really knows what year White Buffalo Calf Woman appeared before the two Lakota warriors, but it was a very long time ago. What is important is that she responded to their needs. Unlike most prophecies, White Buffalo Calf Woman appeared in a nonhuman form. The apparition surely startled the warriors, who were not at first certain what they saw. In such situations, fear is the first human response because people fear the unknown, and the ghostly image initially frightened the two warriors.

When White Buffalo Calf Woman appeared, she did so as a spiritual prophet. She gave a warning to the warriors and their people, instructing them what to do and what would happen. She is a culture hero to the Lakota people. Her powers are not doubted for she demonstrated her powers to them when she transformed from a white buffalo into a beautiful woman.

Codes for living a good life were an integral part of the message in the vision. As a part of her instructions, White Buffalo Calf Woman gave the sacred pipe to the Lakotas. When used by leaders of the Lakotas, they would learn about life and teach this philosophy to their people. This gift led to the way the Lakotas worship and give thanks to the earth. The White Buffalo is a sacred being to the Lakotas as a result of the visit from the White Buffalo Calf Woman. Its importance is representative of the Lakota value system, which embraces the supernatural and having faith in visions. Every white buffalo is a sign of fortune and well-being for the Lakotas and they pay homage to it.

The compelling part of this prophecy is that White Buffalo Calf Woman came to earth as a deity, appearing in physical and then spiritual form. She changed her form within seconds in the presence of the two starving warriors. She appeared to them in human form so that they would understand her, and she responded to the needs of the Lakota people. While other Native prophecies typically involved a human acting as a teacher or interpreter, this story of the Lakota oral tradition demonstrates the metaphysical existence of the Other Side and how it comes to the assistance of Native people. Understandings of nature within the oral tradition include the spiritual world in addition to the physical world.

This Other Side of Life has helped Indian people constantly, although other people of different cultures might find this hard to believe. However, although the Other Side's involvement in life is clear, what is not known is how much control individuals have in shaping their own future. Or is the future already set, but we do not know about it? Even if we do not know how much influence we have on the future, among Native peoples, seers and prophets have existed—and are present today—to provide insight about how to navigate the present and future. Seers are people who can interpret past events; some of these individuals can detect what is important in a person's life. They are blessed with a special intuition and this gift is to be used to help counsel others who ask for their insights and advise. Prophets have greater power; they can see far into the future. They predict events to come and their forecasts can influence the present actions of people, leaders, and communities. The life of a prophet is not an easy one. Their ability to see derives from visions that dictate their life. This was the situation faced by Lame Deer, a Lakota.[2] Lame Deer described his vision quest as a young man: "I was all alone on the hilltop. I sat there in the vision pit, a hole dug into the hill, my arms hugging my knees as I watched old man Chest, the medicine man who had brought me there, disappear among the pines, and soon he was gone altogether. . . . I was sixteen then, still had my boy's name and, let me tell you, I was scared. I was shivering and not only from the cold. The nearest human being was many miles away, and four days and nights is a long, long time."[3] Receiving a vision or visions made a person special, with community expectations to meet; it defined a role for the individual to carry out in life.

Prophecy comes to us sometimes through prophets who are not really people. They are beings from the metaphysical world, like Coyote, and these prophetic encounters have been recorded via oral traditions in the form of stories involving actors looked like people but were not always human who intervened for the good of their people. All of these prophets had in common a connection with the metaphysical world. For many Indians, this connection with the metaphysical continues to exist.

The metaphysical influences the conscious mind via dreams, visions, or the cultivation of a distinct but hard-to-explain atmosphere. This connection with the metaphysical is evident where many *Ihanktonwan* (Lakota spirits) are buried near the river of what is currently Greenwood, South Dakota. Their graves are unmarked and lost forever; their ghosts or spirits dwell there. The area is marked by tall grass that seems to connect with the sky. It is hard to ignore the certain presence of the area, which cannot be explained by Eurocentric reasoning.[4] The metaphysical is often among Native people who believe and it possesses the power to convince skeptics.

Spirituality is a part of Indian life and it should not be denied. Spirits are real to Native people. It is not just matter of believing in them because some Indians do not, but sometimes the spirits convince a person to believe in spirits.

Without them, a Native person is missing a part of his or her identity because this abstract nature is a part of Indigenous life. The spiritual dimension is just as real as the physical dimension.

Spirits can affect the living and they often do so without the realization of people. In order to deal with spirits, the Navajos have set up a series of codes. These guidelines must be followed accordingly, or the protective measures put in place through the use of medicine are broken. How and when they are broken depends on the degree of power exercised by the spirits. For example, a person with a gift of prophecy should not use it for personal gain. If a person misuses his or her prophecy, they will find their ability to prophesize become ineffective. In response, metaphysical beings bestowed upon Native prophets the gift of seeing to help guide the people. The prophets of the past had visions and some of the visions were extraordinarily powerful.

The Shawnee Prophet, Tenskwatawa

Over the years, I have been four or five times to Prophet's Rock and the Tippecanoe Battlefield Park in Indiana. They are near each other in the western part of Indiana. According to legend, the Shawnee Prophet went to his spiritual place, now known as Prophet's Rock, which is actually a shallow cave, prior to the Battle of Tippecanoe. One can imagine him sitting there in deep prayer before a small fire and asked for the assistance of supernatural powers to help him empower the warriors that his brother Tecumseh had persuaded to gather at Tippecanoe.

In early 1775, a Mvskoke Creek mother, Methoatsake (Turtle Laying Its Eggs), gave birth to triplets at Old Piqua, a Shawnee village on the Mad River in western Ohio. The father was Puckeshinwa, an important war leader of the Kispokotha division of the Shawnees. The two parents had several children together, including Tecumseh, who had been born earlier. In all, the couple had three daughters and three sons. Several months before the birth of Lalawethika, Puckeshinwa fell in the battle of Point Pleasant. Without her husband, for whatever reason, Methoatsake abandoned her children.[5]

In his early life during the late 1700s, the Shawnee Prophet was called Lalawethika, the "Noisemaker" or "Rattle." Later, he would become known as Tenskwatawa, "The Open Door." In his early life, he was a boaster of many false deeds and he was a drunkard. Lalawethika lived his childhood without parents, overshadowed by his older siblings. Given this situation, Lalawethika likely felt abandoned and tried to get the attention of his elders by telling exaggerated tales. During his young life of uncertainty, an incident added to his misery: an iron-tipped arrow poked his right eye, causing him to lose his sight in that eye.[6]

In his lodge one day, the Noisemaker fell to the ground. His wife became alarmed and rushed to get help. People in the village thought he was drunk again. When Lalawethika's wife tried to revive him, he did not immediately respond; his body seemed lifeless and without its spirit. The people prepared his body for a two-day burial ceremony, but then he stirred. Lalawethika told his listeners about a surreal journey he experienced in which he met the Master of Life and visited the spirit world. There he saw the Other Side of Life where the fertile earth grew corn and game was abundant in the forest and fish filled the streams. There was no want in this land. He also saw death with all of its horror for all those who had lived a bad life on earth and now lived in an enormous lodge of eternal fire. In order for his people to live in paradise, Lalawethika was instructed to teach them the proper way of living so that they might live in the spiritual world of plenty.[7]

He played an important unifying role in his brother Tecumseh's effort to unite all Indian people against the white man.[8] The Prophet's powers and his introduction of the Dance of the Lakes in 1804 had a charismatic effect on Native people.[9] The dance brought Indians of various languages together and unified them. Convinced of his supernatural powers, many Indians believed in the Prophet and joined Tecumseh in his war effort to unite all Indians and tribes against the United States in a final battle to reacquire the homeland of the Shawnees and the homelands of other tribes. The Shawnee Prophet declared that he would use the medicine weapons of the underworld. He said, "We shall conquer if we are brave. The water will wash them away, the wind will blow them down, darkness will come upon them, & the earth will cover them."[10] From under the earth, he would use a black fog to blind his enemies so that they could be destroyed.

After receiving his first visions, the Shawnee Prophet challenged the leadership of the Shawnee Black Hoof and the Delawares, who had several powerful medicine makers and prophets of their own. He called them wicked and denounced them for signing the Treaty of Greenville that ceded the Ohio Country to the U.S. government. In response to the agreement with the white man, the Prophet had conspired to build a town at Greenville. But he was not satisfied.[11] As more settlers moved into the area, the Prophet realized to his annoyance that he would need to build a community farther west. For now, turmoil existed. In March 1806 and for the next several months, the Prophet lived among the Delawares near Woapikamunk, a village on the White River. Medicine fought medicine when other medicine makers accused the newly arisen Shawnee Prophet of doing evil. In turn, his converts grew in numbers and the Prophet accused certain Delawares of sorcery.[12]

The power of the Prophet peaked on the morning of June 16, 1806. At this time, William Henry Harrison, governor of Indiana Territory, challenged the Shawnee Prophet about his supernatural powers. The Prophet responded by correctly predicting that an eclipse would shortly occur. Shouting at his skeptics, the Prophet yelled, "Did I not speak the truth? See, the sun is dark!"[13] Stories spread quickly to other Native communities of the Prophet's powers and he became legendary and more new followers believed he had powers to rule the sun. Near the confluence of the Tippecanoe and Wabash Rivers in modern-day western Indiana, the Prophet built Prophetstown and many believers arrived to listen and observe his mysterious powers at work.

Other events believed to be supernatural, such as tornados and showers of shooting stars, occurred and believers accredited them to the powers of the Shawnee Prophet. In the spring of 1808, the Prophet led his followers to the campsite at the Wabash near Tippecanoe that once belonged to the Miamis. Miami leader Little Turtle and Five Medals of the Potawatomis threatened to kill the Prophet if he settled there. The Prophet responded by denouncing them as "government chiefs" for signing away Indian land.[14]

Before sunrise on November 7, 1811, eager warriors of Prophetstown attacked William Henry Harrison's camp. Without the presence of Tecumseh, who was away campaigning for more warriors to join his ranks, Harrison's men defeated the Indians in one of the most strategically important battles to open this part of the country to white settlement. With fighting over by midmorning, Harrison ordered his soldiers to burn Prophetstown, forcing Tecumseh to reassemble his force after his return months later.

The Battle of Tippecanoe and sacking of Prophetstown led to the fall of the Shawnee Prophet from power. Without divine protection, Tecumseh was killed on October 5, 1813, at the Battle of the Thames in Canada, causing more frustration for Indians. This final defeat marked the end of this Native movement of the Lakes Indians and the failure of Tecumseh's campaign to drive back the white settlers.

The story of the Shawnee Prophet is a part of the bigger story of Tecumseh's campaign to defeat the Americans. Power played an important role in various forms—supernatural, political, and military. Individually, power was a part of the Shawnee Prophet's life and of Tecumseh's life, and the combined story of both is a part of the oral tradition among the Shawnees. Near the battle site stands the Prophet's Rock, a place of refuge where the Shawnee Prophet supposedly went to pray and ask for divine help. When you see the site, you see that it is not a single rock. It is an inset of rocks that creates the entrance of a cave, like an open door to the Other Side of Life, and this is a good place to end the story about the Shawnee Prophet.

Black Elk of the Oglala Lakotas

In August 2004, my son, Keytha, and I visited the Black Hills and made a special effort to see Black Elk Peak, which was known as Harney Peak at the time and named after General William S. Harney who massacred Lakotas. Nine years old at the time and fidgety, even my energetic son realized the cultural significance of Black Elk being at the peak during a good part of an afternoon. The Lakotas regarded Black Elk as a holy man, and he made his pilgrimage to the top of the Black Hills and described what he saw. Visions were also part of the Mvskoke-Seminole tradition that I grew up with. I contemplated the power of these visions as I tried to imagine how Black Elk felt standing at the top of the tall peak.

On the same trip to the Black Hills, Keytha and I arrived at the bottom of the peak one rainy afternoon. We parked our car and made our way closer to the peak, with hesitation on my part. I began to have doubts, fearing that we would not make it to the top before we ran out of daylight. I surveyed the hiking trail that went to the right in the woods for a while and then doglegged to the left at the top. I looked at my watch and muttered to myself that hike was a four-letter word. In the same moment, my impetuous son exclaimed, "We can make it, Dad!"[15] In that moment of indecision, youthful, adventurous energy won over cautious wisdom. So we started up at the bottom of a wet trail with clouds starting to roll away as the last part of the afternoon's sun glistened off the raindrops of the trees. Enticed and wanting to see where Black Elk stood to see during his vision, we started on our pilgrimage to the top.

Many people have visions and they probably would not admit it. The Oglala holy man of the Lakotas, Black Elk, was such an example. He was afraid at a tender age during the late nineteenth century to confess his visions for fear of not being believed. His father was also called Black Elk and his father before him had the same name and his father before him, so that he was the fourth person to carry the proud name. At the time of his first encounter, he was four years old; he remembered it must have been summer when he first heard voices. He was playing alone when he heard someone calling him and he thought it was his mother, but no one was there. The name-calling happened again and began frightening him. The voice said for him to listen. Then he looked up at the clouds and two men were coming down headfirst like slanting arrows. As they came down, they sang a sacred song and the thunder was like drumming. Black Elk was afraid to tell anyone about his vision.[16]

Black Elk experienced visions and dreams, and many people doubted him. But there were many who believed. Native people who are close to their traditions believe that dreams are a part of reality as the subconscious and conscious form one mind. Dreams are taken seriously as signs and messages that may connect the dreamer to the metaphysical deities and the Other Side of Life. In this way, precious insight into the metaphysical side becomes knowledge for all of us on earth.

Black Elk overcame his fear of sharing his visions and accepted his mission to help his people through those visions. According to Joseph Epes Brown in *The Sacred Pipe*, Black Elk had "a special quality of power and kindliness and a sense of mission that was unique."[17] He possessed this power even among his well-known Lakota peers, Crazy Horse, Sitting Bull, Red Cloud, and American Horse. In time, Black Elk became one of the *wakan* (sacred) leaders. Following his training of prayer, fasting, and the pipe's way of life, which were like a conduit he obtained sacred knowledge. His mission was to serve his people with his gifts from the Other Side. His words carried the weight of special wisdom. He described peace upon earth and the Great Spirit. In his story, he recalled that all things were the works of the Great Spirit. He said that people should know that "He is within all things: the trees, the grasses, the rivers, the mountains, and all the four-legged animals, and the winged peoples; and even more important, we should understand that He is also above all these things and peoples."[18]

One of Black Elk's greatest visions occurred at the top of the peak. At the end of his pilgrimage to the top, Black Elk saw the world in the shape of a sacred hoop. His vision included the future and the past simultaneously. It included the flora and fauna. Black Elk recalled being on top of the peak in the Black Hills. In his famous account, he said,

> Then I was standing on the highest mountain of them all [Black Elk Peak], and round about beneath me was the whole hoop of the world. And while I stood there I saw more than I can tell and I understood more that I saw; for I was seeing in a sacred manner these shapes of all things in the spirit, and the shape of all shapes as they must live together like one being. And I saw that the sacred hoop of my people was one of many hoops that made one circle, wide as daylight and as starlight, and in the center grew one mighty flowering tree to shelter all the children of one mother and one father. And I saw that it was holy.[19]

With his powers matured, Black Elk could see in the broadest sense. He could see all that was meant to be revealed and he understood the vision. He was grateful for the revelation.

For many Indian groups, a high point of the earth offers the opportunity for prayers and vision quests. At the top of a high point, a person might witness the Other Side of Life momentarily through a vision, dream, or trance. This moment, when the physical and metaphysical meet, enables the fortunate person to see the Other Side, which has no chronological sequence of time. The past can reveal itself within the present or future. It is most important to realize this opportunity and not to fear this experience. What happens to an individual is powerful and can alter the person's life.

When two entities of power, such as the physical reality and the metaphysical, meet, an ultimate balance develops. It is like a door that allows Native people to momentarily see into other spaces or worlds. Through this timeless portal, we must realize this is actually one existence, consisting of many existences. This is the Medicine Way.

In early September 2013, I returned to Black Elk Peak with hiker friend Michelle. I wanted to revisit where Black Elk made his prophetic observation about all things being connected and I thought about his vision while making the arduous three-mile hike. It was a crowded weekend, with many people making the same trek, but not one percent of all of the hikers that day knew about the holy man of the Lakotas, Black Elk. At the base of the trail, small rocks of mica, granite, and quartz glistened in the sunlight, making the pathway shine like the yellow brick road. A seventy-degree late morning with a few

Black Elk Peak in Black Hills, South Dakota. Courtesy Michelle M. Martin.

clouds made the beginning of the hike pleasant as we paused. The path turned into a shaded trail; then it became steep. We rested, finally completing the long dogleg climb to the stone structure at the top.

This visit made me think that Black Elk Peak was not really a sacred site. Rather, a sacred person made this pilgrimage many years earlier and he had a sacred moment when he had his vision. At such a high point — 7,242 feet tall — the highest point east of the Rockies, visitors experience the same vista that Black Elk saw. But Black Elk saw the earth in a holy manner in his vision. Considering the context of Black Elk's vision, it is up so high that looking around for 360 degrees does make earth look like a circle or hoop. In this philosophical realm, you can sense that everything does seem connected because everything is encircled. In any direction you look, the horizon is filled with blue and darker blue horizons and clouds fill the sky. From this high vantage point, you see the earth below you with rows of rolling trees, green earth, and waves of hills. Black Elk's vision was prophetic as he described the goodness of all things being connected in a sacred relationship with the earth. This is what life is meant to be. The wind blows through the pine trees, sending a message that I believe we can actually understand, if we listen with our hearts. This is so, if we can learn nature's discourse with our spirits and see with our spiritual eyes all that is good like Black Elk did. We can experience a similar sacred moment of being thankful for life and of self-examination about how we can make our own lives better. As we began the descent from Black Elk Peak, I periodically looked back, imagining seeing Black Elk having his vision. I thought that all visitors who are at the top have the opportunity to have a sacred moment, if they are willing to free their minds and listen to the wind so they can be connected to the earth.

Black Elk's vision of the world in a sacred way expressed his understanding of life on earth. His philosophical view has been incorporated into oral tradition among the Lakotas. He struck a chord with many who have read *Black Elk Speaks* as they think about his words and begin to understand the importance of oral tradition among the Lakotas and other Indigenous groups.

Sweet Medicine of the Cheyennes

On the last day of August in 2013, Michelle and I began our morning quest to hike up Bear Butte. Bear Butte rests on the northern edge of the Black Hills, near present-day Sturgis, South Dakota. This is where the Cheyenne prophet Sweet Medicine visited several times as he received visions that he shared with his people. The morning felt right, although I forgot my tennis shoes that I was going to wear on the hike. So I was wearing my black dress shoes, oxfords that have been half-soled three or four times and have traveled much of the world. I am not much of a hiker, reminding Michelle that "hike" is a four-letter word. We turned the Ford Focus rental car into the entrance to read a sign, "Buffalo can be dangerous; please stay in your car." Our car was burgundy, a good color, but Michelle was miffed that we rented a Ford because she grew up with Chevys. Of the two or three buffalo actually mingling with two longhorn cattle, one buffalo enjoyed being photographed, thus stopping all the cars in front of and behind us. We stopped at the education center, learning more about how many tribal groups from the northern and southern plains visited Bear Butte. This was my second time to Bear Butte, but I had not climbed it the first time.

With the introduction of the horse to the Cheyennes about 1760, their way of life changed radically as they learned to ride horses to hunt buffalo. Until then, for an unknown length of time, the Cheyennes had been without guidance. The Cheyennes had found life to be hard and meaningless. Only survival seemed important to them. Other Native groups prospered, but not the Cheyennes. A young boy among the Cheyennes began to draw attention to his community. Strange by comparison with other Native youth, he had mysterious habits. He preferred to be alone and sought out only elders for conversations. He became known as Sweet Medicine.

We stopped at the Education Center and walked through the gallery of history and photographs. The park ranger knew all about the history of the area. My last question to him was how long it would take to make the climb to the top. He replied about an hour and a half. When he said this, I winced, followed by a sigh, then a groan. I began to think that the sign about the buffalo was trying to tell us something. Michelle looked at me and said, "Come on, wimp, you can make it." I thought it was generous for the park to have a water fountain and restrooms at the base. That was a good sign. A cool morning encouraged us to start our ascent; however, we had vastly underestimated what was to come. The trail at the base had numerous prayer ties asking for personal blessings or for blessings of other people. The ties, of kaleidoscopic colors and sizes, were tied to the lower branches of the pine trees, reminding us of the many Native people who had paid their respects to Bear Butte. Many Native people had made the climb to the top of this sacred site. I began to wonder if some of the prayer ties were for those who did not return from the hike.

We started our hike that would turn into a climb and I began to think about how many people died trying to climb Mount Everest. Maybe more than two hundred? I kept thinking about the water fountain because we had no water with us. As the climb became steeper, sharp rhyolite volcanic shards filled the path, which I could feel through the soles of my oxfords. It was a big mistake to forget my tennis shoes. I kept thinking that I would be glad when we got out of the sun, which was beating down on us. The trail curved around the butte where there was nice-looking shade. I could not wait to get there.

The late morning sun arrived, its heat quickly dehydrating all climbers. The trail took us to the other side of the butte and what a surprise! A blowing wind greeted us with a cool force that soon became difficult to tolerate. The cool north wind felt like it was going to blow us off the trail, which had become narrower and a little dangerous. I kept thinking that if Sweet Medicine made this trek many times, I could make it at least once. Keep going, I told myself,

Bear Butte in South Dakota. Courtesy Michelle M. Martin.

one foot in front of the other. To my surprise, the wimp passed Michelle, and I reached the top first. I stood on the windy platform, at the top of Bear Butte, 1,253 feet in height.

The wind blew at least thirty-five miles per hour, making it hard to hold onto anything. I stayed on the wooden platform for several minutes and decided to start back down when Michelle reached the top. We walked around on the platform for several minutes looking at the view in different directions before starting back down. One can imagine a young Cheyenne teenager making the arduous climb on his own or visiting the caves on the north side of Bear Butte. At the top or in the caves, the young man spent a lot of time by himself, listening to the wind and the insect and bird wildlife that makes Bear Butte almost a planet of its own. The young prophet had many solitary experiences as he solidified his relationship with the earth and its powers. At the top, you see the earth in a different way, with its long horizons in all directions, even up and down, and the longest direction is the seventh, the inward direction in all of us—the heart. The longest journey is your life, moving toward the inner direction of personal identity and learning who you are and living a good life. In his heart, Sweet Medicine sought to find himself, to learn more about himself in the seventh direction, and to learn his purpose in life. While they are a proud people, the Cheyennes are also humble people who believe in a greater power than their own as human beings. In the oral tradition, Sweet Medicine is a culture hero for he gave instruction and protection to the Cheyennes. He shared his knowledge, which became the Cheyenne Way.

Sweet Medicine taught the Cheyennes much of their way of life—traditional ceremonies, language, and tribal laws that governed the people as they progressed. As a young man, he became a prophet and took refuge at the sacred mountain known as Bear Butte. He stayed inside of a cave for four years, receiving gifts of supernatural power from the spirits that guided him. These spirits appeared as old people—men and women who Sweet Medicine befriended. But the Old Ones were really spirits.[20] They told him that these lifeways were intended for the Cheyenne people. The Cheyennes were eager to receive the instructions, and these practices are carried out to this day in the traditional manner. One such practice is the giveaway, where people give small gifts and money to a person or a family. This act of kindness became a cultural practice of generosity and the people recognized individuals for their sharing virtue and their accomplishments in performing great deeds in war and during peace.

As he grew older, the young man married and with his wife, he traveled to the Black Hills. There, in a great cave, he attended a council called by Maiyun, known to the Cheyennes as the Creator, who chose only the wisest men as delegates. Sweet Medicine became a pupil of Maiyun, who gave four arrows to Sweet Medicine and instructed him in their purpose and care. Two of the arrows held power over buffalo and when pointed at the animals, they became confused and helpless. The other two arrows were to be carried into battle; when pointed at the enemy warriors, the arrows caused them to become blind and mixed up in their actions. Such power then enabled the Cheyennes to surround their enemy to defeat them.[21]

The Sacred Arrows were the soul of the Cheyennes, according to Sweet Medicine. They had to be cared for in a proper way, or if the arrows were neglected, the Cheyennes would meet a similar fate. If the arrows felt secure, the Cheyennes would be safe and prosper. In his teaching, Sweet Medicine spoke of the spirits. They told him that the Cheyennes were going to face certain things and that the current generation would know the future. The spirits also told him of different animals that would be introduced to the Cheyennes. Before the arrival of the white man, another message, in addition to Sweet Medicine's guidance, conveyed that a different people would come to the Cheyennes. One strange person with long hair on his chin and on his legs would carry with him sickness of all kinds. This individual was the white man. He would put the Cheyennes through atrocities and depredations. An animal accompanying the white man had flashy eyes and a tail that touched the ground and one hoof on each foot and it would be restless like the white man. With him, the hairy person would bring a spotted animal with horns and with big eyes. The animal would live on dirt and eat anything. The Cheyennes would do the same; they would become like the new animals and eat almost anything. Sweet Medicine warned the Cheyennes not to be like the hairy person.

He prophesied the future of the Cheyennes, saying that all the people of this earth should listen and remember his words for they were true and sharp as the points of the Sacred Arrows. In this prophecy, he told the people to always keep in mind his prophecies about the future and to remember that as long as the earth lasted, the Cheyenne people would never become extinct. He said, "As long as the blue heavens, the sun, moon, and earth last, you will always be here. Please do not forget the Sacred Arrows. Remember them always and no other. You are instructed to renew the Sacred Arrow sticks annually."[22]

The Cheyennes have followed these instructions and still hold the renewal ceremony every year. They continue this in order to remain Cheyenne, upholding their traditions, songs, language, and ceremonies. With all of this intact, according to the prophecy, they "will always be Cheyenne and there will always be Cheyenne."[23] The Cheyenne chiefs were also a part of Sweet Medicine's prophecy. He received instructions about how the chiefs should conduct themselves, how they should organize so that there would be leadership within the tribe. Thus the Council of Forty-Four remains as the traditional peacemaker of the Cheyennes. Four representatives from each of the ten bands of the tribe meet in council at the annual Sun Dance with four respected leaders at large also included.

Sweet Medicine directed the Cheyennes toward a meaningful life governed by the Council of Forty-Four and preserved by the care of the Four Sacred Arrows. With both of these came the responsibility for the Cheyennes to live their lives in a sacred way. The Cheyenne people talk about their prophet Sweet Medicine with great reverence. I had heard Cheyennes like Peace Chief

Lawrence Hart talk about Sweet Medicine and the ancient way of peace among the Cheyennes, who were also modern warriors. Lawrence had dreamed about becoming and he became a Navy fighter pilot, but when asked to become a peace chief, he decided to pledge his life to peace. Prophecy is about looking for the balance in life and with the natural world, and the Cheyenne Way is one that has found the path to peace. Elders like Peace Chief Hart and other elders continue telling the accounts of Sweet Medicine. This is a part of the Cheyenne oral tradition with the emphasis on peace over war.

Wovoka of the Paiutes

During the Labor Day weekend in 2016, Michelle and I arrived at the airport in Reno, Nevada, in our quest to visit the sacred land of Wovoka, the Paiute messiah. We rented a bright silver Nissan Juke that has a front end that looked like a bug. On Saturday mid-morning we headed out on a 140-mile drive on Highway 80 north, then going south to the Walker River Paiute Reservation. As we kept going higher in the barren mountains, the third sign really got my attention, "Flashing Light: Chains or Snow Tires Required." I was glad it was early September as Michelle remarked it was an overcast day. Michelle checked her phone and the closest Starbucks was forty miles away. For me, a Mountain Dew and M&M's were at my side. We finally reached the town of Schurz about noon and found the tribal cemetery with Wovoka's grave located in the middle. The day had started out strangely with a 5.6 earthquake in Pawnee, Oklahoma, which was felt in half a dozen states; then another 5.6 quake occurred off the coast near Ferndale in northern California. As we sat on the two benches at the foot of Wovoka's and his wife's graves, we could hear a hawk circling overhead behind us. It was hunting and it went into a dive to chase away another hawk from its prey; then two more hawks appeared. We stopped gazing at the hawks, and I returned to my thoughts, reflecting on the mysterious Wovoka.

In 1869, Wodziwob, a Paiute shaman, entered a trance and experienced a vision. His vision depicted an eternal paradise for all Indians with the absence of whites.[24] He shared his vision with others, but they showed little interest. This first Ghost Dance held was not unique in its quest for a return to the traditional ways of life. Previously, at least half a dozen Indian prophets and minor ones lost in history have predicted destruction for the Native race if people failed to follow their prophetic teachings. Another Paiute called Wovoka continued Wodziwob's teachings with different results.

Wovoka, the Paiute Prophet. Courtesy Nevada Historical Society.

Wovoka's father, Tavibo, was a disciple of Wodziwob, the original Paiute messiah. Wovoka worked for a rancher by the name of Wilson, and learned much about Christianity, especially strong in that part of the country with the Mormon presence. In the white man's way, he took the additional name of Jack Wilson. Later, he changed his name to Big Rumbling Belly.[25] In 1886 or 1887, supernatural forces touched Wovoka's life, invoking a visionary message to warn the people of the coming destruction of the white man and the renewed earth.[26]

During his time, Wovoka rose to greatness among Native people in the West. He lived in the barren land of what became Nevada. People claimed he could see the future and that it was a better time for Indians, a time like it used to be before the white man came. This gifted person of the Paiute people was called Wovoka, meaning "wood cutter" in his Native language, and his vision became the dream of many Indian people who were in great need of hope. Wovoka's vision created a momentum that brought forth the Ghost Dance, calling for the dancers to hold hands and form a circle like the earth. He instructed them to dance forward and backward, constricting the circle in order to focus on the fire of life. The vision required for the people to commit themselves to the Ghost Dance, and if they did the world would return to the original way with its abundance before the arrival of the white man. This spiritual energy brought power to Indian tribes and fear among whites as this hypnotic feeling swept through many Indian communities in the West.

Ethnologist James Mooney described Wovoka, the one called the Messiah, as "a young man, a dark full-blood, compactly built, and taller than the Paiute generally, being nearly six feet in height. He was well dressed in white man's clothes, with the broad-brimmed white felt hat common in the West, secured on his head by means of a beaded ribbon under his chin."[27] Ed Dyer, a neighbor who had daily contact with Wovoka, portrayed him as "a tall, well proportioned man with piercing eyes, regular features, a deep voice and a calm and dignified mien. He stood straight as a ramrod, spoke slowly, and by sheer projection of personality commanded the attention of any listener. He visibly stood out among his fellow Indians."[28] In photographs of the Ghost Dance prophet, he is seen wearing suit pants and jackets, white shirts, neckerchiefs, gold watches, vests with fobs, long black coats, and Stetson hats: "he always has on that black suit coat." He had a love for eagle feathers and Stetson hats.[29] He appeared distinguished, but other things would make him distinct.

On January 1, 1889, a total solar eclipse of the American West and central Canada occurred. And during the darkness Wovoka experienced a spiritual journey to heaven and saw God and people who had passed away.[30] In his vision, the Creator instructed Wovoka to share a message with people who would listen. From his reservation in Nevada, Wovoka warned local Indians about the destruction in the Indians' future. His words of warning spread to other reservations in the Great Basin area, then to tribes further away.[31] Wovoka soon became a messiah to many people; even some Mormons thought that he might be the Son of God returned. His words were of peace and seemed righteous for all people. "Do not harm anyone," he advised, "do right always."[32] His message described a world renewed by avoiding the evil ways of the white man, who was deemed responsible for the plight of the Indian race. Peace and devotion to the Ghost Dance doctrine would bring harmony and a utopia to traditional Indian life. In the following months, the Ghost Dance panicked white settlers and brought the military against ghost dancers. The Lakotas were a special concern since Sitting Bull held considerable influence over them due to his leadership. Indian agents on reservations witnessed the growing momentum of the Ghost Dance and viewed it as leading to Indian attacks against whites. As the military ordered the ghost dancers to return to reservations, the infamous massacre at Wounded Knee occurred on December 29, 1890, when the Seventh Cavalry slaughtered Big Foot and 150 followers and wounded another 50.

Wovoka's visions contained transformations of the world being recreated to the state that it once had been for the Paiutes and other Indians. His renewed world—like a paradise with plentiful wild game to hunt, with flowing rivers and rich valleys—did not include the white man. Doubters and skeptics wanted proof from the prophet, and they asked him to exhibit his powers to foretell the future. Two Indians, Tall Bull and Black Coyote, visited the prophet and asked him to prove he had supernatural powers. According to Tall Bull's account, the three of them were sitting on the ground. Wovoka sat facing them with his sombrero held upside down between them, with his eagle feathers in his hands. With a quick movement, he put his hand into the empty hat and drew out something black. Tall Bull saw nothing. But Black Coyote looked into the hat as if in a trance and he saw the whole world going through a renewal of transformation.[33]

Wovoka described the earth that would be renewed on New Year's Day, 1889. In his vision, he had died and so had the sun. According to his vision, "he met with God, they talked and God told him he was the messiah. Tell my children, the Indians—God directed—always to do the right thing, tell no lies and live in peace with everyone. And that's what he told all the Arapahos and Sioux who came to him. That and nothing more."[34]

Wovoka and his medicine making involved the eagle, one of the most powerful animals in the Paiute world. When he doctored the sick, he used an eagle feather to help draw the poison from the ill person's body. Powerful, he was indeed. In one case, he brought a deceased child back to life and many people saw him perform this miracle.[35]

The Paiute messiah's messages warned the people to follow his teachings, which called for their cooperation and promised a world renewed. Wovoka sparked intrigue and aroused the curious nature in people, both Indians and whites, who heard about him. His words spread as a message of hope against the despair of reservation poverty, and the Ghost Dance spread like a prairie fire converting Native communities. This spiritual movement hosted many gatherings of Indians, including the largest Native following ever in the nineteenth century throughout sixteen states. Wovoka's teachings persuaded some thirty tribes, including the Kiowa, Caddo, and Wichita, who learned about it from the Cheyennes. The Osages, Otoes, Cherokees, and others learned from the Caddos. On the northern plains, the Crows, Northern Cheyennes, Arapahos, Shoshonis, and Lakotas took up the Dance of the Ghosts.[36] To the south, the Southern Paiutes introduced the Ghost Dance to the Pai tribes of Arizona. First, the Walapais took up the dance in May of 1889, and they likely introduced it to western bands of the Pais; then eastern bands such as the Havasupai and Chemehuevi joined the movement.[37]

Wovoka, the Indian messiah, continued his life with respect from his community. Isabelle Creighton, a neighbor in Mason, Nevada, in 1915 said, "Yes, Jack [Wovoka] smiled, and could laugh, but I can also remember, that a great deal of the time, it was a sad and discouraged smile. A look of resignation, shall we say. . . . To us children, he was always kind and gentle, but boy if he told us to mind, we minded." She continued, "If he had any chance for an education in the white man's language and ways he would have gone far, and also might I say, he was a grand person and neighbor."[38] In 1917, Jack Wilson, the Ghost Dance prophet, lived with his wife, Mary Wilson, three or four miles from Mason in a small farmhouse built on an earthen floor. And he abstained from gambling and alcohol throughout his life.

On September 29, 1932, the Ghost Dance prophet died at the age of seventy-four, and the Lyon County coroner wrote out the standard death certificate. "The (Wood) Cutter died in his cabin at the southeast end of the Yerington Indian Colony, after having been attended to since September 13 by an Indian agency physician, who noted on the death certificate Wovoka's enlarged prostate cystitis." Nephritis was the cause and death occurred at approximately 1:00 A.M.[39]

In his last prophecy, Wovoka said that when he died he would shake the earth. Exactly three months after his death, Mason Valley residents experienced the most threatening earthquakes on record. The *Mason Valley News* reported on December 23, 1932, that "the most severe earth quake felt by the majority of Mason Valley residents in their lives occurred at ten thirty Tuesday night and was followed by ten or more less severe ones occurring round eleven thirty which nearly started a second stampede shook virtually the entire Western United States and was felt as far north as Canada and as far south as the Mexican border. The first quake, a prolonged tremor, occurred at 10:10 P.M., while a second quake much later was felt at 11:45 P.M. Other minor shocks were felt in Yerington later."[40] Was this the presence of Wovoka? Perhaps it was a sign that the worst was to come when the earth rebelled, according to the prophecy of Wovoka. Among Indian groups of the Great Basin region, the stories about Wovoka are well known and an important part of the Paiute oral tradition.

The older people in the area still remember Wovoka. In Yerington, Nevada, the Paiute Tribe built a six-foot rock memorial to Wovoka and the Lyon County Museum in town has an exhibit of the prophet. The exhibit recounts the history of the Indian messiah and his power. One day he made ice flow in the Walker River. On another occasion, Wovoka was walking down the road and some men haying in a field taunted him. "Rain Maker! Why don't you make it rain?" Wovoka kept walking, thinking the men might be thirsty. It began to rain very heavily only on the spot where the men were working.

The afternoon on that Labor Day weekend was a fulfilling one as we headed the Juke toward Reno to return it. I felt gratified having finally visited Wovoka in his homeland. The overcast morning had turned into a sunny early afternoon, but before our trip ended the overcast skies returned with a 20 percent chance of rain.

Medicine Wheel

On a Friday afternoon in 2013 during the Labor Day weekend, Michelle and I made the trek to Medicine Wheel in the Bighorn Mountains of Wyoming. The Medicine Wheel is considered by scholars to be a sacred map of the cosmos revealing how early Indians understood astronomy. Some people suggest that its true meaning is not known. As we drove along Highway 90 to Sheridan, we turned west on Highway 14. Dark clouds loomed high above and I thought nature might not allow a visit to Medicine Wheel. Highway 14 climbed, going up a thousand feet until we would be at ten thousand feet all together. We could see rain shafts in the distance and minutes later it rained slightly on us. We stopped at a scenic turnout and a rainbow was behind us, a good sign. Signs are important to me, especially in this kind of situation. In my mind, I remembered what my grandmother Lena had told me about always looking up at the sky when you wake up and when you are traveling. The rain had stopped, and light shafts broke through the clouds against the dark blue sky. Finally we reached the parking area and a tall park ranger greeted us and asked where we were from. I asked how far the hike was to Medicine Wheel, and before I could remind Michelle, she said, "Yes, I know, 'hike' is a four-letter word." I had been to Medicine Wheel before and knew it was well worth the effort. And I reminded myself that at 6:00 P.M. we would be at the Holiday Inn. Yep, if I do anything like a hike at any time, I want to be at a Holiday Inn by the end of the day. The park ranger smiled and said that it was a mile and a half. He added that that there was a park cultural interpreter at the Medicine Wheel. Along the way, we found out from other visitors that the interpreter was a young woman. After we walked about a mile resting at the log benches and taking photographs of the landscape, I suggested to Michelle that both of us get three guesses what the interpreter's name was. Anything to take my mind off the hike, although the scenery was breathtaking, like the trail. I was the closest as I guessed Emily and her named turned out to be Lee.

Medicine Wheel was constructed by earlier Indians, so long ago that no one really knows who they were for certain. The circle of the wheel originally had twelve spokes and later someone of the Cheyenne added sixteen more, according to Lee. Her information was from a story told to her by a Cheyenne elderly woman. Originally five rock cairns as tall as five feet tall with rock slabs on them were located at various points of the circle, but scavengers looted the cairns.

Medicine Wheel evokes positive energy, a kind of healing power that uplifts your spirit, making you feel better. The spiritual power would make you less depressed, if depression was a problem. Many Indians visit Medicine Wheel on personal quests as a plethora of prayer ties and red tobacco offerings tied in red cloth decorate the wire fence protecting the sacred circle. As you stand pondering the Medicine Wheel, the wind blows, almost singing, as it passes through the tops of pine trees. The wind constantly blew that day as if letting us know that spirits suffuse this empowered place. Seemingly the wind connects you to the Wheel because it is the Medicine Way when people recognize that greater forces in the universe control our very existence. Symbolically, the Medicine Way is a philosophical approach that enumerates the various tribal beliefs about the right way for people to live.

Many ask, what is the Medicine Wheel? It resembles a cosmological map. This suggestion has prodded scholars, who have concluded that some of the cairns resemble certain constellations in the sky at night. For certain, there is something special about the Medicine Wheel. It is an ancient presence and

Medicine Wheel in Bighorn Mountains of Wyoming. Author's collection.

Native people have used the site for vision quests and personal pilgrimages. As I walked the two hundred steps around the Medicine Wheel, I realized that it was Indigenous human beings working with ecuna, the earth, to construct a specific project for a deliberate reason. But the question still remained: What was their objective? I am sure the prophecy is there, and we need to be patient when the Medicine Wheel reveals the future to us.

We left this ancient shire at the approaching power time of the day's end, when dark and light intersect, when dusk looks the same as early dawn. Leaving Medicine Wheel was a powerful moment—feeling that the long drive and hike to get there had been rewarding. This part of Indian Country, so spaciously vast with rolling high hills after leaving the Bighorns, makes you realize the preciousness of life for yourself, all people, and all things. The true meaning of the Medicine Wheel is uncertain since it was constructed about two thousand years ago of rocks laid out in the pattern of a wagon wheel. Stories about its purpose surround it, and there are about seventy-five such wheels of various sizes in the United States and Canada. All of them hold the same mystery of their purposes, but one thing for certain is that they are held sacred by Indians in their regions. Most likely, ancient Indians charted the sky at night, watching the movement of the moon and mapping the stars and comets like ancient astronomers did. If this guess is correct, surely their stories about the stars and moon relate to more current Indian oral traditions of stories about the constellations and the moon. Some people have even suggested that the Medicine Wheel and other wheels hold prophetic information about the future that we are not yet able to decipher. Such Indigenous knowledge is all around us if we stop, look and listen, and try to understand ecuna, the earth.

Much of the challenge for American Indian prophecy has been the inability of mainstream Americans to believe in the traditional Indian ways. Some Indian religious beliefs sharply conflict with Christianity. In times of stress, Native people asked the help of a prophet or a "seer," sometimes called a fortuneteller by the Mvskoke Creek and other tribes like the Cherokee. In many cases, this endowed person was called a visionary. The usual protocol involved offering the gifted seer or prophet some tobacco in exchange for the use of the seer's talent. Such a person with this ability saw visions on an irregular basis. He or she was like a door to the Other Side of Life—the spiritual side.

Such individuals were called upon often, and the extent of their gift from the Creator did not usually permit them to work like most people. Their work rested in their calling to use their given talent to help others. "Seeing" in the traditional way means envisioning the totality of the universe due to the mental sight that the seer possesses. Such seeing and understanding does not occur immediately. Patience and an uncomplicated life are essential for seeing and for the way these gifted people think about such things. The point of knowledge or an idea may not be apparent at the moment of observing the mental picture, but with patience the message becomes clear. Sometimes, understanding what one sees takes several minutes, days, or perhaps years.

Learning to see requires the help of a wiser elder or special person who is gifted at interpreting insightful experiences. For example, such helpers can interpret dreams and visions. Among the Mvskoke Creeks, a gifted person who sees is called a Kerrata "Key tha." Most tribes have such a person whose role is that of a metaphysical interpreter or translator. The well-known Lakota seer Black Elk described his power vision as a young boy, saying, "It was the pictures I remembered and the words that went with them; for nothing I have ever seen with my eyes was so clear and bright as what my vision showed me; and no words that I have ever heard with my ears were like the words I heard. I did not have to remember these things; they have remembered themselves all these years."[41] Others could tell that Black Elk could see into the future as a prophet, and that he was sensitive to all things in his understanding of the universe. His role was to serve and protect his people. His special ability to see things connected with the metaphysical world made him valuable to his community as a threshold between the two realities of the physical and metaphysical.

Certain individuals are given this power to serve their people or to risk having the gift taken away from them. In this way, they do not serve only themselves. This call in life is hard because communities and leaders depend on them. The Other Side of Life is in communication with Native prophets, assisting them to comprehend visions accurately. During the last part of the nineteenth century, the Pacific Northwest experienced nearly a dozen renegade dreamers who had nearly two thousand followers.[42] What does the future hold for Indian people? For all of us?

On August 20, 1994, a white buffalo calf named Miracle was born in Janesville, Wisconsin. The Lakotas and other Indians took it as a significant sign. Many Lakotas and other Indians renewed their faith in their traditions. More signs have appeared with the birth of other white buffalo that serve as reminders to the Lakotas and other tribes of the prophecy given a long time ago. Like many Indians and non-Indians, I journeyed to Janesville to see the white buffalo calf. I had known the white buffalo calf prophet story for a long time and I respect the Lakotas for their beliefs. What struck me during this visit was the distance that many traveled to see white buffalo calf with many kinds of prayer ties and medicine items fastened to a fence close to where Miracle was kept. Many Lakotas had made the pilgrimage to see the white buffalo calf that was a part of Lakota destiny. Then, a second white buffalo calf was born at the same ranch in Janesville on August 25 in 2006 and died three months later. On September 19, 2004, Miracle died to the sadness of many Native people.[43]

Many people were not sure what to conclude about the birth and death of Miracle within their lifetimes. It was not supposed to happen this way. Did this mean that the Lakota prophecy was wrong? Yet the outpouring of grief and sadness at Miracle's deaths represents the continuing belief in the power and values of the prophecy and maybe that is what is most important. For the prophecy about the White Buffalo Calf Woman also helped to give identity and strength to the Lakota people, and perhaps above all — hope.

The nature of Native prophecy addresses all things about the future and is not restricted to events concerning solely Indians. For example, Black Elk's prophecies included dangers arising from contact with the white man. Other tribes like the Yaquis of Mexico have a similar prophecy. In their myth of the "Talking Tree," the Yaquis predicted the coming of the Spanish and the dangers of colonization that would follow.[44] In these interpretations, the prophecies include Indians and other people. How meaningful are the stories about a future on a shared earth? Are they as powerful as the ancient fire that made Carl a believer in what he heard — Indians singing and dancing vividly yet he could not see them?

Among the Mvskokes and Seminoles, a prophet is called *owalv* (pronounced o wall ah). Typically they are medicine people, but they have an extra special gift that includes conversing with animals, plants, and nonliving things that they understand and gather their knowledge about the future. They have the ability to *owaletv* (to prophesize), that's what they used to say, to see things happening before they do.

Prophets have played critical roles in decision-making among Indian communities. They advised their leaders who came to depend on them as people watched for signs about the future. Native reality combines the metaphysical and the physical, enabling an inclusive ethos of seeing things and understanding life and the universe. These prophecies have been retold to the young who gathered to listen to an elder telling stories in the oral tradition. These stories are still being told. They are lessons about how to live the good life, raise families, and fulfill one's role in communities. While it may be comforting to believe a prophecy, it may be equally important to believe that it is important. People need to believe in something relevant to their lives and continuing to tell the stories in the oral tradition brings together people in a spiritual way whether they are Indian or not. Many other cultures experience the same spirituality of togetherness when stories, legends, and myths are shared in the oral tradition.

Conclusion

Grandma Lena never went to school, but she formed the foundation of my values while teaching me many things, mostly four very important virtues. She prized family, hard work, cleanliness, and respect. I remember people coming to visit—many of them relatives—and my grandmother made me greet them as I shyly looked at the ground while reaching up to shake hands. This was respect: always respect strangers, especially elders, hvmakimata.

I wanted to end this book with some concluding thoughts and three personal stories that might be interesting and amusing. I have attempted to use stories I have grown up with and personal accounts to demonstrate the powerful energy of American Indian oral traditions. Stories are alive and they bring Indians together in such a spiritual way that story time has a dimension of its own when the past, present, and future become one reality. Each combined physical and metaphysical reality is according to a Seneca worldview, a Comanche worldview, a Mvskoke worldview, or other tribal worldviews of the earth and universe. Sharing stories creates a surreal inside the lodge realism where storytellers and listeners experience spiritual energy that unites them and makes them a part of the story, like they are there. In this cultural psychological sense, they are there at the place where the story happened. This is the internal identity of togetherness—of being inside the lodge—that some may call social identity, but it goes well beyond this. This spiritual feeling creates a kinship of belonging and knowing the new knowledge obtained from each story told. Feeling this spiritual energy is being Indian, whether you actually are or not.

Stories told in a hypnotic way are powerful, appealing forces that persuade us to believe that what has been told is true. Whether a story is true or not, what is most significant is the story's effect, message, and purpose. These shared stories in this volume are meant to convince you that you too can experience being Indian inside the lodge and that open-minded acceptance of the story permits spiritual energy to flow. When listeners open their minds, anything is possible, hvmakimata.

The first story begins with my Mvskoke Creek grandmother, Lena Fixico. My grandmother has been gone since February 1989, but she played an influential role in my upbringing. My Seminole grandfather, Jonas Fixico, passed away when I was seven years old, and I remember it like it was yesterday. We lived out in the country west of Shawnee on Route 4, according to the U.S. mail service. We rented a shotgun house with a small concrete porch. In the living room, next to the front door, an uncomfortable chair leaned forward. My mother had placed it there. Most of the time no one sat there except for my grandfather. The second night after he died, we heard the chair move against the wooden floor, like it always did when grandfather sat down. My grandfather had a very large funeral at the Snake Creek Church cemetery with traditionalists and Christian Indians attending.

My dad worked in Oklahoma City and his drive home took about an hour. As tired as he was, after dinner, he worked at night under a light with a round metal shade that he had rigged up. He began to build what I thought was a long playhouse, and I was excited for me and my brother Ron. The next night as I handed my father nails, my seven-year-old mind decided that he was building a doghouse, but our dogs already had one. The third night, Uncle Telmond, my dad's older brother, showed up to help. My dad and Uncle Telmond loaded the long house onto my uncle's pickup. I soon found out that they had built a burial house for my grandfather's grave in the old way, for his spirit and to protect the buried body.

I remember spending small parts of summers at the Old Place on my grandfather's land allotment north of Seminole in Oklahoma where my grandparents lived. I developed many treasured memories there. My grandfather received his allotment when the Dawes Commission allotted the Seminoles their individual lands following an amendment to the Dawes Act of 1887.[1] Initially, Congress had excluded the so-called Five Civilized Tribes from the original allotment act. The land on my grandparents' farm was of poor soil and so full of rocks that

Jonas Fixico and Lena Spencer Fixico. Author's collection.

even a jackrabbit would be hungry most of the time. This was a grand time in my young life. My younger brother, Ron, our cousins, and I liked to go barefoot when we played. My grandfather would turn the soil with a plow pulled by a horse, and I would help by picking up rocks I could carry and moved them out of the way as the adults planted a large garden to grow small crops of potatoes, tomatoes, green beans, and lots of corn.

Grandmother made *osafke* (boiled corn with ash and lye) on a regular basis; it tasted like bad grits with a smell. When you grow up with it, you learn to like it. You might say it is an acquired taste, like learning to drink fine wine. But the worse it smells, the better it is.

My Grandmother, Lena Spencer Now Fixico

My grandmother Lena Spencer had married my grandfather many years earlier. She was Mvskoke Creek and he was Seminole, so their marriage made a lot of sense. Back in the 1920s, many Mvskoke and Seminole marriages were arranged, but I never heard that theirs was. My grandmother never went to school, but she could write her name. I always break into a grin when I recall my father telling how my grandmother would sign her name most of the time as "Lena Spencer now Fixico."

Grandmother Fixico was dedicated to her family and grandchildren. We were small, skinny Indian kids, as I recall. My grandmother was such a firm believer in being clean and ironing. She ironed everything that she could wash—shirts, pillowcases, sheets, my jeans with patches on them. Everything! All of my brothers and my cousins learned to be clean from our granny.

Life was hard and Grandma believed that everyone should work hard. She believed that nothing got done that was worthwhile that did not require hard work. When you became an adult, she did not care what kind of a job you had, as long as you worked hard at it. Grandma believed that nobody should be lazy.

Family was always important to Grandmother Fixico. Look after family members; take care of them, even when they did not appreciate what you did for them. She was a proud Indian woman and wanted everyone related to her to stand up straight and stay out of trouble so the rest of the family would be proud of you.

Grandmother would put us on the back porch to take a bath. Yes, there was running water in the house, but being bathed on the back porch meant that we had to run outside to draw water from the well and carry it inside. As kids, we played a lot and got dirty, but after our baths, we were not red or brown. We were pink. My grandmother would fill a round number 3 washtub about the diameter of a full-grown oak tree. She would fill the number 3 tub with hot water from the wood stove, and when it was our turn make us stand in the water, and she would scrub and scrub us until we turned pink from our skin being scrubbed so hard! That was my grandmother Lena Spencer now Fixico.

Granny and the Chitto

It was a warm summer day, many years ago. I was a kid growing up in rural Oklahoma. Summers in Oklahoma can get very hot and these were years when no one had air conditioners—at least I did not know any families who had one. When you lived out in the country, who needed an air conditioner? There was plenty of fresh air and sunshine, plus more than enough room to run and explore and play. Having an air conditioner during those days made just about as much sense as a screen door on a submarine.

One summer afternoon at the Old Place on my grandfather's allotment, we kids—my brother and I and a cousin or two—were playing in the backyard having a great time. We were playing tag and chasing each other around. We were oblivious to anything outside of our sphere of the enjoyment of being kids.

Our grandmother always kept a hoe leaning against the wall next to the back door. I never questioned this habit. I would never question my grandmother about anything that she thought was important. She said and we did. My grandmother kept the blade of the hoe sharp. I assumed this was to chop the weeds in her garden more effectively. But this was not the only reason, as my cousins, my brother, and I learned.

On that warm afternoon in 1957, we kids played merrily until we stopped, frozen with fear. Less than ten feet away, a chitto crawled swiftly, zigzagging back and forth. Someone must have yelled or screamed! I do not remember that part, but I still can see the chitto's long black body and menacing appearance as it wiggled back and forth. That image is forever etched in my mind. At that moment, in a single breath my granny rushed past us and with one swinging motion with her sharp hoe, she cut the chitto in half in a flash! I never knew that my granny could move so fast!

I also did not know that a chitto could keep going. The first half of chitto kept going like a young man in a big hurry; it crawled into a hole that we did not know was there. The other half of the chitto did not know what to do and wiggled out of control for several minutes until it stopped!

Always look up (*em vnvtaksetv*) when you are traveling to watch the weather, and always look down where you are walking, hvmakimata.

Vyoposketv (Revenge)

In the fall of 1930 or 1931, during the Great Depression, killing and revenge occurred deep in the country of the Mvskoke Creeks and Seminoles. Johnny Fixico was the younger brother of Jonas Fixico, and Porter Bear was the half-brother of Lena Spencer Fixico. This made Johnny and Porter brothers-in-law. My father is named after this Johnny Fixico. At some point, a disagreement occurred with a Seminole family who had three sons. The family lived on the

Dawes land allotment nearby. Matters became worse when the families began to quarrel. Finally, the quarrels got out of hand; it seemed the Seminole family was jealous of my grandparents.

One evening Johnny and Porter went to find the family's milk cows. It was getting late and the cows needed milking, but they could not be found. The three Seminole brothers hid in a ravine, waiting. Johnny and Porter entered the ravine, not knowing death was waiting for them. As Johnny and Porter looked for the cows in the ravine, the three Seminole brothers shot them. They killed Johnny, but a bullet lodged near Porter's heart. The Seminoles believed that their deed was done and tried to hide the bodies. However, Porter was still alive.

In the dark of the evening, my aunt Pauline Fixico, then a little girl, heard gunshots, as did the rest of the family. Carrying coal oil lanterns in the dark, members of the family—including Pauline, who was barefoot—rushed to look for Johnny and Porter. They found Porter first. Nearby, Pauline almost stepped on the hand of Johnny Fixico, who they found dead in some bushes. Porter was taken back to the house and a medicine man was summoned.

Weeks passed, then months. Porter got well and stronger. Porter and Roman Spencer planned *vyoposketv* against the three Seminole brothers. This happened in the barnyard of the family of the Seminole brothers, whose names are not known. Porter and Roman confronted the three brothers and a fight broke out. Roman hit one of the brothers with part of the tongue of a wagon, killing him. Porter, a huge man, standing about six foot four or six foot six, killed the other two brothers with his bare hands.

The Seminole family reported the murders to the local sheriff and his men came to arrest the two brothers-in-law, Porter Bear and Roman Spencer. A court sentenced Porter and Roman to the Oklahoma State Penitentiary in McAlester for killing the three Seminole brothers.

In prison, the two brothers-in-law planned to escape. They dug a hole under the fence of the prison and ran. They planned to get help and had to travel about sixty miles to reach a relative who lived southeast of Dustin, a small town. Prison officials soon learned of their escape, and the sheriff and his men began to hunt for Porter and Roman. The two escapees caught rides when they could, but stayed in the backwoods as much as possible. Porter and Roman had a big head start in making their escape, but they also knew they were not safe. They were sure that they had been seen. The sheriff and prison officials picked up the men's trail using four bloodhounds. With the bloodhounds chasing them, Porter and Roman moved deeper into the woods. They could hear the bloodhounds getting closer. They hoped that a heles hayv, a relative named Sam Butler, would help them.

They reached the medicine maker's small house, consisting of only a large front room and kitchen. Porter and Roman asked Sam Butler to hide them. The medicine maker instructed them to stand in the middle of the front room back-to-back, one facing east and the other facing west, and to not make a sound. The bloodhounds reached the house and the sheriff knew this was the end. The brothers-in-law were inside. The medicine maker reminded Porter and Roman to stand very still, back-to-back. The sheriff was on the front porch. He knocked at the door. The dogs barked, running back and forth excitedly. Sam Butler told Porter and Roman to close their eyes and not make the slightest sound.

The sheriff entered the small house, but could not see the brothers-in-law standing there in the middle of the room. He went into the kitchen, then checked the back porch. Satisfied, but mystified, the sheriff left. The dogs began to chase a rabbit. Porter and Roman were safe and made their way home. Sam Butler had used the power of ehosa on the sheriff, so that he became confused and not sure where he was. Porter and Roman never returned to prison. That's how it happened, hvmakimata.

German Prisoners of War in Seminole, Oklahoma

During World War II, the country and Oklahoma endured difficult times of sacrifice. My grandparents Jonas and Lena saw their eldest son, Telmond, go off to war. After my uncle Telmond returned home from the war, he never talked much about being in the army. His nickname was Fox. He served in the 101st Airborne Division, which so many Indian boys from Oklahoma joined to help the country during World War II. On the home front, there were meatless Tuesdays and other days of the week that President Roosevelt ordered. All citizens had to sacrifice. There was rationing of gasoline and other items because the United States was losing the war during the early 1940s. The gasoline rationing did not affect Grandma and Grandpa, since they did not have a car anyway.

Of all the strange places, Seminole, Oklahoma, became a holding place for German prisoners of war. Local officials kept the German prisoners at the old courthouse in downtown Seminole; there was not much of a main street, although the town is much bigger now. Seminole was such a rural town that after a while the authorities figured there was no need to put a fence around the German prisoners because where would they go? They did not know where they were, but they did know that they were safe from the war.

Every two weeks or so, my grandmother would inform my grandfather that it was time to go to town. My father was about thirteen years old at the time and he looked forward to trips into town. There were always exciting things to do and people to see, especially through the eyes of a young Indian boy. To him, Seminole was a big town and the only town he knew until his late teens. My grandfather would hitch up the two horses to the wagon, just as my grandmother finished up in the kitchen. One horse was a bay and his name was Bill, and the white horse was named Jim. Then, all three—my grandparents and my dad—left for the long ride into town.

As my grandparents stopped at their regular place to tie the horses, the German prisoners would see them and they knew what was to come. They began to line up, forming one line. My grandmother would take her basket of now semi-warm biscuits to the German soldiers and hand them out one by one, trying to make sure that each one got a biscuit.

As I heard this story for the first time, I thought how ironic it was that my grandmother fed German soldiers who might have tried to kill her son, my uncle Telmond. I asked my dad, why did Grandma do this? He had asked his mom why she did this many years ago when he was barely a teenager. There was a pause, and then my dad spoke quietly with a saddened, serious tone. He said that his mother said in her broken English, "Them soldiers have mothers too. Right now they can't be with them."

In 2008, my father and I drove to Seminole. He showed me the courthouse and how it had been enlarged. We walked across the courthouse yard and I touched the old building's faded yellow bricks. The same trees were there, but they had grown much taller. My father showed me where his dad would hitch the horses and wagon to a post across the street from the courthouse, about a block east, when he drove the wagon into town. My father pointed in that direction. My father is now with his parents, passed away, and I have precious memories and stories about them, other people, and some things most people would not believe. But this is being *este chate* (Indian), when the physical reality is combined with the metaphysical Other Side of Life. It has always been this way, hvmakimata.

Your patience is appreciated for my indulgence in telling these stories from my life and my family on the Fixico side. There are more from my mother's Wakolee side, of Sac and Fox and Shawnees, especially involving Moccasin Trail, located north of Shawnee and south of Prague in Oklahoma. Telling these stories has made me feel right in completing this book, as sometimes such work can be too academic. Telling these stories makes me feel fulfilled in my goal to write such a book that addresses why oral tradition is so important among Indians.

Many Indians live a dual life in which they must balance being among only Indians and living in the mainstream society. Being Indian among other Indians who are friends and relatives is often a common feeling of togetherness. That common ground of being emotionally connected by the oral tradition is that reality of inside the lodge that I have tried to share with everyone reading and pondering these pages. Where Indian oral tradition intersects with the mainstream is revealing, as in the German POW story. Most people probably do not know that most states in the United States, especially in the South, had POW camps during World War II. There were in fact about 175 branch camps that served 511 area camps, hosting an estimated 425,000 prisoners of war. In Seminole, Oklahoma, the POW camp opened on October 11, 1943, and held at times as many as forty POWs.[2] Many people also do not know that more than 25,000 American Indian men and several hundred Indian women served in World War II, just as my uncle Telmond did. When Telmond came home, he did not want to talk much about the war. He just wanted to get on with his life because now he was home safe.

Undoubtedly my uncle preferred the "old ways," as we refer to them. By this we mean the tribal ways that we have traditionally practiced and in which we continue to believe. I hope that this volume, *That's What They Used to Say*, has shared some of Indian life and how Native people understand things. Like a heavy weight of burden removed from my shoulders, at least I have put on paper what I think needs to be said about Indian oral traditions. While this has been a personal quest, I hope that it also fills a void in helping to articulate an Indian voice through various forms of oral traditions. And, now you know a little more about Indians. I hope that you have enjoyed the stories, as I have been told that I am an *emvpanayv* (storyteller).

    MVTO.

Notes

Introduction

1. Fixico, *Call for Change.*
2. Castile and Kushner, *Persistent Peoples*, xv–xxii.
3. "That's what they used to say," and in the Mvskoke Creek language, *hvmakimata.* This familiar phrase is pronounced as "ha ma ki ma ta."
4. My father, John Fixico, told me this hunting story in May 2006, in Sapulpa, Oklahoma.
5. In the Museum of Man in San Diego, there was an exhibit until spring 2016 that displayed a creature like the Tall Man that used to exist many years ago, and I viewed the exhibit on January 22, 2016. Early primates and humans are discussed in Von Koenigswald, *Meeting Prehistoric Man* and *Evolution of Man.*
6. *Este capcvke* is the spelling of "Tall Man" in Chaudhuri and Chaudhuri, *Sacred Path*, 128–29.
7. Willie Lena's father reported that he had seen a Tall Man many years ago, in the early decades of the twentieth century, in Howard in collaboration with Lena, *Oklahoma Seminoles*, 211.
8. Frazer, *Myths of the Origins of Fire*, vi.
9. Krupat, *For Those Who Come After* and *Red Matters.*
10. McWhorter, *Yellow Wolf*, 291.
11. Dorson, *American Folklore and the Historian*, 171.

Chapter 1

1. Tecumseh, "Sleep Not Longer, O Choctaws and Chickasaws," 62–63, 65.
2. McGaa, *Native Wisdom*; Suzuki and Knudtson, *Wisdom of the Elders*; and Wilmer, *Indigenous Voice in World Politics.*

3. Edmunds, *Shawnee Prophet*, 49.

4. Toelken, *Anguish of Snails*, 6.

5. See in the introduction that a Chinese student noted that he saw the world as a circle and that Westerners see it as a line, in Nisbett, *Geography of Thought*, xiii.

6. See Finnegan, "Note on Oral Tradition and Historical Evidence," 195–201; Finnegan, "How Oral is Oral Literature?," 52–64; Cohen, "Undefining of Oral Tradition," 9–18; Henige, *Oral Historiography*; Hutton, "Problem of Oral Tradition," 3–23; and Lang, "Herodotus," 93–103.

7. Tecumseh, "Sleep Not Longer, O Choctaws and Chickasaws," 62–63, 65.

8. See Thompson, *The Voice of the Past*.

9. Terkel, *"The Good War."*

10. Brown, *Bury My Heart at Wounded Knee*.

11. See Vansina's two works, *Oral Tradition* and *Oral Tradition as History*; refer also to West, "Oral Tradition," 348–52.

12. For helpful information on tribal history, see Hale, *Researching and Writing Tribal Histories*.

13. See Blatz, "Craftsmanship and Flexibility in Oral History, 7–22; Tonkin, "Implications of Oracy," 41–49; Tonkin, "Boundaries of History in Oral Performance," 273–84; Tonkin, *Narrating Our Pasts*; Grele, *Envelopes of Sound*; Gudschinsky, *How to Learn an Unwritten Language*; Seligman, "Is Oral History a Valid Research Instrument?" 175–82; Allen Smith, *Directory of Oral History Collections*; Harms, "Oral Tradition and Ethnicity," 61–85; Heintze, "Oral Tradition," 47–56; and Philip D. Curtin, "Field Techniques for Collecting and Processing Oral Data," 367–86; Dunaway, "Oral Biography," 256–66; Faris, "Narrative Form and Oral History, 159–80.

14. Indian nations accounting for their own histories begin with the oral tradition, thus providing an oral history of legends and myths, which accounted for creations and metaphorical stories for morals and values among the people. Vansina's *Oral Tradition as History* and Ritchie's more recent *Doing Oral History* provide instruction on how to interview people in collecting oral history. The difficulties of collecting Indian oral history are told by a frustrated Fred McTaggart in his insightful experience, recounted in *Wolf That I Am*.

15. Cunningham, *American Indians' Kitchen-Table Stories*, 36.

16. The life of William Tecumseh Sherman is told in McDonough, *William Tecumseh Sherman*, and in O'Connell, *Fierce Patriot*.

17. Ruoff, "American Indian Oral Literature," 309–26.

18. Fixico, *American Indian Mind in a Linear World*, 24.

19. Chaudhuri and Chaudhuri, *Sacred Path*, 4.

20. Tecumseh, "Sleep Not Longer, O Choctaws and Chickasaws," 63.

21. Fixico, *American Indian Mind*, 25.

22. Nelson, *Place and Vision*, 8.

23. In describing the Yaqui homeland and homeplace, Kirstin Erickson noted homeland "stories are about the ways that these places embody memory; they are about

identification with a particular landscape." Erickson, *Yaqui Homeland and Homeplace*, 69.

24. In regard to the role of the listener and interpretation of oral history, see Campisi and Hauptman, "Talking Back," 441–48; Finnegan, *Oral Tradition and Verbal Arts*; Hill and Irvine, *Responsibility and Evidence in Oral Discourse*; Lummis, *Listening to History*; and Mercer, "Oral Tradition in the Pacific, 130–53.

25. The famed Chickasaw storyteller Te Ata modulated her voice to speak the words of human and animal characters with "grace and fluidity," and she often shook a gourd rattle or beat a drum while gesturing to release the power in her stories and make the characters believable. Richard Green, *Te Ata*, xii.

26. King, *Truth of Stories*, 10.

27. "December 16, 1811: Earthquake Rocks the American Wilderness," *This Day in History*, History.com, 2010.

28. Swisher, "Why Indian People Should Be the Ones," 83–90.

29. Zumthor, *Oral Poetry*, 9.

30. Fixico, *American Indian Mind*, 41–62.

31. Neihardt, *Black Elk Speaks*, 36.

32. Bradshaw, "Oral Transmission and Human Memory," 303–7; Figlio, "Oral History and the Unconscious," 120–32; Henige, "Oral Tradition and Chronology," 371–89; Kemnitz, "Hand of Memory," 175–89; Rips and Stubbs, "Genealogy and Memory," 705–21; and Thelen, *Memory and American History*.

33. Thelen, *Memory and American History*, vii.

34. See Moss, "Oral History," 429–39; O'Danachair, "Oral Tradition and the Printed Word," 31–41; Oliver, "Oral and Other History," 99–103; and Goody, *Interface Between the Written and the Oral*.

35. See Bahr, "On the Complexity of Southwest Indian Emergence Myths," 317–49, and Jay Miller, *Earthmaker*.

36. As an example, for the Diné (Navajo), see Kelley and Harris, "Places Important to Navajo People," 151–70.

37. Gallagher, *Power of Place*, 23, 96.

38. Thurman, "Plains Indian Winter Counts," 173–75.

39. For insight into the difference of gender in storytelling, see Gluck and Patai, *Women's Words*.

40. This information is from personal experiences as a Native person of Mvskoke Creek and Seminole backgrounds in Oklahoma. See also Fixico, "Muscogee Creeks," 30–43.

41. Cobb, *Listening to Our Grandmothers' Stories*, xvii.

42. See Fixico, *Call for Change*, 11–12, 111–13, 180–82.

43. Thomas B. Marquis, *Memoirs of a White Crow Indian*, 91.

44. Information about the Doris Duke Indian Oral History Project is in Ellis, "Duke Indian Oral History Collection," 259–63.

Chapter 2

1. For the origin of the Mvskoke Creeks, see Swanton, *Early History of the Creek Indians* and "Social History and Usages of the Creek Confederacy."
2. Debo, *Road to Disappearance*, 15.
3. For discussion of Mvskoke Creek traditions and the traditions of other members of the Five Civilized Tribes in the late nineteenth century, see Perdue, *Nations Remembered*, 87–115. For history and cultural information about the Creeks, see Debo, *Road to Disappearance*; Green, *Politics of Indian Removal*; J. Leitch Wright, Jr., *Creeks and Seminoles*. For cultural information on the Seminoles of Oklahoma, refer to Howard in collaboration with Lena, *Oklahoma Seminoles*.
4. The full version is "Rabbit Steals Fire," in Swanton, *Myths and Tales of the Southeastern Indians*, 46.
5. Matthews, *Navaho Legends*, 104–59.
6. See Rooth, "Creation Myths of the North American Indians," 497–508.
7. Nelson, *Place and Vision*, 8.
8. MacDonald with Schwarz, *Last Warrior*, 1.
9. Brant, *Jim Whitewolf*, 123.
10. Konrad Lorenz's quote is found in Thomas, *Talking with the Animals*, 27.
11. Alvord and Van Pelt, *Scalpel and the Silver Bear*, 84.
12. *Times Atlas of the World*, 34.
13. Oklahoma Climatological Survey, "The Climate of Oklahoma."
14. Flora of North America, *Flora of North America* 28, pt. 2:xvi–xviii.
15. Ibid., xvi–xviii.
16. Katz, ed., *I Am the Fire of Time*, xvii.
17. In describing the grandmother's role, Patricia Monture-Angus, a Mohawk scholar, stated, "This grandmother is the oldest woman in the community. . . . Woman is the only one who is the giver of life. Once a woman has entered her advanced years (that is past menopause), she has almost walked a full circle." This statement is analogous to the cycles and patterns described earlier involving the nature of animals and plants. Life on earth is cyclical. Monture-Angus, *Thunder in My Soul*, 242.
18. Vogel, *American Indian Medicine*, 3–12.
19. A comprehensive work is Hahn, *The Invention of the Creek Nation*.
20. Swanton, "Social History and Usages of the Creek Confederacy."
21. Howard, *Shawnee!*, 163. Originally the account is in Trowbridge, *Shawnese Traditions*, 40.
22. A thorough study of Shawnee culture is found in Howard, *Shawnee!*
23. Howard, *Shawnee!*, 164. Originally the account is in Trowbridge, *Shawnese Traditions*, 41.
24. Howard, *Shawnee!*, 163. Originally the account was found in Voegelin and Voegelin, "Shawnee Female Deity in Historical Perspective," 371.
25. Callender, "Sauk," 648.

26. A classic study of the Sac and Fox is Hagan, *The Sac and Fox Indians*.

27. Edmunds and Peyser, *Fox Wars*, 31; Jones, "Episodes in the Culture-Hero Myth of the Sauks and Foxes," 237–39, and Jones, "Notes on the Fox Indians," 74–75.

28. Fixico, "Wei Wir Black Hawk vom Volk der Sac und Fox Erinnern," 139–47.

29. Edmunds and Peyser, *The Fox Wars*, 61–182.

Chapter 3

1. Kenoi, "A Chiricahua Apache's Account," 71–72.

2. Hiskey, "Where the Tradition of Yelling 'Geronimo,'" *Today I Found Out: Feed Your Brain*, TodayIFoundOut.com, January 20, 2011, www.todayifoundout.com/index.php /2011/01/where-the-tradition-of-yelling-geronimo-when-jumping-out-of-a-plane -came-from/.

3. For biographies about Geronimo, see Adams, *Geronimo*; Aleshire, *Fox and the Whirl-wind*; Barrett, *Geronimo*; Debo, *Geronimo*; Faulk, *Geronimo Campaign*; Roberts, *Once They Moved Like the Wind*; Schwarz, *Geronimo*; Sonnichsen, *Geronimo and the End of the Apache Wars*.

4. Paul Andrew Hutton, *Apache Wars*, 71–246.

5. Basso, *Wisdom Sits in Places*.

6. Alvord and Van Pelt, *Scalpel and the Silver Bear*, 12.

7. Hassrick, *Sioux*, 57–73, 151–180.

8. Quote in Eby, *"That Disgraceful Affair,"* 39.

9. Edmunds, "Black Hawk," 25.

10. Treadway, "Triumph in Defeat," 6.

11. Massey, "Sac and Fox in Indian Territory," 6; "Treaty with the Sauk and Foxes, 1804," 74–77.

12. Black Hawk, quoted in Vanderwerth, *Indian Oratory*, 89.

13. Edmunds, "Black Hawk," 27.

14. Black Hawk, quoted in Froncek, "I Was Once a Great Warrior," 98.

15. Froncek, "I Was Once a Great Warrior," 99.

16. Volkman, "Lorado Taft."

17. Citizens to Preserve Black Hawk Park Foundation, letter to the editor, February 2010, *Sac and Fox News* (Stroud, Okla.) 31, no. 4 (April 2010), 11.

18. Black Hawk, *Autobiography of Black Hawk*, ed. by Patterson (2007); Black Hawk, *Life of Black Hawk*, ed. by Kennedy (2008); Black Hawk, *Autobiography of Ma-ka-tai-me-she-kia-kiak*, interpreted by LeClair (2009); Drake, *Great Indian Chief of the West*; Cole, *I Am a Man*; Jackson, *Black Hawk*; Lawson, *Proud Warrior*; Beckhard, *Black Hawk*; Oppenheim, *Black Hawk, Frontier Warrior*; Thayer, *Hunting a Shadow*; Nichols, *Black Hawk and the Warrior's Path*; Trask, *Black Hawk*; Bowes, *Black Hawk and the War of 1832*.

19. For biographies about Osceola, see Hartley and Hartley, *Osceola, the Unconquered Indian*; Oppenheim, *Osceola, Seminole Warrior*; and Wickman, *Osceola's Legacy*.

20. Tustennuck Hajo is how the name is spelled on the list although both first and last names have been spelled differently over the years. List of Seminole Prisoners, Seminoles, Coe Hadjo's people, folder–ca. 15 December 1837, List of Seminole and Other Prisoners, Saint Augustine Historical Society Library, Saint Augustine, Fla.
21. Fixico, *Call for Change*, 108.
22. Nabokov, *Native American Testimony*, 125.
23. GreatSchools.net.
24. State of Florida, Division of Corporations, SunBiz.org.
25. United States Census, American FactFinder, www.factfinder.census.gov.
26. For biographies about Crazy Horse, see Ambrose, *Crazy Horse and Custer*; Bray, *Crazy Horse*; Hollihan, *Crazy Horse*; Marshall, *Journey of Crazy Horse*; McMurtry, *Crazy Horse*; Sajna, *Crazy Horse*; and Sandoz, *Crazy Horse*.
27. Crazy Horse, "We Preferred Our Own Way," 147.
28. Crazy Horse, "We Preferred Our Own Way," 147. Original source is Wheeler, *Buffalo Days*, 199–200.
29. Winsell, "Crazy Horse 1840(?)–1877," p. 97. See also more recent works, Bray, *Crazy Horse*; Hedren, *Great Sioux War Orders of Battle*; and Moulton, *Valentine T. McGillycuddy*.

Chapter 4

1. An example of the Mvskoke welcome speech and protocol is given by Tallahassee town speaker Edward Marshall, "Muscogee Creek Festival—2 Stomp Dancing."
2. Before tomato soup or tomato paste cans, sets of cans were made from Pet milk cans and river gravel as I was told by my grandmother they made the best sound. The phrase "shaking shells" is the same as the women shaking cans.
3. Willie Lena describes the scratching (*sapke*) ceremony in detail in Howard, *Oklahoma Seminoles*, 136–38.
4. Hymes, *Foundations in Sociolinguistics*, 52.
5. Morgan, *League of the Ho-de'-No-Sau-Nee*, 102.
6. Ibid.
7. Young Bear and Theisz, *Standing in the Light*, 33.
8. Littlefield and Underhill, "Crazy Snake Uprising of 1909," 309.
9. "Testimony of Chitto Harjo," November 23, 1906, Elks Lodge, Tulsa, Oklahoma Territory, Alfred Mitchell, 1895–1910, Papers, Box 1, Western History Collections, University of Oklahoma, Norman.
10. Federal officials refused the delegation's request to sell the allotted lands of the members of the Four Mothers. In return, the Four Mothers wanted to take the proceeds from the sale to purchase land in Mexico. The Four Mothers Society had made an agreement with Mexico to buy land, but the United States government rejected this proposal. See Debo, *History of Indians*, 308–9.
11. For an autobiography of Dennis Banks, see Banks with Erdoes, *Ojibwa Warrior*.

12. Peltier, *Prison Writings*, 93.

13. Means with Wolf, *Where White Men Fear to Tread*, 152–53.

14. Banks with Erdoes, *Ojibwa Warrior*, 171.

15. In his own many stories, Leonard Peltier has written his version of the Oglala Firefight in 1975, Arden, *Prison Writings*, 121–36.

16. "Termination of the Menominee," P.L. 399, June 17, 1954, *U.S. Statutes at Large*, 68:250–52.

17. Ulrich, *American Indian Nations from Termination to Restoration*, 247.

18. Deer, "Statement of Ada E. Deer," 105–8.

19. "Wilma P. Mankiller (1945–)" in *Native North American Almanac*, 1098–99; Leonard, "Wilma Mankiller," *The Daily O'Collegian* (Stillwater, Oklahoma), February 2, 2000, www.ocolly.com; Hafften, "Wilma Mankiller Speaks at Women of ELCA Convention," Minneapolis, Minn., ELCA News Service, July 11, 1996, http://archive.wfn.org/1996/07/msg00197.html; and Trahant, "Wilma Mankiller Talks Straight," *Seattle Times*, May 21, 2000; and "Former Cherokee Chief Cites Tenacity, Courage," *Lawrence (Kan.) Journal-World*, December 25, 1999, 10B.

20. Mankiller, "Rebuilding the Cherokee Nation," text of speech, April 2, 1993, Sweet Briar College, Sweet Briar, Va., http://gos.sbc.edu/m/mankillerlhtml.

Chapter 5

1. See Smith, *Prominent American Ghosts*; El-Zein, *Islam, Arabs, and the Intelligent World of the Jinn*; Mann, *Spirits of Blood, Spirits of Breath*; McDaniel, *Lovelorn Ghost and the Magical Monk*; Schmitt, *Ghosts in the Middle Ages*; and Thieselton, *Holy Spirit*.

2. *Holy Bible*, Luke 24:13.

3. For some discussion on people attempting to interact with their own spirits, see Brown, *Voices of Earth and Sky*, 42–43.

4. Smith, *Prominent American Ghosts*, vii.

5. Ibid.

6. Hungry Wolf, *Ways of My Grandmothers*, 50.

7. Crockett, *Angels of the Lord*, 14–15.

8. Hultkrantz, *Shamanic Healing and Ritual Drama*, 30.

9. Smith, *Prominent American Ghosts*, viii.

10. "Dr. John Roberts Completes Half Century of Missionary Work with Indians," February 8, 1933, *Wyoming State Journal* (Lander, Wyo.), Folder open, Box 4, John Roberts Papers, American Heritage Center, University of Wyoming, Laramie.

11. "The Death Trail (Choctaw)," in Judson, *Native American Legends of the Great Lakes and the Mississippi Valley*, 91.

12. Ibid.

13. Spence, *Myths and Legends of the North American Indians*, 131–32.

14. Bastian and Mitchell, *Handbook of Native American Mythology*, 106.

15. Brown, *Sacred Pipe*, xx.
16. For the Navajo worldview, see McPherson, *Sacred Land, Sacred View*, 11–76.
17. See the children's book, Lossiah, *Cherokee Little People*.
18. Lavine, *Ghosts the Indians Feared*, 18.
19. Ibid.
20. Spence, *Myths and Legends of the North American Indians*, 121.
21. "The Little People (Cherokee)," in Judson, *Native American Legends of the Great Lakes and the Mississippi Valley*, 192.
22. Among the Mvskoke Creeks, the term *ehosa* is used often to describe when a spiritual being makes you temporarily lost in your mind as you forget where you are and what you are doing.
23. Linderman, *Old Man Coyote*, 35.
24. Ibid., 43.
25. "The Little People of the Senecas," in Hardin, *Legends & Lore of the American Indians*, 82.
26. Ibid.
27. McTaggart, *Wolf That I Am*, 107.
28. Jones, *Sanapia*, 67.
29. Ibid., 66.
30. Momaday, *Names*, 136.
31. Quirk, *When Spirits Touch the Red Path*, 178–79.
32. MacDonald with Schwarz, *Last Warrior*, 22.
33. Alvord and Van Pelt, *Scalpel and the Silver Bear*, 84. See also Shepard, *Thinking Animals: Animals*.
34. Spence, *Myths and Legends of the North American Indians*, 151.

Chapter 6

1. McDonald, *Shawnee OK Naval Air Station*, 31–36.
2. Soden, "City of Shawnee History," www.shawneeok.org/History/.

Chapter 7

1. Fixico, *Urban Indian Experience in America*, 188–89.
2. Imitating the routine manner of another culture, but retaining your own manner is mimicry, in Bhabha, *Location of Culture*, 121–31.
3. "Westerners live in a simpler, more deterministic world; they focus on salient objects or people instead of the larger picture; and they think they can control events because they know the rules that govern the behavior of objects [and other people]," Nisbett, *Geography of Thought*, xiii.
4. Fixico, *Daily Life of Native Americans*, 171.
5. Berkhofer, *White Man's Indian*.

6. Lincoln, *Indi'n Humor*, 5.

7. Creating misunderstandings about other people due to presumptions is a part of "othering," as explained in Said, *Orientalism*, 166–221.

8. Deloria, *Custer Died for Your Sins*, 146.

9. Fixico, *Daily Life*, 173.

10. Ibid.

11. Robert Lowie described "extreme culture relativism" in his book, *Culture and Ethnology*. The importance of culture relativism has been attributed to Boas, *The Mind of Primitive Man*.

12. Silverheels (as Tonto), interview by Johnny Carson, September 9, 1969, *Tonight Show*, www.casttv.com/video/c8ipod/johnny-carson-jay-silverheels-1969-the-tonight-show-video. Available on YouTube.

13. Osawa, *On and Off the Res' with Charlie Hill*, www.iupui.edu/~mstd/narep/chill.html, accessed February 29, 2016.

14. Fixico, *Daily Life*, 175.

15. "Quotes [of Will Rogers]," Will Rogers Memorial Museums, Claremore and Oologah, Oklahoma, www.willrogers.com/says/will-says.html.

16. Yagoda, *Will Rogers*, ii.

17. Flores, *Coyote America*, 209–32; Trafzer, *Grandmother, Grandfather, and Old Wolf*, 89–133; and Trafzer and Scheuerman, *Mourning Dove Stories*, 51–111.

18. Jones, *Chuck Amuck*, 302.

19. Hassrick, *Sioux*, 136–37.

20. Banks with Erdoes, *Ojibwa Warrior*, 136.

21. Fixico, *Daily Life*, 178.

22. It was actually an Apache Longbow attack helicopter that we saw. McDonnell Douglas developed the Apache helicopter and the U.S. army used it for the first time in 1984; then Boeing took over making it.

23. Fixico, *Daily Life*, 178.

24. Ibid., 179.

25. Ibid.

26. Ibid.

27. Ibid.

28. Ibid.

29. Ibid., 180.

30. Ibid., 181.

31. Deloria, *Custer Died for Your Sins*, 78.

32. Ibid., 79.

33. See the chapter on humor in Deloria's *Custer Died for Your Sins*.

34. Fixico, *Daily Life*, 182.

35. Ibid.

36. Basso, *Portraits of 'The Whiteman,'* 4.

37. Fixico, *Daily Life*, 182.

Chapter 8

1. Caduto and Bruchac, *Native American Stories*, 127–30.

2. Carmody and Carmody, *Original Visions*, 13.

3. Lame Deer and Erdoes, *Lame Deer, Seeker of Visions*, 11.

4. Means with Wolf, *Where White Men Fear to Tread*, 4.

5. Edmunds, *Shawnee Prophet*, 28–29.

6. Ibid., 30.

7. Ibid., 33.

8. See Cave, "Failure of the Shawnee Prophet's Witch-Hunt," 445–75; Edmunds, "Tecumseh, The Shawnee Prophet, and American History," 261–76; Edmunds, "The Thin Red Line," 2–19; Hall, "Open Door Recognizes a Window of Opportunity," 232–35; Thurman, "Shawnee Prophet's Movement and the Origins of the Prophet Dance," 530–31.

9. Dowd, *Spirited Resistance*, 128.

10. Ibid., 11.

11. Dowd, *Spirited Resistance*, 136.

12. Edmunds, *Shawnee Prophet*, 47, and Dowd, *Spirited Resistance*, 137.

13. Edmunds, *Shawnee Prophet*, 48–49.

14. Dowd, *Spirited Resistance*, 138, 143.

15. Fixico, *Call for Change*, 39.

16. Neihardt, *Black Elk Speaks*, 6, 15–16.

17. Joseph Epes Brown, *Sacred Pipe*, xx.

18. Neihardt, *Black Elk Speaks*, 36.

19. Ibid., 43.

20. Bastian and Mitchell, *Handbook of Native American Mythology*, 189–91. See also Stands In Timber and Liberty, *Cheyenne Memories*.

21. Hoebel, *Cheyennes*, 8.

22. Ibid., and Yellowman, "Turtle Island Storyteller Gordon Yellowman, Sr.," Wisdom of the Elders, Turtle Island Storytellers Network. www.turtleislandstorytells.met/tis _oklahoma/transcript_g_yellowman.htm.

23. Ibid.

24. Thornton, *We Shall Live Again*, 2.

25. Rex Alan Smith, *Moon of Popping Trees*, 65; and Utley and Washburn, *Indian Wars*, 294.

26. Thornton, *We Shall Live Again*, 6.

27. Hittman, *Wovoka and the Ghost Dance*, 107.

28. Ibid., 108.

29. Ibid., 110–11.

30. Mooney, *Ghost-Dance Religion and the Sioux Outbreak of 1890*, 764.

31. Rex Alan Smith, *Moon of Popping Trees*, 74.

32. Utley and Washburn, *Indian Wars*, 294.

33. Ibid., 113.

34. Ibid., 132.

35. Ibid., 144, 148.

36. Miller, *Ghost Dance*, 36.

37. Dobyns and Euler, *Ghost Dance of 1889*, 14–28.

38. Lynch, *Wovoka and the Ghost Dance*, 110–11.

39. Ibid., 168.

40. Ibid., 172–73.

41. Neihardt, *Black Elk Speaks*, 41.

42. Ruby and Brown, *Dreamer Prophets of the Columbia Plateau*, 66.

43. "Miraculous White Buffalo Dies," *Madison Wisconsin State Journal*, September 25, 2004; and Kucka, "A 2nd Chance for a Miracle," *Chicago Tribune*, October 1, 2006.

44. Spicer, *Yaquis*; and Erickson, *Yaqui Homeland and Homeplace*, 24.

Conclusion

1. "General Allotment Act," February 8, 1887, *U.S. Statutes at Large*, 24:388–91.

2. "Work Camp," *Seminole (Okla.) Producer*, May 4, 1944.

Bibliography

Manuscript and Archival Sources

Annual Report of the Secretary of War for the Fiscal Year Ending June 30, 1877, 630–31.

"Dr. John Roberts Completes Half Century of Missionary Work with Indians." *Wyoming State Journal* (Lander, Wyo.), February 8, 1933. Folder open, Box 4, John Roberts Papers, American Heritage Center, University of Wyoming, Laramie.

"General Allotment Act," February 8, 1887. *U.S. Statutes at Large* 24:388–91.

"Illinois, Louisiana, Iroquois, Lower Canada, 1702–1712." *Jesuit Relations* 66 (1882), Theodore Hesburgh Library, University of Notre Dame, Notre Dame, Indiana.

List of Seminole Prisoners, Seminoles, Coe Hadjo's People. Folder–ca. 15 December 1837. List of Seminole and Other Prisoners. Saint Augustine Historical Society Library, Saint Augustine, Fla.

Moulton, Gary E., ed. *The Papers of Chief John Ross.* 2 vols. Norman: University of Oklahoma Press, 1985.

Roberts, John, Papers. Special Collections, American Heritage Center, University of Wyoming, Laramie.

Swanton, John R. *Early History of the Creek Indians and Their Neighbors.* Bureau of American Ethnology Bulletin 73. Washington, D.C.: Government Printing Office, 1922.

————. "The Social History and Usages of the Creek Confederacy." *Forty-Second Annual Report of the Bureau of American Ethnology.* Washington, D.C.: United States Government Printing Office. 1928.

"Termination of the Menominee." P.L. 399, June 17, 1954, *U.S. Statutes at Large* 68:250–52.

"Testimony of Chitto Harjo." November 23, 1906, Elks Lodge, Tulsa, Oklahoma Territory. Alfred Mitchell Papers, 1895–1910, Western History Collections, University of Oklahoma, Norman.

"Treaty with the Arapaho and Cheyenne, 1861." February 18, 1861. In Charles J. Kappler, ed., *Indian Treaties, 1778–1883*, New York: Interland, 1972, 807–11.

"Treaty with the Sauk and Foxes, 1804." November 3, 1804. In Charles J. Kappler, ed., *Indian Treaties, 1778–1883*, New York: Interland, 1972, 74–77.

"Treaty with the Wyandot, Etc., 1795." August 3, 1795. In Charles J. Kappler, ed., *Indian Treaties, 1778–1883*, New York: Interland, 1972, 39–45.

Books and Articles

Adams, Alexander B. *Geronimo: A Biography*. New York: Putnam, 1971.

Aleshire, Peter. *The Fox and the Whirlwind: General George Crook and Geronimo; A Paired Biography*. New York: John Wiley, 2000.

———. *Warrior Woman: The Story of Lozen, Apache Warrior and Shaman*. New York: St. Martin's, 2001.

Alvord, Lori Arviso, and Elizabeth Cohen Van Pelt. *The Scalpel and the Silver Bear: The First Navajo Woman Surgeon Combines Western Medicine and Traditional Healing*. New York: Bantam Books, 1999.

Ambrose, Stephen E. *Crazy Horse and Custer: The Parallel Lives of Two American Warriors*. New York: New American Library, 1986.

Bahr, Donald M. "On the Complexity of Southwest Indian Emergence Myths." *Journal of Anthropological Research* 33, no. 3 (Fall 1977): 317–49.

Banks, Dennis, with Richard Erdoes. *Ojibwa Warrior: Dennis Banks and the Rise of the American Indian Movement*. Norman: University of Oklahoma Press, 2004.

Barrett, S. M., ed. *Geronimo: His Own Story*. New York: Meridian, 1996. First published 1906.

Basso, Keith H. *Portraits of 'The Whiteman': Linguistic Play and Cultural Symbols among the Western Apache*. Cambridge: Cambridge University Press, 1979. Reprinted 1980.

———. *Wisdom Sits in Places: Landscape and Language among the Western Apache*. Albuquerque: University of New Mexico Press, 1996.

Bastian, Dawn E., and Judy K. Mitchell. *Handbook of Native American Mythology*. New York: Oxford University Press, 2004.

Baum, L. Frank. "The Death of Sitting Bull." *The Aberdeen (S.D.) Pioneer*, December 15, 1890.

Beckhard, Arthur J. *Black Hawk*. New York: Julian Messner, 1968.

Berkhofer, Jr., Robert F. *The White Man's Indian: Images of the American Indian from Columbus to the Present*. New York: Alfred A. Knopf, 1978.

Bhabha, Homi. *The Location of Culture*. New York: Routledge, 1994.

Bierhorst, John, ed. *Myths and Tales of the American Indians*. New York: Indian Head Books, 1992.

Black Hawk. *The Autobiography of Black Hawk*. Edited by J. B. Patterson. New York: Cosmo Classics, 2007. First published 1834.

———. *Autobiography of Ma-ka-tai-me-she-kia-kiak, or Black Hawk, Dictated by Himself,* interpreted by Antoine LeClair. Rock Island, Ill., 1833. Project Gutenberg, 2009. www.gutenberg.org/dirs/etext04/bhawk10.txt.

———. *Life of Black Hawk, or Ma-ka-tai-me-she-kia-kiak: Narrated by Himself.* Edited by J. Gerald Kennedy. New York: Penguin Classics, 2008. First published 1834.

Blatz, Perry K. "Craftsmanship and Flexibility in Oral History: A Pluralistic Approach to Methodology and Theory." *Public Historian* 12 (Fall 1990): 7–22.

Boas, Franz. *The Mind of Primitive Man.* New York: Collier Books, 1963. First published 1911.

Bowes, John P. *Black Hawk and the War of 1832: Removal in the North.* New York: Chelsea House, 2007.

Bradshaw, J. "Oral Transmission and Human Memory." *Expository Times* 92 (1981): 303–7.

Brant, Charles S., ed. *Jim Whitewolf: The Life of a Kiowa Apache Indian.* New York: Dover, 1969.

Bray, Kingsley M. *Crazy Horse: A Lakota Life.* Norman: University of Oklahoma Press, 2006.

Brown, Dee. *Bury My Heart At Wounded Knee: An Indian History of the American West.* New York: Henry Holt, 1970.

Brown, Joseph Epes, ed. *The Sacred Pipe: Black Elk's Account of the Seven Rites of the Oglala Sioux.* New York: Penguin Books, 1971. First published 1953 by University of Oklahoma Press.

———. *The Spiritual Legacy of the American Indian.* New York: Crossroad, 1982.

Brown, Vinson. *Voices of Earth and Sky: The Vision Life of Native Americans.* Happy Camp, Calif.: Naturegraph, 1989. First published 1974.

Buchanan, Kimberly Moore. *Apache Women Warriors.* El Paso: Texas Western, 1986.

Caduto, Michael J., and Joseph Bruchac. *Native American Stories Told by Joseph Bruchac.* Golden, Colo.: Fulcrum, 1991.

Caldwell, E. K., ed. *Dreaming the Dawn: Conversations with Native Artists and Activists.* Lincoln: University of Nebraska Press, 1999.

Callender, Charles. "Sauk." In Bruce G. Trigger, ed., *Handbook of the North American Indian: Northeast* 15, Washington, D.C.: Smithsonian Institution, 1978, 648–55.

Calloway, Colin G., ed. *The World Turned Upside Down: Indian Voices from Early America.* Boston: St. Martin's, 1994.

Campisi, Jack, and Laurence M. Hauptman. "Talking Back: the Oneida Language and Folklore Project, 1938–1941." *Proceedings of the American Philosophical Society* 125, no. 6 (1981): 441–48.

Carmack, W. C., ed. *Indian Oratory: Famous Speeches by Noted Indian Chieftains.* Norman: University of Oklahoma Press, 1971.

Carmody, Denise Lardner, and John Tully Carmody. *Original Visions: The Religions of Oral Peoples.* New York: Macmillan, 1993.

Cartaino, Carol. *Myths and Truths About Coyotes: What You Need to Know to Know About America's Most Misunderstood Predator.* Birmingham, Ala.: Menasha Ridge, 2011.

Carter, Harvey Lewis. *The Life and Times of Little Turtle: First Sagamore of the Wabash.* Urbana: University of Illinois Press, 1987.

Castile, George Pierre, and Gilbert Kushner, eds., *Persistent Peoples: Cultural Enclaves in Perspective.* Tucson: University of Arizona Press, 1981.

Cave, Alfred A. "The Failure of the Shawnee Prophet's Witch-Hunt." *Ethnohistory* 42, no. 3 (Summer 1995): 445–75.

———. *Prophets of the Great Spirit: Native American Revitalization Movements in Eastern North America.* Lincoln: University of Nebraska Press, 2006.

Chaudhuri, Jean, and Joyotpaul Chaudhuri. *A Sacred Path: The Way of the Muscogee Creeks.* Los Angeles: UCLA American Indian Studies Center, 2001.

The Citizens to Preserve Black Hawk Park Foundation, letter to the editor, February 2010, *Sac & Fox News* (Stroud, Okla.) 31, no. 4 (April 2010): 11.

Clements, William M. *Oratory in Native North America.* Tucson: University of Arizona Press, 2002.

Cobb, Amanda J. *Listening to Our Grandmothers' Stories: The Bloomfield Academy for Chickasaw Females, 1852–1949.* Lincoln: University of Nebraska Press, 2000.

Coe, Charles. *Red Patriots: The Story of the Seminoles.* Gainesville: University Press of Florida, 1974. Facsimile of the 1898 edition.

Cohen, David William. "The Undefining of Oral Tradition." *Ethnohistory* 36, no. 1 (Winter 1989): 9–18.

Cole, Cyrenus. *I Am a Man: The Indian Black Hawk.* Whitefish, Mont.: Kessinger, 2010. Facsimile of the 1938 edition.

Courlander, Harold. *The Fourth World of the Hopis: The Epic Story of the Hopi Indians as Preserved in their Legends and Traditions.* New York: Crown, 1971.

Crazy Bull, Cheryl. "A Native Conversation about Research and Scholarship." *Tribal College Journal* 9, no. 1 (Summer 1997): 17–23.

Crazy Horse, Tashunka Witco (Oglala Sioux). "We Preferred Our Own Way of Living, September 5, 1877." In Bob Blaisdell, ed., *Great Speeches by Native Americans,* Mineola, N.Y.: Dover, 2000, 147.

Crockett, Arthur. *Angels of the Lord: Calling Upon Your Guardian Angel for Guidance and Protection.* New Brunswick, N.J.: Inner Light, 1982.

Cunningham, Keith. *American Indians' Kitchen-Table Stories: Contemporary Conversations with Cherokee, Sioux, Hopi, Osage, Navajo, Zuni, and Members of Other Nations.* Little Rock, Ark.: August House, 1992.

Curtin, Philip D. "Field Techniques for Collecting and Processing Oral Data." *Journal of African History* 9, no. 3 (1968): 367–85.

Cushing, Frank Hamilton, comp. *Zuni Coyote Tales.* Tucson: University of Arizona Press, 1998.

Debo, Angie. *Geronimo: The Man, His Time, His Place.* Norman: University of Oklahoma Press, 1976.

———. *A History of the Indians of the United States.* Norman: University of Oklahoma Press, 1971.

———. *The Road to Disappearance: A History of the Creek Indians*. Norman: University of Oklahoma Press, 1941.

"December 16, 1811: Earthquake Rocks the American Wilderness," *This Day in History*. History.com, 2010. www.history.com/this-day-in-history/earthquake-rocks-the -american-wilderness.

Deer, Ada. "Statement of Ada E. Deer Before the Senate Committee of Indian Affairs, July 15, 1993." *Wicazo Sa Review* 9, no. 2 (Autumn 1993): 105–8.

Deloria, Vine, Jr. *Custer Died For Your Sins: An Indian Manifesto*. Norman: University of Oklahoma Press, 1988. First published 1969 by Avon.

Denetdale, Jennifer Nez. *Reclaiming Diné History: The Legacies of Navajo Chief Manuelito and Juanita*. Tucson: University of Arizona Press, 2007.

Densmore, Frances. *Chippewa Customs*. Saint Paul: Minnesota Historical Society, 1979.

Diedrich, Mark, ed. *Sitting Bull: The Collected Speeches*. Rochester, Minn.: Coyote Books, 1998.

Dobie, J. Frank. *The Voice of the Coyote*. Lincoln: University of Nebraska Press, 1961.

Dobyns, Henry F., and Robert C. Euler. *The Ghost Dance of 1889: Among the Pai Indians of Northwestern Arizona*. Prescott, Ariz.: Prescott College Press, 1967.

Dorson, Richard M. *American Folklore and the Historian*. Chicago: University of Chicago Press, 1971.

Dowd, Gregory Evans. *A Spirited Resistance: The North American Indian Struggle for Unity, 1745–1815*. Baltimore: Johns Hopkins University Press, 1992.

Drake, Benjamin. *The Great Indian Chief of the West; or, the Life and Adventures of Black Hawk*. Cincinnati: Applegate, 1854.

———. *Life of Tecumseh, and of His Brother the Prophet; with a Historical Sketch of the Shawanoe Indians*. Cincinnati: E. Morgan, 1841.

Dunaway, David King. "The Oral Biography." *Biography* 14 (1991): 256–66.

Eastman, Charles A. *From the Deep Woods to Civilization*. Boston: Little, Brown, 1916.

———. *Indian Boyhood*. Garden City, N.Y.: Doubleday, Page, 1915.

———. *The Soul of the Indian: An Interpretation*. Boston: Houghton Mifflin, 1911.

Eby, Cecil D. *"That Disgraceful Affair," the Black Hawk War*. New York: W. W. Norton, 1975.

Edmonds, Margot, and Ella E. Clark, eds. *Voices of the Winds: Native American Legends*. New York: Facts on File, 1989.

Edmunds, R. David. "Black Hawk." *Timeline* 5, no. 2 (April–May 1988): 24–27.

———. *The Potawatomis: Keepers of the Fire*. Norman: University of Oklahoma Press, 1978

———. *The Shawnee Prophet*. Lincoln: University of Nebraska Press, 1983.

———. *Tecumseh and the Quest for Indian Leadership*. Boston: Little, Brown, 1984.

———. "Tecumseh, The Shawnee Prophet, and American History: A Reassessment." *Western Historical Quarterly* 14, no. 3 (1983): 261–76.

———. "The Thin Red Line: Tecumseh, the Prophet, and Shawnee Resistance." *Timeline* 4, no. 6 (December 1987–January 1988): 2–19.

Edmunds, R. David, and Joseph L. Peyser. *The Fox Wars: The Mesquakie Challenge to New France*. Norman: University of Oklahoma Press, 1993.

Ellis, Richard. "The Duke Indian Oral History Collection Project." *New Mexico Historical Review* 48, (Summer 1973): 259–63.

Elm, Demus, and Harvey Adams. *The Oneida Creation Story*. Columbia, S.C.: Yorkshire, 2000.

El-Zein, Amira. *Islam, Arabs, and the Intelligent World of the Jinn*. Syracuse, N.Y.: Syracuse University Press, 2009.

Erdoes, Richard, and Alfonso Ortiz, eds. *American Indian Myths and Legends*. New York: Pantheon Books, 1984.

Erickson, Kirstin C. *Yaqui Homeland and Homeplace: The Everyday Production of Ethnic Identity*. Tucson: University of Arizona Press, 2008.

Faris, David E. "Narrative Form and Oral History: Some Problems and Possibilities." *International Journal of Oral History* 1 (1980): 159–80.

Faulk, Odie B. *The Geronimo Campaign*. New York: Oxford University Press, 1993.

Fenton, William N. *The Great Law and the Longhouse: A Political History of the Iroquois Confederacy*. Norman: University of Oklahoma Press, 1998.

Figlio, Karl. "Oral History and the Unconscious." *History Workshop Journal*, no. 26 (1988): 120–32.

Finnegan, Ruth. "How Oral Is Oral Literature?" *Bulletin of the School and African Studies* 37, no. 2 (1974): 52–64.

———. "A Note on Oral Tradition and Historical Evidence." *History and Theory* 9 (1970): 195–201.

———. *Oral Traditions and the Verbal Arts: A Guide to Research Practices*. New York: Routledge, 1991.

"First Americans Are Last; Pro and Con Discussion." *Senior Scholastic* 62 (March 4, 1953): 5–6.

Fixico, Donald L. *The American Indian Mind in a Linear World: American Indian Studies and Traditional Knowledge*. New York: Routledge, 2003.

———. *Call for Change: The Medicine Way of American Indian History, Ethos, and Reality*. Lincoln: University of Nebraska Press, 2013.

———. *Daily Life of Native Americans in the Twentieth Century*. Westport, Conn.: Greenwood, 2006.

———. "The Muscogee Creeks: A Nativistic People." In *Between Two Worlds: The Survival of Twentieth Century Indians*, edited by Arrell M. Gibson, 30–43. Oklahoma City: Oklahoma Historical Society, 1986.

———. *The Urban Indian Experience in America*. Albuquerque: University of New Mexico Press, 2000.

———. "Wei Wir Black Hawk vom Volk der Sac und Fox Erinnern [How we remember Black Hawk of the Sac and Fox]." In Iris Edenheiser, ed., *Tecumseh, Keokuk, Black Hawk: Indianerbildnisse in Zeiten von Verträgen und Vertreibung* [Portrayals of Native Americans in times of treaties and removal], Stuttgart, Germany: Arnoldsche Art, 2013, 139–47.

Flora of North America Editorial Committee, eds. *Flora of North America North of Mexico.* Vol. 28, Bryophyta: Mosses, pt. 2. New York: Oxford University Press, 2014.

Flores, Dan. *Coyote America: A Natural and Supernatural History.* New York: Basic Books, 2016.

"Former Cherokee Chief Cites Tenacity, Courage." *Lawrence (Kan.) Journal-World,* December 25, 1999, p. 10B.

Frazer, J. G. *Myths of the Origins of Fire: An Essay.* London: Macmillan, 1930.

Froncek, Thomas. "I Was Once a Great Warrior." *American Heritage.* 24, no. 1 (1972): 16–21, 97–99.

Furtwangler, Albert. *Answering Chief Seattle.* Seattle: University of Washington Press, 1997.

Gallagher, Winifred. *The Power of Place: How Our Surroundings Shape Our Thoughts, Emotions, and Actions.* New York: Harper Perennial, 1993.

Geronimo. *Geronimo: His Own Story.* As told to S. M. Barrett. New York: Meridian, 1996. First published 1906.

Gill, Sam D. *Native American Religions: An Introduction.* Belmont, Calif.: Wadsworth, 1982.

Gluck, Sherna Berger, and Daphne Patai, eds. *Women's Words: The Feminist Practice of Oral History.* New York: Routledge, 1991.

Goody, Jack. *The Interface Between the Written and the Oral.* Cambridge: Cambridge University Press, 1987.

GreatSchools.net. Accessed January 14, 2007.

Green, Michael. *The Politics of Indian Removal: Creek Government and Society.* Lincoln: University of Nebraska Press, 1982.

Green, Richard. *Te Ata: Chickasaw Storyteller, American Treasure.* Norman: University of Oklahoma Press, 2002.

Grele, Ronald J., ed. *Envelopes of Sound: Six Practitioners Discuss the Method, Theory and Practice of Oral History and Oral Testimony.* Chicago: Precedent, 1975.

Grinnell, George Bird. *Blackfoot Lodge Tales: The Story of a Prairie People.* New York: Charles Scribner's Sons, 1892.

Gudschinsky, Sarah C. *How to Learn an Unwritten Language.* New York: Holt, Rinehart and Winston, 1967.

Hafften, Ann. "Wilma Mankiller Speaks at Women of ELCA Convention," Minneapolis, Minn. ELCA News Service, July 11, 1996. http://archive.wfn.org/1996/07/msg00197.html.

Hagan, William T. *The Sac and Fox Indians.* Norman: University of Oklahoma Press, 1958.

Hahn, Steven C. *The Invention of the Creek Nation, 1670–1763.* Lincoln: University of Nebraska Press, 2004.

Haile, Berard. *Navajo Coyote Tales: The Curly Tó Aheedíinii Version.* Lincoln: University of Nebraska Press, 1984.

Hale, Duane Kendall. *Researching and Writing Tribal Histories.* Grand Rapids: Michigan Indian Press and Grand Rapids Inter-Tribal Council, 1991.

Hall, Robert L. "The Open Door Recognizes a Window of Opportunity and Other Tales of Suns Turned Black." *Wisconsin Archeologist* 79, no. 1 (1998): 232–35.

Hallowell, A. Irving. "Ojibway Ontology, Behavior, and World View." In Stanley Diamond, ed., *Primitive Views of the World: Essays from Culture in History*, New York: Columbia University Press, 1964.

Hardin, Terri, ed. *Legends and Lore of the American Indians.* New York: Barnes & Noble Books, 1993.

Harms, Robert. "Oral Tradition and Ethnicity." *Journal of Interdisciplinary History* 10, no. 1 (1979): 61–85.

Harrod, Howard L. *Renewing the World: Plains Indian Religion and Morality.* Tucson: University of Arizona Press, 1987.

Hartley, William B., and Ellen Hartley. *Osceola, the Unconquered Indian.* New York: Hawthorn Books, 1973.

Hassrick, Royal B. *The Sioux: Life and Customs of a Warrior Society.* Norman: University of Oklahoma Press, 1964.

Hatch, Thom. *Black Kettle: The Cheyenne Chief Who Sought Peace but Found War.* Hoboken, N.J.: John Wiley, 2004.

Hedren, Paul L. *Great Sioux War Orders of Battle: How the United States Army Waged War on the Northern Plains, 1876–1877.* Norman: University of Oklahoma Press, 2010.

Heintze, Beatrix. "Oral Tradition: Primary Source Only for the Collector?" *History in Africa* 3 (1976): 47–56.

Henige, David P. *Oral Historiography.* London: Longman, 1982.

———. "Oral Tradition and Chronology." *Journal of Africa History* 12 (1971): 371–90.

Herring, Joseph B. *Kenekuk, the Kickapoo Prophet.* Lawrence: University Press of Kansas, 1988.

Hertzberg, Hazel W. *The Great Tree and the Longhouse: The Culture of the Iroquois.* New York: Macmillan, 1966.

Hill, Jane H., and Judith T. Irvine, eds. *Responsibility and Evidence in Oral Discourse.* New York: Cambridge University Press, 1993.

Hill, Michael J. "Science Should Serve the Community." *Tribal College Journal* 7, no. 4 (Spring 1996): 12.

Hirschfelder, Arlene, ed. *Native Heritage: Personal Accounts by American Indians, 1790 to Present.* New York: Macmillan, 1995.

Hiskey, Daven. "Where the Tradition of Yelling 'Geronimo' When Jumping Out of a Plane Came From." *Today I Found Out: Feed Your Brain.* TodayIFoundOut.com, January 20, 2011. www.todayifoundout.com/index.php/2011/01/where-the-tradition -of-yelling-geronimo-when-jumping-out-of-a-plane-came-from.

Hittman, Michael. *Wovoka and the Ghost Dance.* Edited by Don Lynch. Lincoln: University of Nebraska Press, 1990.

Hoebel, E. Adamson. *The Cheyennes: Indians of the Great Plains.* New York: Holt, Rinehart and Winston, 1960.

Hogan, Linda. *The Woman Who Watches Over the World*. New York: W. W. Norton, 2001.

Hollihan, Tony. *Crazy Horse: Warrior Spirit of the Sioux*. Edmonton, Alta.: Folklore, 2003.

Hollman, Clide. *Pontiac, King of the Great Lakes*. New York: Hastings House, 1968.

The Holy Bible. New York: Oxford University Press, 1917. King James version.

Hoover, Herbert T. "Sitting Bull." In R. David Edmunds, ed., *American Indian Leaders: Studies in Diversity*, Lincoln: University of Nebraska Press, 1980, 152–72.

Hopkins, Sarah Winnemucca. *Life Among the Piutes: Their Wrongs and Claims*. New York: G. P. Putnam's Sons, 1883.

Howard, James H. *Shawnee! The Ceremonialism of a Native American Tribe and Its Cultural Background*. Athens: Ohio University Press, 1981.

Howard, James H., in collaboration with Willie Lena. *Oklahoma Seminoles: Medicine, Magic and Religion*. Norman: University of Oklahoma Press, 1984.

Hultkrantz, Ake. *Shamanic Healing and Ritual Drama: Health and Medicine in Native North American Religious Traditions*. New York: Crossroad, 1992.

Hungry Wolf, Beverly. *The Ways of My Grandmothers*. New York: Quill, 1982.

Hunter, Charles. "The Delaware Nativist Revival of the Mid-Eighteenth Century." *Ethnohistory* 18 (1971): 39–49.

Hutton, Patrick H. "The Problem of Oral Tradition in Vico's Historical Scholarship." *Journal of the History of Ideas* 53, no. 1 (1992): 3–23.

Hutton, Paul Andrew. *The Apache Wars: The Hunt for Geronimo, the Apache Kid, and the Captive Boy Who Started the Longest War in American History*. New York: Crown, 2016.

Hymes, Dell. *Foundations in Sociolinguistics: An Ethnographic Approach*. Philadelphia: University of Pennsylvania Press, 1974.

Inter Press Service, comp. *Story Earth: Native Voices on the Environment*. San Francisco: Mercury House, 1993.

Iverson, Peter. *The Navajo Nation*. Albuquerque: University of New Mexico Press, 1981.

Jackson, Donald Dean, ed. *Black Hawk: An Autobiography*. Urbana: University of Illinois Press, 1955.

Jacobs, Melville. *Badger and Coyote Were Neighbors*. Corvallis: Oregon State University Press, 2000.

Johnston, Basil H. *The Manitous: The Supernatural World of the Ojibway*. New York: Harper Perennial, 1995.

Jones, Chuck. *Chuck Amuck: The Life and Times of an Animated Cartoonist*. New York: Farrar, Straus and Giroux, 1999.

Jones, David E., ed. *Sanapia: Comanche Medicine Woman*. Prospect Heights, Ill.: Waveland, 1984.

Jones, William. "Episodes in the Culture-Hero Myth of the Sauks and Foxes." *Journal of American Folklore* 14 (October–December 1901): 237–39.

———. "Notes on the Fox Indians." *Iowa Journal of History and Politics* 10 (January 1912): 74–75.

Judson, Katharine B., ed. *Native American Legends of the Great Lakes and the Missis-sippi Valley.* DeKalb: Northern Illinois University Press, 2000.

Katz, Jane N., ed. *I Am the Fire of Time: The Voices of Native American Women.* New York: E. P. Dutton, 1977.

Kearney, Michael. *World View.* Novato, Calif.: Chandler & Sharp, 1984.

Kelley, Klara, and Francis Harris. "Places Important to Navajo People." *American Indian Quarterly* 17, no. 2 (Spring 1993): 151–70.

Kemnitz, Charles. "The Hand of Memory: Forging Personal Narrative." *Genre* 16 (1983): 175–89.

Kennekuk to Superintendent of Indian Affairs William Clark, 1827. "Prairie Stories." Early American Museum, The Heritage Center of Champaign County. www.early americanmuseum.org/prairienative10.htm. Accessed October 22, 2010.

Kenoi, Samuel E. "A Chiricahua Apache's Account of the Geronimo Campaign of 1886." In C. L. Sonnichsen, ed., *Geronimo and the End of the Apache Wars,* Lincoln: University of Nebraska Press, 1986, 71–72.

King, Thomas. *The Truth of Stories: A Native Narrative.* Toronto: House of Anansi, 2003.

Klinck, C. F. *Tecumseh: Fact and Fiction in Early Records.* Ottawa, Ont.: Tecumseh Press, 1978.

Kluckhohn, Clyde, and Dorothea Leighton. *The Navajo.* Cambridge, Mass.: Harvard University Press, 1974.

Krupat, Arnold. *For Those Who Come After: A Study of Native American Autobiography.* Berkeley: University of California Press, 1985.

———. *Red Matters: Native American Studies.* Philadelphia: University of Pennsylvania Press, 2002.

Kucka, Susan. "A 2nd Chance for a Miracle: New Birth of a White Buffalo on a Wisconsin Farm Renews Hope among Native Americans," *Chicago Tribune,* October 1, 2006.

Lame Deer, John (Fire), and Richard Erdoes. *Lame Deer, Seeker of Visions.* New York: Touchstone, 1972.

Lang, Mabel L. "Herodotus: Oral History with a Difference." *Proceedings of the American Philosophical Society,* no. 128 (1984): 93–103.

Lavine, Sigmund A. *The Ghosts the Indians Feared.* New York: Dodd, Mead, 1975.

Lawson, Marion. *Proud Warrior: The Story of Black Hawk.* New York: Hawthorn Books, 1968.

Leonard, Quannah. "Wilma Mankiller." *Daily O'Collegian* (Stillwater, Okla.), February 2, 2000. www.ocolly.com.

Lincoln, Kenneth. *Indi'n Humor: Bicultural Play in Native America.* New York: Oxford University Press, 1993.

Linderman, Frank B., ed. *Old Man Coyote.* Lincoln: University of Nebraska Press, 1996. First published 1931 by John Day.

Littlefield, Daniel F., Jr., and Lonnie E. Underhill. "The Crazy Snake Uprising of 1909: A Red, Black, or White Affair?" *Arizona and the West* 20, no. 4 (Winter 1978): 309.

Lossiah, Lynn. *Cherokee Little People: The Secrets and Mysteries of the Yunwi Tsunsdi.* Cherokee, N.C.: Cherokee, 1998.

Lowie, Robert. *Culture and Ethnology*. New York: D. C. McMurtrie, 1917.

Lummis, Trevor. *Listening to History: The Authenticity of Oral Evidence*. Totowa, N.J.: Barnes & Noble Books, 1988.

Lurie, Nancy O., ed. *Mountain Wolf Woman, Sister of Crashing Thunder: The Autobiography of a Winnebago Indian*. Ann Arbor: University of Michigan Press, 1961.

MacDonald, Peter, with Ted Schwarz. *The Last Warrior: Peter MacDonald and the Navajo Nation*. New York: Orion Books, 1993.

Malotki, Ekkehart, and Michael Lomatuway'ma. *Hopi Coyote Tales: Istutuwutsi*. Lincoln: University of Nebraska Press, 1984.

Mankiller, Wilma. "Rebuilding the Cherokee Nation." Gifts of Speech. Text of Speech, April 2, 1993, Sweet Briar College, Sweet Briar, Va. http://gos.sbc.edu/m/mankiller .html.

Mann, Barbara Alice. *Spirits of Blood, Spirits of Breath: The Twinned Cosmos of Indigenous America*. Oxford: Oxford University Press, 2016.

Marquis, Thomas B., ed. *Memoirs of a White Crow Indian (Thomas H. Leforge)*. Lincoln: University of Nebraska Press, 1974. First published 1924 by The Century Company.

Marquis, Thomas Guthrie. *The War Chief of the Ottawas: A Chronicle of the Pontiac War*. Toronto: Glasgow, Brook, 1935.

Marshall, Edward. "Muscogee Creek Festival–2 Stomp Dancing." Smithsonian National Museum of the American Indian, December 17, 2014. www.youtube.com/watch?v =hJjzlIp77wc.

Marshall, Joseph M. *The Journey of Crazy Horse: A Lakota History*. New York: Viking, 2004.

Martínez, David. *Dakota Philosopher: Charles Eastman and American Indian Thought*. Saint Paul: Minnesota Historical Society, 2009.

Massey, Stacey. "The Sac and Fox in Indian Territory." *Sac and Fox News* (Stroud, Okla.) 30, no. 12 (December 2009): 6.

Matthews, Washington, ed., comp., and trans. *Navaho Legends*. Boston: Houghton, Mifflin, 1897.

McConnell, Michael N. *A Country Between: The Upper Ohio Valley and Its Peoples, 1724–1774*. Lincoln: University of Nebraska Press, 1992.

McDaniel, Justin Thomas. *The Lovelorn Ghost and the Magical Monk: Practicing Buddhism in Modern Thailand*. New York: Columbia University Press, 2014.

McDonald, Ann Lanier. *Shawnee OK Naval Air Station*. Shawnee, Okla.: Shawnee OK History Books, 2014.

McDonough, James Lee. *William Tecumseh Sherman: In the Service of My Country; A Life*. New York: W. W. Norton, 2016.

McGaa, Ed. *Native Wisdom: Perceptions of the Natural Way*. Minneapolis: Four Directions, 1995.

McMurtry, Larry. *Crazy Horse*. New York: Viking, 1999.

McPherson, Robert S. *Sacred Land, Sacred View: Navajo Perceptions of the Four Corners Region*. Provo, Utah: Brigham Young University, Charles Redd Center for Western Studies, 1992.

McTaggart, Fred. *Wolf That I Am: In Search of the Red Earth People.* Norman: University of Oklahoma Press, 1984. First published 1976 by Houghton Mifflin.

McWhorter, L. V., ed., *Yellow Wolf: His Own Story.* Caldwell, Idaho: Caxton, 2000.

Means, Russell, with Marvin J. Wolf. *Where White Men Fear to Tread: The Autobiography of Russell Means.* New York: St. Martin's, 1995.

Medal of Honor Citation for Ernest Childers. HomeofHeroes.com. www.homeofheroes .com/moh/citations_living. Accessed January 17, 2008.

Mercer, P. M. "Oral Tradition in the Pacific: Problems of Interpretation." *Journal of Pacific History* 14 (1979): 130–53.

Miller, David Humphreys. *Ghost Dance.* New York: Duell, Sloan and Pearce, 1959.

Miller, Jay. *Earthmaker, Tribal Stories from Native North America.* New York: Perigee Books, 1992.

Mintz, Steven, ed. *Native American Voices: A History and Anthology.* Saint James, N.Y.: Brandywine, 1995.

"Miraculous White Buffalo Dies on Farm in Janesville; The Buffalo, Miracle, Was Considered a Sacred Sign by American Indians," *Madison Wisconsin State Journal,* September 25, 2004.

Momaday, N. Scott. *The Names: A Memoir.* New York: Harper & Row, 1976.

Monture-Angus, Patricia. *Thunder in My Soul: A Mohawk Woman Speaks.* Halifax, N.S.: Fernwood, 1995.

Mooney, James. *The Ghost-Dance Religion and the Sioux Outbreak of 1890.* Lincoln: University of Nebraska Press, 1991.

———. *History, Myths, and Sacred Formulas of the Cherokees.* Asheville, N.C.: Historical Images, 1992. First published 1891 and 1900 by Bureau of American Ethnology.

Morgan, Lewis H. *League of the Ho-de'-No-Sau-Nee or Iroquois.* North Dighton, Mass.: JG Press, 1995.

———. *League of the Iroquois.* New York: Citadel, 1993.

Moss, William W. "Oral History: An Appreciation." *American Archivist* 40, no. 4 (October 1977): 429–39.

Moulton, Candy. *Valentine T. McGillycuddy: Army Surgeon, Agent to the Sioux.* Norman: University of Oklahoma Press, 2010.

Mourning Dove (Humishuma). *Coyote Stories.* Lincoln: University of Nebraska Press, 1990. First published by Caxton Printers, 1933.

Nabokov, Peter, ed. *Native American Testimony: A Chronicle of Indian-White Relations from Prophecy to the Present, 1492–1992.* New York: Penguin Books, 1991.

Neihardt, John, ed. *Black Elk Speaks: Being the Life Story of a Holy Man of the Oglala Sioux.* 7th ed. New York: Pocket Books, 1973. First published 1932.

Nelson, Robert B. *Place and Vision: The Function of Landscape in Native American Fiction.* New York: Peter Lang, 1993.

Nichols, Roger. *Black Hawk and the Warrior's Path.* Hoboken, N.J.: Wiley-Blackwell, 1991.

Nisbett, Richard E. *The Geography of Thought: How Asians and Westerners Think Differently . . . and Why.* New York: Simon and Schuster, 2003.

O'Connell, Robert L. *Fierce Patriot: The Tangled Lives of William Tecumseh Sherman*. New York: Random House, 2014.

O'Danachair, Caoimhim. "Oral Tradition and the Printed Word." *Irish University Review: A Journal of Irish Studies* 9 (1979): 31–41.

Oklahoma Climatological Survey. "The Climate of Oklahoma." http://climate.ok.gov /index.php/site/page/climate_of_oklahoma. Accessed December 26, 2015.

Oliver, W. H. "Oral and Other History." *New Zealand Journal of History* 12 (1978): 99–103.

Oppenheim, Joanne. *Black Hawk, Frontier Warrior*. Mahwah, N.J.: Troll, 1979.

———. *Osceola, Seminole Warrior*. Mahwah, N.J.: Troll, 1979.

Osawa, Sandy, dir. *On and Off the Res' with Charlie Hill*. Upstream Productions, 2000, color, 58 mins. www.iupui.edu/~mstd/narep/chill.html.

Parkman, Francis. *The Conspiracy of Pontiac and the Indian War after the Conquest of Canada*. 2 vols. Lincoln: University of Nebraska Press, 1994. First published 1851.

Parmenter, Jon. *The Edge of the Woods: Iroquoia, 1534–1701*. East Lansing: Michigan State University Press, 2010.

Peckham, Howard H. *Pontiac and the Indian Uprising*. Princeton, N.J.: Princeton University Press, 1947.

Peltier, Leonard. *Prison Writings: My Life Is My Sun Dance*. Edited by Harvey Arden. New York: St. Martin's, 1999.

Perdue, Theda. *Nations Remembered: An Oral History of the Five Civilized Tribes, 1865–1907*. Westport, Conn.: Greenwood, 1980.

Quirk, Patrick Edward. *When Spirits Touch the Red Path*. Salt Lake City: Northwest, 1993.

"Quotes from Chief Sitting Bull." Powerful People. www.powersource.com/gallery/people /sittbull.html. Accessed July 2, 2009.

"Quotes [of Will Rogers]." Will Rogers Memorial Museums. www.willrogers.com/says /will-says.html. Accessed June 23, 2012.

Radin, Paul. *The Trickster: A Study in American Indian Mythology*. New York: Philosophical Library, 1956.

Relander, Click. *Drummers and Dreamers*. Seattle: Caxton, 1986.

Rips, Lance J., and Margaret E. Stubbs. "Genealogy and Memory." *Journal of Verbal Learning and Verbal Behavior* 19 (1980): 705–21.

Ritchie, Donald A. *Doing Oral History*. New York: Twayne, 1995.

Roberts, David. *Once They Moved Like the Wind: Cochise, Geronimo, and the Apache Wars*. New York: Simon and Schuster, 1993.

Rooth, Anna Birgitta. "The Creation Myths of the North American Indians." *Anthropos* 52 (1957): 497–508.

Ruby, Robert H., and John A. Brown. *Dreamer Prophets of the Columbia Plateau: Smohalla and Skolaskin*. Norman: University of Oklahoma Press, 1989.

Ruoff, A. Lavonne Brown. "American Indian Oral Literature." *American Quarterly* 33 (1981): 309–26.

Sajna, Mike. *Crazy Horse: The Life Behind the Legend*. New York: John Wiley, 2000.

Said, Edward. *Orientalism*. New York: Vintage Books, 1978.

Sandoz, Mari. *Crazy Horse: The Strange Man of the Oglalas*. Lincoln: University of Nebraska Press, 1992.

Schmitt, Jean-Claude. *Ghosts in the Middle Ages: The Living and the Dead in Medieval Society*. Chicago: University of Chicago Press, 1999.

Schwarz, Melissa. *Geronimo: Apache Warrior*. New York: Chelsea House, 1992.

Seligman, Haim. "Is Oral History a Valid Research Instrument?" *International Journal of Oral History* 10, no. 3 (1989): 175–82.

Shepard, Paul. *Thinking Animals: Animals and the Development of Human Intelligence*. New York: Viking, 1978.

Smith, Allen, ed. *Directory of Oral History Collections*. Phoenix: Oryx, 1988.

Smith, Rex Alan. *Moon of Popping Trees*. Lincoln: University of Nebraska Press, 1981.

Smith, Susy. *Prominent American Ghosts*. Cleveland: World, 1967.

Soden, Dale. "City of Shawnee History." ShawneeOk.org. www.shawneeok.org/History/. Accessed July 25, 2016.

Sonnichsen, C. L., ed. *Geronimo and the End of the Apache Wars*. Lincoln: University of Nebraska Press, 1986.

Spence, Lewis. *Myths and Legends of the North American Indians*. London: CRW, 2004.

Spicer, Edward. *The Yaquis: A Cultural History*. Tucson: University of Arizona Press, 1980.

Standing Bear, Luther. *Land of the Spotted Eagle*. Lincoln: University of Nebraska Press, 1978. First published 1933.

"Standing Bear's Speech." Timeless Truths Free Online Library. Speech by Standing Bear. http://library.timelesstruths.org/texts/Stories_Worth_Rereading/Standing_Bears_speech. Accessed July 2, 2009.

Stands In Timber, John, and Margot Liberty. *Cheyenne Memories*. 2nd ed. New Haven, Conn.: Yale University Press, 1998.

State of Florida, Division of Corporations. SunBiz.org. Accessed January 14, 2007.

Stockel, Henrietta H., ed. *LaDonna Harris: A Comanche Life*. Lincoln: University of Nebraska Press, 2000.

Sugden, John. *Tecumseh's Last Stand*. Norman: University of Oklahoma Press, 1985.

Suzuki, David, and Peter Knudtson. *Wisdom of the Elders: Honoring Sacred Native Visions of Nature*. New York: Bantam Books, 1992.

Swanton, John. *Myths and Tales of the Southeastern Indians*. Norman: University of Oklahoma Press, 1991. First published 1929.

Swisher, Karen. "Why Indian People Should Be the Ones to Write about Indian Education." *American Indian Quarterly* 20, no. 1 (Winter 1996): 83–90.

Tecumseh. "Sleep Not Longer, O Choctaws and Chickasaws." In W. C. Vanderwerth, ed., *Indian Oratory: Famous Speeches by Noted Indian Chieftains*, Norman: University of Oklahoma Press, 1971, 62–66.

Terkel, Studs. *"The Good War": An Oral History of World War Two*. New York: Ballantine Books, 1984.

Thayer, Crawford B. *Hunting a Shadow: The Search for Black Hawk.* Madison: University of Wisconsin–Madison, 1981.

Thelen, David, ed. *Memory and American History.* Bloomington: Indiana University Press, 1990. Collection first appeared as special issue of *Journal of American History* 75, no. 4 (1989).

Thieselton, Anthony C. *The Holy Spirit: In Biblical Teachings, Through the Centuries, and Today.* Grand Rapids, Mich.: William B. Eerdmans, 2013.

Thomas, Bill. *Talking with the Animals: How to Communicate with Wildlife.* New York: William Morrow, 1985.

Thompson, Gerald. *The Army and the Navajo: The Bosque Redondo Reservation Experiment, 1863–1868.* Tucson: University of Arizona Press, 1976.

Thompson, Paul. *The Voice of the Past: Oral History.* London: Oxford University Press, 1978.

Thompson, Stith. *Folk Tales of the North American Indians.* North Dighton, Mass.: JG Press, 1995.

Thornton, Russell. *We Shall Live Again: The 1870 and 1890 Ghost Dance Movements as Demographic Revitalizations.* New York: Cambridge University Press, 1986.

Thurman, Melburn D. "Plains Indian Winter Counts and the New Ethnohistory." *Plains Anthropologist* 27 (1982): 173–75.

———. "The Shawnee Prophet's Movement and the Origins of the Prophet Dance." *Current Anthropology* 25, no. 4 (August–October 1984): 530–31.

Tibbles, Thomas Henry. *Buckskin and Blanket Days: Memoirs of a Friend of the Indians.* Lincoln: University of Nebraska Press, 1969.

The Times Atlas of the World. 10th ed. New York: Random House, 1999.

Toelken, Barre. *The Anguish of Snails: Native American Folklore in the West.* Logan: Utah State University Press, 2003.

Tonkin, Elizabeth. "The Boundaries of History in Oral Performance." *History in Africa* 9 (1982): 273–84.

———. "Implications of Oracy: An Anthropological View." *Oral History* 3, nos. 1–2 (1975): 41–49.

———. *Narrating Our Pasts: the Social Construction of Oral History.* Cambridge: Cambridge University Press, 1992.

Trafzer, Clifford E. ed., *Grandmother, Grandfather, and Old Wolf: Tamanwit Ku Sukat and Traditional Native American Narratives from the Columbia Plateau.* East Lansing: Michigan State University Press. 1998.

Trafzer, Clifford E., and Richard D. Scheuerman, eds. *Mourning Dove's Stories.* San Diego: San Diego State University, 1991.

Trahant, Mark. "Wilma Mankiller Talks Straight but Makes Mischief, Too." *Seattle Times,* May 21, 2000.

Trask, Kerry A. *Black Hawk: The Battle for the Heart of America.* New York: Henry Holt, 2006.

Treadway, Sandra Gioia. "Triumph in Defeat: Black Hawk's 1833 Visit to Virginia." *Virginia Cavalcade*. 35, no. 1 (Summer 1985): 4–17.

Treuer, Anton, ed. *Living Our Language: Ojibwe Tales & Oral Histories*. Saint Paul: Minnesota Historical Society, 2001.

Trowbridge, C. C. *Shawnese Traditions*. Edited by Vernon Kinietz. *Occasional Contributions from the Museum of Anthropology*, University of Michigan, no. 7. Ann Arbor: University of Michigan Press, 1938.

Ulrich, Roberta. *American Indian Nations from Termination to Restoration, 1953–2006*. Lincoln: University of Nebraska Press, 2010.

United States Census. American FactFinder. www.factfinder.census.gov. Accessed January 14, 2007.

Utley, Robert M., and Wilcomb E. Washburn. *Indian Wars*. Boston: Houghton Mifflin, 1977.

Vanderwerth, W. C., ed. *Indian Oratory: Famous Speeches by Noted Indian Chieftains*. Norman: University of Oklahoma Press, 1971.

Vansina, Jan. *Oral Tradition: A Study in Historical Methodology*. Chicago: Aldine, 1965.

———. *Oral Tradition as History*. Madison: University of Wisconsin Press, 1985.

Voegelin, C. F. *The Shawnee Female Deity*. Yale University Publications in Anthropology 10. New Haven, Conn.: Yale University Press, 1936: 3–21.

Voegelin, C. F., and E. W. Voegelin. "The Shawnee Female Deity in Historical Perspective." *American Anthropologist* 46, no. 3. (July–Sept. 1944): 370–75.

Vogel, Virgil. *American Indian Medicine*. Norman: University of Oklahoma Press, 1970.

Volkmann, Carl. "Lorado Taft: The Prairie State Sculptor." April 16, 2012. http://loradotaft theprairiestatesculptor.blogspot.com/2012/04/eternal-indian.html.

Von Koenigswald, G. R. R. *The Evolution of Man*. Rev. ed. Ann Arbor: University of Michigan Press, 1976.

———. *Meeting Prehistoric Man*. New York: Harper, 1956.

Walker, Deward E., Jr., in collaboration with Daniel N. Matthews. *Nez Perce Coyote Tales: The Myth Cycle*. Norman: University of Oklahoma Press, 1998.

Wallace, Anthony F. C. *The Death and Rebirth of the Seneca*. New York: Vintage Books, 1969.

West, Francis. "Oral Tradition." *History and Theory* 5 (1966): 348–52.

Wheeler, Homer W. *Buffalo Days*. Indianapolis: Bobbs-Merrill, 1905.

Whickar, J. Wesley. "Shabonee's Account of Tippecanoe." *Indiana Magazine of History* 17, no. 4 (December 1921): 362.

Wickman, Patricia Riles. *Osceola's Legacy*. Tuscaloosa: University of Alabama Press, 1991.

Wile E. Coyote Fan Club Website and Ten Rules. www.geocities.com/televisioncity /3081/-14k. Accessed January 16, 2008.

"Wilma P. Mankiller (1945–)." In Duane Champagne, ed., *The Native North American Almanac: A Reference Work on Native North Americans in the United States and Canada*, Detroit: Gale, 1994, 1098–99.

Wilmer, Franke. *Indigenous Voice in World Politics*. Newbury Park, Calif.: Sage, 1993.

Winsell, Keith A. "Crazy Horse 1840(?)–1877." In Sharon Malinowski, ed., *Notable Native Americans*, New York: Gale, 1995, 97.

Wood, Charles Erskine Scott. "The Pursuit and Capture of Chief Joseph." Archives of the West, 1874–1877, episode 6. *New Perspectives on the West*. PBS. www.pbs.org/weta /thewest/resources/archives/six/. Accessed January 14, 2008.

"Work Camp." *Seminole (Okla.) Producer*, May 4, 1944.

Wright, J. Leitch, Jr. *Creeks and Seminoles: The Destruction and Regeneration of the Muscogulgee People*. Lincoln: University of Nebraska Press, 1986.

Wright, Muriel H. "Pawnee." In Muriel H. Wright, ed., *A Guide to the Indian Tribes of Oklahoma*, Norman: University of Oklahoma Press, 1951.

Yagoda, Ben. *Will Rogers: A Biography*. Norman: University of Oklahoma Press, 2000. First published 1993.

Yellowman, Gordon. "Turtle Island Storyteller Gordon Yellowman, Sr." Wisdom of the Elders. Turtle Island Storytellers Network. www.turtleislandstorytells.met/tis _oklahoma/transcript_g_yellowman.htm. Accessed September 9, 2011.

Young Bear, Severt, and R. D. Theisz. *Standing in the Light: A Lakota Way of Seeing*. Lincoln: University of Nebraska Press, 1994.

Zah, Peterson, and Peter Iverson. *We Will Secure Our Future: Empowering the Navajo Nation*. Tucson: University of Arizona Press, 2012.

Zumthor, Paul. *Oral Poetry: An Introduction*. Minneapolis: University of Minnesota Press, 1990.

Interviews

Begay, Manuelito (Navajo). Interview by Tom Ration, November 1968. Tape 167, side 1, p. 1. Oral History Collection, Labriola National Data Center, Carl Hayden Library, Arizona State University, Tempe.

Big Horse, Laura (Cheyenne), and Gladys Mann (Cheyenne). Interview by David Jones, February 1968. T-251-1, pp. 6–7. Doris Duke Oral History Collection, Western History Collections, University of Oklahoma, Norman.

Johnson, Jack (Navajo). Interview by Tom Ration, October 1968. Tape 185, side 1, p. 1. Oral History Collection, Labriola National Data Center, Carl Hayden Library, Arizona State University, Tempe.

Little Jim, Webb (Shawnee). Interview by Julia Jordan, February 2, 1969. Vol. 52, tape M-14. Doris Duke Indian Oral History Collection, Western History Collections, University of Oklahoma, Norman.

Silverheels, Jay (as Tonto). Interview by Johnny Carson, September 9, 1969. *The Tonight Show Starring Johnny Carson*, https://www.youtube.com/watch?v=1X1zOytr2MU.

Whistler, Tom (Ottawa). Interview by J. W. Tyner, September 16, 1969. T-535-1, p. 5. Doris Duke Indian Oral History Collection, Western History Collections, University of Oklahoma, Norman.

Index

Page numbers in *italics* refer to illustrations.

Printed in the USA
CPSIA information can be obtained
at www.ICGtesting.com
CBHW022126170424
7121CB00001B/51